THE CERTIFIED SIX SIGMA YELLOW BELT HANDBOOK

Also available from ASQ Quality Press:

The Certified Six Sigma Green Belt Handbook, Second Edition
Roderick A. Munro, Govindarajan Ramu, and Daniel J. Zrymiak

The Certified Six Sigma Black Belt Handbook, Third Edition
T.M. Kubiak and Donald W. Benbow

Practical Engineering, Process, and Reliability Statistics
Mark Allen Durivage

The ASQ Pocket Guide for the Certified Six Sigma Black Belt
T.M. Kubiak

Process Improvement Using Six Sigma: A DMAIC Guide
Rama Shankar

Statistics for Six Sigma Black Belts
Matthew Barsalou

The ASQ Pocket Guide to Statistics for Six Sigma Black Belts
Matthew Barsalou

The Certified Six Sigma Master Black Belt Handbook
T.M. Kubiak

The Certified Quality Engineer Handbook, Third Edition
Connie M. Borror, editor

The Quality Toolbox, Second Edition
Nancy R. Tague

Root Cause Analysis: Simplified Tools and Techniques, Second Edition
Bjørn Andersen and Tom Fagerhaug

The Certified Manager of Quality/Organizational Excellence Handbook, Fourth Edition
Russell T. Westcott, editor

The ASQ Quality Improvement Pocket Guide: Basic History, Concepts, Tools, and Relationships
Grace L. Duffy, editor

To request a complimentary catalog of ASQ Quality Press publications, call
800-248-1946, or visit our website at http://www.asq.org/quality-press.

THE CERTIFIED SIX SIGMA YELLOW BELT HANDBOOK

Govind Ramu

ASQ Quality Press
Milwaukee, Wisconsin

American Society for Quality, Quality Press, Milwaukee 53203
© 2017 by ASQ. Printed in 2016
All rights reserved.
Printed in the United States of America
21 20 19   5 4

Library of Congress Cataloging-in-Publication Data
Names: Ramu, Govindarajan, author.
Title: The certified Six Sigma yellow belt handbook / Govindarajan Ramu.
Description: Milwaukee : ASQ Quality Press, 2016. | Includes bibliographical
    references and index.
Identifiers: LCCN 2016022355 | ISBN 9780873899345 (hardcover : alk. paper)
Subjects: LCSH: Six sigma (Quality control standard)—Handbooks, manuals,
    etc. | Production management--Handbooks, manuals, etc. | Quality
    control—Statistical methods—Handbooks, manuals, etc
Classification: LCC TS156.17.S59 R36 2016 | DDC 658.5/620218—dc23
LC record available at https://lccn.loc.gov/2016022355

Publisher: Seiche Sanders
Acquisitions Editor: Matt Meinholz
Managing Editor: Paul Daniel O'Mara
Production Administrator: Randall Benson

ASQ Mission: The American Society for Quality advances individual, organizational, and community excellence worldwide through learning, quality improvement, and knowledge exchange.

Attention Bookstores, Wholesalers, Schools, and Corporations: ASQ Quality Press books, video, audio, and software are available at quantity discounts with bulk purchases for business, educational, or instructional use. For information, please contact ASQ Quality Press at 800-248-1946, or write to ASQ Quality Press, P.O. Box 3005, Milwaukee, WI 53201–3005.

To place orders or to request a free copy of the ASQ Quality Press Publications Catalog, visit our website at http://www.asq.org/quality-press.

 Printed on acid-free paper

Quality Press
600 N. Plankinton Ave.
Milwaukee, WI 53203-2914
E-mail: authors@asq.org
ASQ The Global Voice of Quality®

I thank my mom, Vasantha, for her unconditional love and encouragement. My dad, Ramu, would have been so proud to see this book come out. The morals and principles that he taught me keep me grounded. Thanks to my wife, Anitha, and my children, Vibha and Vivek, for their patience and sacrifice of countless evenings and weekends. Without their support, this book would not have been possible.

Table of Contents

List of Figures and Tables

Part V

CD-ROM Contents*

ASQ certification materials

ASQ webinars

History of quality

Simulated exam—Note that these questions are not the questions that will appear on the exam. The sample questions are intended to represent the style of the exam questions and are offered for practice.

Tools and templates

Useful publications

Worked out examples

*Please see the CD-ROM for a complete listing of the contents in each folder.

Preface

Welcome to *The Certified Six Sigma Yellow Belt Handbook*. This reference manual is designed to help both those interested in passing the certification exam of the American Society for Quality (ASQ) for the Six Sigma Yellow Belt and those who want a handy reference to the appropriate materials needed for successful Six Sigma projects. I have made a sincere attempt to make this book a reference for both beginners in Six Sigma and those who are already knowledgeable about process improvement and variation reduction.

The primary layout of the handbook follows ASQ's Body of Knowledge (BoK) for the Certified Six Sigma Yellow Belt (CSSYB) released in 2015. I have utilized feedback from Six Sigma practitioners and knowledge gained through helping others prepare for exams to create a handbook that I hope will be beneficial to anyone seeking to pass the ASQ CSSYB or other Six Sigma exams. In addition to the primary text, the handbook contains numerous appendixes, a comprehensive list of abbreviations, and practice exam questions; a CD-ROM accompanying the book contains additional materials. One caution—you are not allowed to take any of the exam questions from the CD-ROM or from any other simulation into the ASQ exam.

While most ASQ certification exams use solely a multiple-choice question format (ASQ CMQOE and CSSMBB are exceptions), many users of ASQ handbooks on the academic side prefer essay-type questions for the chapters to test the comprehension of students using this book at colleges and universities. I would advise the ASQ exam takers to make a note of this but not be too concerned. The essay questions were added to challenge the users. The difficulty level of the essay questions is likely higher than that of the questions in the ASQ certification exam. Six Sigma trainers for organizations may find this additional feature useful, as they want their trainees (staff) to not only pass ASQ Six Sigma exams but have a comprehensive understanding of the Body of Knowledge that will allow them to support real Six Sigma projects in their roles.

I intend to start an ASQ CSSYB handbook users group in LinkedIn (a web-based social media application for professionals) and would greatly appreciate readers' comments and feedback on how the handbook can be improved. Constructive and respectful posts are encouraged. Users will be acknowledged if their input and feedback are found useful and incorporated into the next edition.

I encourage users of the handbook to read the ASQ *Quality Progress* publication "Test Run" to obtain tips for passing the ASQ exam (http://asq.org/quality-progress/2010/01/certification-asq/test-run.html and also located on this book's CD-ROM).

Test-takers will also find useful the CSSYB keyword search located on the CD-ROM. This lists the terms and phrases in the BoK and where they are located within the handbook, since in an open-book exam it is useful to the test-taker to be able to quickly find these within the book. It is recommended you print this out to use in conjunction with the handbook during the exam.

WHERE ARE YOU IN YOUR CAREER?

Over the course of your professional career, you have learned to use many tools. Certification as a Six Sigma Yellow Belt is the beginning of your journey of achieving higher levels of accomplishments and potentially lifelong learning. Consider this as laying the foundation. The following career pyramid provides guidance on reaching additional certifications. It is *not* a representation of ASQ certification exam requirements or prerequisites; rather, it presents a logical order of how one would progress.

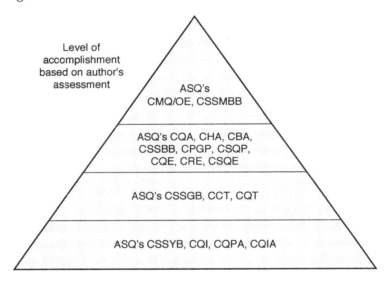

Best wishes as you embark on your Six Sigma journey!

Acknowledgments

I would like to thank the numerous individuals who have taught me technical and management acumen, and hard and soft skills; have provided opportunities for me; and have been coaches and mentors to me. I would like to acknowledge Noel Wilson from the ASQ Knowledge Center for her guidance and support of my publications since 2006. Noel is an asset to ASQ and a gift to quality professionals like me.

We all learn a lot from our managers. Over my 30 years in quality management I have had lots of bosses and I have learned a lot about critical thinking. My very first manager taught me attention to details. Another manager explained to me that when my requirement is one, learn to live with half. Another one famously repeated "check, recheck, and cross check." I learned to be empathetic to my colleagues and respectful to staff. While I was working at JDS Uniphase Corporation (JDSU), Peter Makin and Jordan Freed provided opportunities and support to strengthen my quality skills. Peter was so kind to offer me the opportunity to work for him and provided management visibility to my work. While I was working for Jordan, he continually encouraged me to pursue my ASQ certifications and provided necessary management support to formally launch my Six Sigma career. I am forever grateful to these individuals. Dan Courtney (formerly JDSU) provided guidance and mentoring during my early Six Sigma career. His decision to hire me in the JDSU Six Sigma organization was a great turning point for me. The hands-on experience of coaching and mentoring Black Belts and Green Belts, and setting up a global Design for Six Sigma program further strengthened my knowledge and experience. I would like to acknowledge the SunPower Corporation management team for its support of my continued professional development. I have always been fortunate to have managers who support my development.

I would like to thank Quality Press staff Paul O'Mara and Matt Meinholz for their incredible patience, understanding, and support in this project, and John Noguera, CTO and cofounder of SigmaXL, Inc. I would also like to thank my coauthors from my previous publication on Six Sigma. I learned a lot working with Roderick Munro and Daniel Zrymiak on the second edition of *The Certified Six Sigma Green Belt Handbook*. Contents of that handbook provided a baseline for my authoring of *The Certified Six Sigma Yellow Belt Handbook*.

I would like to thank the following Lean Six Sigma professionals who performed careful reviews at different stages of the book: S. Anilkumar, David S. Foxx, Eric Gemunder, and Chad Walters.

Finally, there are many I am not addressing here. They all have my respect for their professionalism and continued support.

Introduction:
The ASQ Certification Process

This section contains information about the exam process itself. Although not part of the exam material, this is useful information to give you background and help you understand the ASQ Certification process. You are encouraged to read this section.

THE TEST DEVELOPMENT PROCESS

Many exams, whether tests or certifications, are written by a very few people (sometimes only one person) based on what they think an examinee should know to meet the criteria of some training materials (like nearly all college exams). The American Society for Quality Control (ASQC changed its name to ASQ in 1997) started developing the Certified Quality Engineer (CQE) program in 1967, making it the oldest professional quality certification in the United States. ASQC gathered a small number of quality professionals together for the development cycle of the exam. The first CQE exam developers and a few others were grandfathered in, bypassing the taking of the first exam, which was offered in 1968.

Throughout the 1970s and early 1980s ASQC and others developed more certification exams. During this time, the issue of what the difference is between a professional certification and a state license (for example, the Professional Engineers exam process) was being raised as some U.S. states and Canada started questioning the professional community about what they were doing. ASQC and other professional organizations started trying to distinguish certifications given by their organizations from state or other governmental certifications. Basically, one is granted by peer recognition (professional organizations), the other by a governmental licensing process.

In response to this growing concern and the possibility of legal litigation as to the fairness of the exam process, ASQC wanted to become proactive about their certification process. After a benchmarking exercise and a search for what was considered the very best exam development process, ASQC partnered with the Educational Testing Service (ETS is the organization that creates and maintains the SAT exams for college-bound students).

The two organizations worked together to develop an exam development process that would be legally defensible both in court and to the various governmental organizations who might choose to challenge the process. The ASQC CQE exam was the first to be redesigned with the new development process. The basic steps include:

- Design of a survey to identify the current tools and methodologies being used in a wide breadth of industries across the United States.

- Targeting ASQ members who are currently certified in a particular discipline, as well as managers and industry leaders who are aware of the needs in the various industry sectors across the country.

- Tabulating the results of the most widely used tools, techniques, and methodologies to create a basic Body of Knowledge (BoK) for the new or redeveloped exam.

- Coordinating exam-writing workshops around the BoK, paying special attention to the demographics of the exam question writers. Each industry and all parts of the country are ensured some participation in the exam-writing process.

- During the exam-writing process the participants are broken up into teams. Each person writes a few questions based on their assigned portion of the BoK and then has two or more other team members review the question for accuracy, references, and fairness.

- The team leader submits the questions to the exam-writing workshop lead person, who also reviews the questions. Others will then review anything that raises any issue at the workshop.

- The questions are then entered into a proposed exam bank based on their relevance to the specified exam's BoK.

- As enough questions are identified in the proposed exam bank, another workshop is called, with new reviewers to look over each question. The questions are accepted, reworked, or rejected for the BoK exam bank.

- About six months before an exam is to be given, a sort of the exam bank is conducted to select a new exam (each exam is different from all other exams) with some alternate questions for each area of the BoK. This exam mockup is then presented to an exam review workshop. These participants review every question and discuss their attributes related to the BoK. At the end of this process the exam is set for the next offering.

- Exams are prepared and distributed to testing centers or ASQ conferences where they will be administered to participants.

- All exams are graded using the identified answers from the exam bank. Once all exams are graded, a statistical cut score is developed to maintain a predetermined level of ongoing knowledge for the BoK field of experience (this is not just a simple 70 percent or some other numerical pass score).

- With the cut score established for a given exam sequence, all exams are then reviewed to determine those who passed. Any examinee that falls below the cut score will receive a Pareto diagram of their exam identifying where they had problems. Those that pass the exam will receive a certification and exam card for their wallet or purse.

- Once an exam has been given, the exam questions are statistically reviewed for how well they discerned the knowledge of the applicants. Any questions that were generally missed or passed by a significant portion of the audience will be discarded. Only a very few of the questions will return to the exam bank for possible use on a future exam.

- Every five years this cycle is repeated for each exam that ASQ offers.

This process is long and tedious, and ASQ spends a lot of time, resources, and volunteer effort to maintain this process to ensure the highest level of professionalism possible for the certifications offered by the Society. Once you pass an exam, you are encouraged to join in this process to help ensure that future exams will be meaningful to the participants.

ONGOING MAINTENANCE

As can be seen in the previous section, ASQ maintains a comprehensive process for ensuring that exams are reviewed every five years and that the exams are of the highest professionalism possible. To this end, security is tight for the entire process, and very few individuals know the entire history of an exam question's life to ensure that questions are not released to exam participants prior to an exam being given.

Some of the general activities that ASQ uses to maintain exam processes are:

- If you are a local section volunteer helping to administer a refresher program or teach a refresher course or other training process, you are not allowed to proctor an exam for the same BoK.

- If you proctor an exam for a section or conference, you are not allowed to teach that BoK.

- If you volunteer to assist with any of the activities listed in the previous section on the exam development cycle, you are not allowed to teach or publish anything related to that BoK.

- ASQ maintains an ASQ National Certification Committee for each exam that is offered through the Society. Each exam is either coordinated through an ASQ division (based on their field of expertise) and/or the ASQ National Headquarters, who coordinates with all ASQ divisions that might have a stake in a specific exam.

- These ASQ National Certification Committees are made up of ASQ member volunteers who meet on a regular basis to ensure that the processes listed above, the ASQ national activities, and other issues related to their specific exam are maintained at the highest possible level of professionalism. This includes recertification activities for those exams that have that requirement.

- These ASQ National Certification Committees ensure that the process listed in the previous section is followed (usually by participating in and/or coordinating the various events) as well as ensure that the BoK is positioned for reevaluation every five years.

After the questions have been used for a certain period of time, they will be put into an archival file with notes on each as to when it was used and statistical results of how the question performed on the exam. These old files can occasionally be used as a basis for writing new or variations of questions. Thus, it would be unlikely to see one of these questions show up on a future exam. While using practice exams (as included on the CD-ROM accompanying this handbook) for study can be useful, the user should realize that these are not the same questions that will be on the ASQ exam.

THE EXAMINATION PROCESS

Given the aforementioned process, the ASQ exam candidate should realize that anyone saying that they have inside information as to what will be on any given exam is either violating the ASQ Code of Ethics (by stealing information, in which case ASQ will prosecute if found out) or stretching the truth in the way that they are presenting the information. The ASQ certification exam process is always evolving and will rarely ever have a question in the same format on any two given exams. The candidate must be prepared to answer questions that could be reasonably extracted from the ASQ Certified Six Sigma Yellow Belt BoK (see Appendix B).

Also, given the number of various industries in the marketplace today, general questions can be asked about a given topic in any number of ways. One example, FMEA (note: acronyms are very rarely used in the actual exam). If you are in the automotive industry you might use the *AIAG Potential Failure Mode and Effects Analysis (FMEA) Reference Manual*, 4th edition (https://www.aiag.org/products/products-list/product-details?ProductCode=FMEA-4) or the SAE J1739:2009 standard (http://standards.sae.org/j1739_200901/). On the other hand, if you are in the medical devices industry, you would have to use BS EN ISO 14971:2007 *Medical devices—Application of risk management to medical devices* (http://shop.bsigroup.com/ProductDetail/?pid=000000000030091423). Still other industries might use the book *Failure Mode Effect Analysis: FMEA from Theory to Execution*, Second Edition. Either way, any question related to FMEA might focus on what the primary function of FMEA is, which is to manage the risk of the product or service that your organization offers to a customer (either internal or external). So, you should not be shaken if a question sounds as if it comes from an industry other than the one in which you work. The point is whether you can decipher the intent of the question as it relates to the Yellow Belt BoK and answer the question using facts and reason. The sample questions on the CD-ROM have been selected from sample exam questions from ASQ Certification pages for you to use for practice. An effort was made to ensure that only the sample questions relevant to the CSSYB BoK were selected.

The *ASQ Certified Six Sigma Yellow Belt Guidelines* booklet starts off the explanation of the BoK with:

> *Included in this body of knowledge (BoK) are explanations (subtext) and cognitive levels for each topic or subtopic in the test. These details will be used by the Examination Development Committee as guidelines for writing test questions and are designed to help candidates prepare for the exam by identifying specific content within each topic that can be tested. Except where specified, the subtext is not intended to limit the subject or be all-inclusive of what might be covered in an exam but is intended to clarify how topics are related to the role of the Certified Six Sigma Yellow Belt (CSSYB). The descriptor in parentheses at the end of each subtext entry refers to the highest cognitive level at which the topic will be tested. A complete description of cognitive levels is provided at the end of this document.*

After the BoK is listed, a description of the meanings of *remember, understand, apply, analyze, evaluate,* and *create* is given. This is important as it tells you the examinee what level of knowledge you will need for that category of the BoK. The ASQ booklet lists the levels of cognition as:

Based on Bloom's Taxonomy—Revised (2001)
In addition to content *specifics, the subtext for each topic in this BoK also indicates the intended* complexity level *of the test questions for that topic. These levels are based on "Levels of Cognition" and are presented below in rank order, from least complex to most complex.*

Remember (Knowledge Level)
Recall or recognize terms, definitions, facts, ideas, materials, patterns, sequences, methods, principles, and so on.

Understand (Comprehension Level)
Read and understand descriptions, communications, reports, tables, diagrams, directions, regulations, and so on.

Apply (Application Level)
Know when and how to use ideas, procedures, methods, formulas, principles, theories, and so on.

Analyze (Analysis Level)
Break down information into its constituent parts and recognize their relationship to one another and how they are organized; identify sublevel factors or salient data from a complex scenario.

Evaluate (Evaluation Level)
Make judgments about the value of proposed ideas, solutions, and so on, by comparing the proposal to specific criteria or standards.

Create (Synthesis Level)
Put parts or elements together in such a way as to reveal a pattern or structure not clearly there before; identify which data or information from a complex set are appropriate to examine further or from which supported conclusions can be drawn.

These words can be kept in mind while reviewing the chapters in this book to get a better sense of the detail of questions that could be asked in that section. This is also why it may appear that some material is covered in more than one section of the BoK.

In preparing for the actual exam, we suggest that you do the following:

- Follow the list of "What Can and Can Not Be Brought into the Exam Site" found on the ASQ certification website—Frequently Asked Questions—"Taking the Exam."

- Select the reference that you have used in preparing for the exam. You should be familiar with how the reference is laid out and how you will use it.

- Create an index of your planned references—you are allowed to use self-prepared information as long as there are no practice exam questions in the material.

- Consider having a good Standard English dictionary available. Sometimes a word might be used in the questions that you may not be familiar with.

- Arrive at the exam site early so that you can set up your materials in a manner that best fits your needs. You might even call the chief proctor ahead of time to learn the room layout if you have not been to the particular exam site before.

- Remember that anything that you write on during the exam (scratch paper, exam pages, answer sheets, and so on) must be turned in to the proctor at the end of the exam. Thus, during the exam do not write in any of your references that you want to take home with you.

- Relax and breathe.

Additional advice given in the ASQ Certified Six Sigma Yellow Belt brochure includes:

Test takers are also advised to keep in mind these general pointers about standardized exams:

- *Read all of the questions on the first page of the test so you realize that you do know the material. In other words, relax.*

- *Read each question thoroughly. Don't assume you know what's being asked.*

- *Eliminate implausible answers and move quickly past the obviously wrong choices.*

- *Keep in mind that an answer may be a correct statement in itself but may not answer the question.*

- *Two answers may say exactly the opposite things or may be very similar. Read them again to decide what makes one correct and the other wrong.*

- *ASQ does not subtract points for incorrect answers. Answer every question. There is no penalty for guessing, so you have a minimum 25 percent chance of getting it right, and even higher if you are successful in eliminating one or two of the answers as incorrect.*

- *Go through and answer the questions you know. Then go through and read the ones you're unsure of.*

- *Mark those you are still uncomfortable with. You will narrow the field down to just a few questions you will need to spend more time on. These are the questions you might want to use your reference books for.*

- *Be aware of the time available for the exam and the remaining time as you work through the exam.*

- *Do not select more than one answer for a question. If you do, it will be scored as a "blank." For example, you think that both A and C are correct answers. Select only one answer and use the comment sheet supplied with your test to point out why you think both A and C are correct. Your comments will be reviewed before results are reported.*

Taking an exam (offered by ASQ or any other organization) is a matter of preparation on the participant's part, and your results will show how well you achieved the exam requirements. We have seen people who based on overall education *should* pass an exam not do well, and the other extreme where a person who we thought might struggle but studied very hard actually passed the exam. Study and use your reference materials, and know where and how to find information when you need it. Few people can memorize everything, so the next best thing is knowing how to find information quickly when needed so that you can finish the exam in a timely manner.

The breadth and scope of material within this handbook is based on the current version of the ASQ BoK for Certified Six Sigma Yellow Belt practitioners. When reviewing the material, there are two considerations: coverage and intensity.

Coverage reflects the material in relation to the expected scope of the exam. ASQ has defined for each BoK category the number of questions expected to be present on the exam. It is important to devote the appropriate time to each section in order to ensure proper preparation. Without considering the coverage of the BoK, there is a risk that certain portions will be inadequately addressed in advance of the exam. One practice is to create a matrix on a spreadsheet indicating the BoK items on one axis, and the study progress made for each item on the other. Maintaining such a matrix would clearly indicate those areas where mastery has been achieved, and where more effort is required.

Intensity refers to the learning level specified by ASQ, as referenced by the Bloom's Taxonomy category.

Those topic areas with the highest knowledge levels require additional effort by the examinee to fully master the concepts to sufficiently select or derive the correct response on the exam. Consequently, more effort should be devoted to those BoK items with the highest levels of knowledge, as these will align with the most complicated and time-consuming questions on the exam. For convenience, those items with the highest levels have been included within the following table for extra attention.

The components of the BoK are explained below with two examples. In the Yellow Belt BoK, only two levels of cognition are used: "Understand" and "Apply."

Section	Subsection	Knowledge area	Knowledge item
I. Six Sigma Fundamentals	D. Team basics	1. Types of teams	Identify the various types of teams that operate within an organization (i.e., continuous improvement, self-managed, and cross-functional) and their value. (Understand)
II. Define Phase	A. Project identification	4. Process inputs and outputs	Use SIPOC (suppliers, inputs, process, outputs, customers) to identify and define important elements of a process. (Apply)

Additional guidance for planning for, preparing for, and taking any ASQ Certification exam is available in *Quality Progress* (http://asq.org/quality-progress/2010/01/certification-asq/test-run.html). Exam takers are encouraged to read this publication prior to planning to take an ASQ Certification exam.

Part I
Six Sigma Fundamentals

Chapter 1
A. Six Sigma Foundations and Principles

> Describe the purpose of six sigma (reducing varia-
> tion), its methodology (DMAIC) and its evolution
> from quality. Describe the value of six sigma to the
> organization as a whole. (Understand)
>
> **Body of Knowledge I.A**

PURPOSE OF SIX SIGMA: REDUCING VARIATION

The main purpose of a for-profit organization is to generate money for operating the business and making profits for shareholders. Even the organization that is not for profit (e.g., American Society for Quality [ASQ]) has to generate enough money to cover operational costs and to fund future programs that bring value to customers (i.e., ASQ members). These organizations generate income by offering products and services to customers. There is no guarantee that every product and service delivered to customers will be identical. There is some variability that is inherent to products and services. What if the variability increases to an extent that it affects the customer? Let's look at some different scenarios. If you purchase a gallon of gas and the gas pump dispenses anywhere from three-fourths of a gallon to one gallon, would you find that acceptable? If a healthcare clinic delivers between 0.25 mL and 1 mL of the flu vaccine against the specification of 0.5 mL ± 0.05 mL, would you still get a flu shot from this clinic? While variability is inherent, organizations strive to keep it as low as possible in order to deliver products and services that meet or exceed customer expectations. Highly variable products and services result in poor quality, and the organization must spend money to correct the defect. If an organization spends more than it takes in, it will be out of business. Thus, the challenge for every organization is to become profitable at whatever it does so that it can continue to do what it does. Managers, employees, suppliers, and customers all have their wants and needs that the business must satisfy in an effective and efficient manner so profit can be achieved. Six Sigma as a disciplined methodology for improvement and problem solving helps achieve just that with a focus on the bottom line.

Six Sigma is a structured and disciplined process designed to consistently deliver perfect products and services. It aims to improve the bottom line by finding and eliminating the causes of mistakes and defects in business processes. *Sigma* (σ) is a statistical term that refers to the standard deviation of a process about its mean.

A wide range of companies have found that when the Six Sigma philosophy is fully embraced, the enterprise thrives. What is this Six Sigma philosophy? Several definitions have been proposed. Common threads of these definitions are the following:

- Use of teams that are assigned to well-defined projects that have direct impact on the organization's bottom line.

- Training in statistical thinking at all levels of the organization and providing key people with extensive training in advanced statistics and project management. These key people are designated Black Belts and Master Black Belts.

- Emphasis on the DMAIC approach to problem solving: define, measure, analyze, improve, and control.

- A management environment that supports these initiatives as a business strategy.

Opinions on the definition of Six Sigma differ:

- *Philosophy.* The philosophical perspective views all work as processes that can be defined, measured, analyzed, improved, and controlled. Processes require inputs and produce outputs. If you can control the inputs, you can control the outputs. This is generally expressed as the $y = f(x)$ concept.

- *Set of tools.* Six Sigma as a set of tools includes all the qualitative and quantitative techniques used by the Six Sigma expert to drive process improvement. These tools include statistical process control charts, failure mode and effects analysis, and process mapping. There is probably little agreement among Six Sigma professionals as to what constitutes the tool set, as it continues to evolve.

- *Methodology.* This view of Six Sigma recognizes the underlying and rigorous approach known as DMAIC. DMAIC defines the steps a Six Sigma practitioner is expected to follow, starting with identifying the problem and ending with the implementation of long-lasting solutions. While DMAIC is not the only Six Sigma methodology in use, it is certainly the most widely adopted and recognized structured approach.

- *Metrics.* In simple terms, Six Sigma quality performance means 3.4 defects per million opportunities (accounting for a 1.5-sigma shift in the mean advocated by Motorola).

At this point, Six Sigma purists are quick to say, "You're not just talking about Six Sigma; you're talking about lean too." Today, the demarcation between Six Sigma and lean is blurred. With greater frequency, we are hearing the term "Lean-Six Sigma" because process improvement requires aspects of both approaches to attain positive results.

Six Sigma focuses on reducing process variation and enhancing process control, while lean—originally known as lean manufacturing and now broadly accepted as lean enterprise—drives out waste (non-value-added activities) through value stream mapping and promotes work standardization. Six Sigma practitioners should be well versed in both lean and Six Sigma methodologies. Most practitioners advocate to implement lean first to remove wastes and standardize processes, and then implement Six Sigma to reduce variability and make the process efficient. **Effectiveness before efficiency**.

METHODOLOGY (DMAIC)

The DMAIC model is very similar to the PDCA (Plan-Do-Check-Act) or PDSA (Plan-Do-Study-Act) model that you may already be using. Table 1.1 shows the alignment between these models.

A key factor is for management to provide the time and resources needed to accomplish each phase in striving for continual improvement. This is one of the driving forces that make Six Sigma different from other quality improvement programs. Other driving forces include getting everyone in the organization involved, getting the resources to supply data to everyone more quickly, and getting financial data (e.g., cost of quality [COQ] analysis).

Everyone in the organization will be asked to get involved with the Six Sigma model and to look for continual improvement opportunities in their work areas. Basically, you will do the following in each step:

Define: Identify an issue causing decreased customer satisfaction, a reduced bottom line, safety incidents, supplier quality failure, and so forth

Measure: Collect data from the process and verify the validity of the data

Analyze: Study the process data to identify root cause(s)

Improve: Act on the root causes to change the process for the better

Control: Monitor the system to sustain the gains

A number of tools and methods can be used in each of the steps of the DMAIC model. The list shown in Table 1.2 is only a quick overview of many of these items. More detailed information can be found in the references that focus solely on quality tools. Please refer to the bibliography of this book.

Table 1.1   Mapping of PDCA with Six Sigma DMAIC model

Plan	Define
Plan	Measure
Plan	Analyze
Do/Check	Improve
Act	Control

Table 1.2   Six Sigma tools overview by stage

Tool	Description
Define	
SIPOC (supplier-input-process-output-customer)	Tool to describe and understand a process more clearly. Supplier can also be interpreted as "source of inputs" or "who supplies the inputs," and customer can be interpreted as the "recipient of the outputs."
Is-is not analysis	Tool helpful in defining a problem. Oftentimes, understanding what is not a problem will help the team zero in on areas that are a problem. This saves a significant amount of time during problem solving.
Timeline of events	Tool used to understand the problem through a sequence of events (one event leads to another)
Trend chart	Tool used to understand process trends (favorable and unfavorable) from historical events of data
Run chart	Tool used to understand process patterns from historical data
Process flowchart	Graphical representation of the sequence of interrelated activities
Current state map	A value stream map that represents the current state of a process
GANTT chart	Management of schedule, resources, cost, and risk used in project management
Stakeholder analysis	Tool used to understand the people who are influential to a project and those who offer resistance coupled with their level of involvement in a project
Measure	
Data collection plan	Plan describing what, why, where, when, who, and how of data collection (5W1H). Prior to collecting data, having a detailed collection plan can help make collection more effective.
Measurement systems analysis (MSA)	Analysis of the capability of a measurement system (tools, methods, people, environment, etc.)
Benchmark	Start by setting the current baseline for the process
Process capability	Ability of the process to meet expected output. Often represented by indices Cp and Cpk (the higher the indices, the better).

(continued)

Table 1.2   Six Sigma tools overview by stage *(Continued)*

Tool	Description
Analyze	
Why-why	Method of continuing to ask "why" on a problem symptom until the root cause is reached
Hypothesis tests	Statistical methods to test hypothesis on process improvement
Statistical sampling	Statistically valid sampling (e.g., power and sample size, acceptance sampling)
Improve	
Design of experiments	Tool for understanding cause and effect in a process and for optimizing process variables to achieve improved performance
Future value stream map	Creates a "should be" future state value stream with non-value-added process steps removed
Theory of constraints	Tool for understanding bottlenecks
FMEA	Tool to evaluate potential risk and prioritize actions
Poka-yoke (mistake proofing)	Concept that prevents errors from happening in processes and products by "designing in" controls
Control	
Process behavior chart	Tool to help understand the behavior of a process by analyzing historical patterns and trends
Control plan	Document that provides basic information on what is required to manage a process during the manufacturing or service delivery
Process audit	Tool to verify compliance of a process as per the specification
Cost of quality	A measure that captures the cost of conformance and the cost of nonconformance; often represented as a ratio comparing to the revenue or cost of goods sold of an organization
Tools applicable to all stages	
Brainstorming	Tool (and a process) for collecting inputs and ideas from team members without making any instant judgments
Seven quality tools	Check sheet, histogram, flowchart, cause and effect diagram, Pareto chart, run chart, scatter diagram (see Chapter 5 for a description and application of these tools)

Note: Some tools are applicable in more than one stage of DMAIC (see Table 5.1 in Chapter 5).

Many will find this process very exciting, as they will have the tools and methods to demonstrate the improvements that they are helping the organization to achieve. In the past, when an employee tried to tell a supervisor that something was wrong with a machine or process, the employee had no means to prove his or her claim. Now we have the means to not only tell what needs to be done but also demonstrate it. Following this process creates a road map for continual improvement and, once started, is a never-ending journey. These tools and methods have proven themselves useful just about everywhere: shop floors, front offices, schools, hospitals, churches, and even at home.

EVOLUTION OF SIX SIGMA FROM QUALITY

Organizations are always looking for ways to keep their customers satisfied and loyal. Many different techniques have been employed over the years to keep customers coming back. Unfortunately for many organizations, people's wants and needs change over time, leaving the organization with the challenge of finding new and better ways of satisfying those needs and wants. Organizations need to keep up with the customer's changing needs and expectations. Two organizations come to mind. A very successful market leader in photographic film development technology lost significant market share after the introduction of the digital camera. A successful cellphone company was reduced to a small-time player after the competition introduced innovative smartphones.

Concepts of quality and waste reduction have been in the minds of people for centuries.[1] The idea of setting standards of work goes back more than a century and was the foundation of the guilds and crafts trades that developed over the years. From the mid-1800s to the early 1900s, separation of work was developed to speed up the production process. Innovators like Frederick Taylor and Henry Ford developed ideas and techniques that are still with us today.

Given these new methods of doing business, the quality control/quality assurance (QC/QA) specialist was created to ensure that standards were established and maintained and that customers were satisfied. In many organizations, however, this also created a separation of tasks, and many people in organizations came to think of the responsibility of satisfying customers as in the hands of those in the QC/QA departments instead of in the hands of the people who actually made the product or provided the service. This was especially true in the United States during the 1950s, 1960s, and 1970s as managers looked for better ways to manage all the resources of the organization. Even today, many organizations still struggle with meeting customer satisfaction.

In the mid-1920s a young engineer named Walter A. Shewhart devised a technique of using graphs to monitor a process to determine whether the process was acting in a predictable manner or whether what he termed "special causes" were affecting the process. These charts became known as quality control charts; today we sometimes call them statistical process control charts or process behavior charts, as we want to look at what the process is doing in relation to statistical probabilities. Many other tools and techniques have been developed since then; these are summarized in Table 1.3.

Table 1.3   Approaches to quality over the years.

Quality approach	Approximate time frame	Short description
Company wide quality control (CWQC)	1960–1980	Introduced by Ishikawa from Japan. Quality is applicable to the entire organization, not just to products.
Quality circles	1979–1981	Quality improvement or self-sustaining improvement study groups composed of a small number of employees (10 or fewer mostly from the shop floor) and their supervisor. Quality circles originated in Japan, where they are called "quality control circles."
Total quality management (TQM)	1980–present	Management approach to long-term success through customer satisfaction.
Statistical process control (SPC)	Mid-1980s	The application of statistical techniques to control a process. Also called "statistical quality control."
ISO 9000 series of quality management systems	1987–present	A set of international standards on quality management and quality assurance developed to help companies effectively document the quality system elements to be implemented to maintain an efficient quality system. The standards, initially published in 1987, are not specific to any particular industry, product, or service. The standards were developed by the International Organization for Standardization (ISO), a specialized international agency for standardization composed of the national standards bodies of 162 member countries. The standards underwent revisions and amendment in 1994, 2000, 2008, and 2015. Related standards include ISO 9000:2015 (definitions), ISO 9001:2015 (requirements), and ISO 9004:2009 (Managing for sustained success).
Baldrige Award criteria	1987–present	An award established by the US Congress in 1987 to raise awareness of quality management and recognize US companies that have implemented successful quality management systems. Awards are given annually in each of the following categories: business, education, healthcare, and nonprofit. The award is named after the late secretary of commerce Malcolm Baldrige, a proponent of quality management. The US Commerce Department's National Institute of Standards and Technology manages the award, and ASQ administers it.
Benchmarking	1988–1996	An improvement process in which a company measures its performance against that of best-in-class companies, determines how those companies achieved their performance levels, and uses the information to improve its own performance. The categories that can be benchmarked include strategies, project, process, products, etc.

Table 1.3 Approaches to quality over the years. *(Continued)*

Quality approach	Approximate time frame	Short description
Balanced scorecard	1990s–present	A management concept that helps managers at all levels monitor their results in key areas.
Six Sigma	1995–present	A structured approach to improvement and problem solving that provides heavy emphasis on business bottom line and sustainability.
Business process reengineering	1996–1997	A breakthrough approach involving the restructuring of an entire organization and its processes.
Lean manufacturing	2000–present	Inspired by Toyota Production System, companies worldwide started to pay attention to process fundamentals of reducing waste, standardization, employee empowerment, etc. This approach works in tandem with Six Sigma.

VALUE OF SIX SIGMA TO THE ORGANIZATION AS A WHOLE

Significance of Six Sigma

"Six Sigma" is just the latest term for the more general concept of continual improvement. Continual improvement can be defined as the use of problem-solving techniques and quick deployment to implement improvements, followed by the use of process behavioral studies to maintain the gains.[2] Six Sigma has been described as a breakthrough system[3] and is used in many organizations today in a variety of applications. Basically, Six Sigma is about collecting data on a process and using that data to analyze and interpret what is happening in the process so that it can be improved to satisfy the customer's requirements.[4] A basic process can be defined as an input, transformation, and output.

Six Sigma was first started at Motorola and was then further developed at General Electric into more of what we know today. Among practitioners, Six Sigma is referred to as "TQM on steroids." By following a prescribed process, the entire organization starts to look at everything it does in the light of reducing variation and reducing waste, with the result of increasing customer satisfaction. Customers could be anyone—from the next person who uses the work we do (internal customer) to the end customer, who uses the products or services that our organization produces (external customer). To assist in this process, the supplier and the customer are added to the basic process definition listed earlier, creating the SIPOC identification: *supplier, input, process, output, customer*. This is used especially to help define the boundaries of what is to be studied. (Some organizations prefer COPIS over SIPOC. Their rationale is that requirements start with putting the customer first.)

For some, the idea of improving a process is a waste of time that should not be bothered with ("We are already working as hard as we can"). But as Joseph Juran once said, "Changes creep up on us week by week, a little bit at a time. Over a year or two, there are 50 or 100 of these bits, which amounts to quite a bit. The skills of the people have not necessarily kept pace, and we wake up to the existence of a wide gap."[5] This is one explanation for why accidents and product rejections happen in our shops. If the root cause is found for any accident or rejection of product or service, it can usually be traced back to many small changes that occurred either within our own organization or at our supplier. We may or may not see these changes. Mostly we tend to ignore them as trivial.

By using Six Sigma methodologies, we will be able to find those bits of changes and determine which ones require process improvement and which ones need to be corrected and controlled. This process is not a magic bullet approach, nor is it meant to be a quick fix. Logical use of the tools over time will save us resources and effort in doing our daily jobs.

A Six Sigma Yellow Belt's Role

As a Six Sigma Yellow Belt, you are new to the world of Six Sigma. You may play a relatively small yet important role in the Six Sigma implementation. You may be interested in strengthening your foundational knowledge. Six Sigma Yellow Belts can be entry-level employees seeking to improve their knowledge or management executives who require an overview of Six Sigma and DMAIC in order to offer support as sponsors or champions. Note that the role of Six Sigma Yellow Belt may vary between organizations.

You may already be familiar with several of the tools and methods used in this problem-solving process, and a few may be new to you. You may very well ask, "How is this any different from what we have been doing?" This will need to be answered by your organization depending on the various programs that have already been tried. For many of us, this process will be part of an ongoing evolution of how we do our work. One of the main things that you should notice is that top management will be more involved with your problem-solving efforts and in the everyday problems found in your work areas. This involvement may be either sponsorship or even participation where appropriate.

You may already have control plans, process sheets, standard operating procedures, or any number of other tools that you use in your daily work. The Six Sigma model for improvement should not replace anything that you are currently doing, but it should be used to review daily work and to look for areas where the process can be improved in light of what your customers want and need. Just because you are doing the same things that you have always done, is that what your customers want?

We are entering a journey of continual improvement that involves not only our work but our lives. Some of us have been on this journey for some time, while others may be just starting. Through the Six Sigma methodology and by using the Six Sigma model for improvement, we should see things around us work better and satisfy our customers more.

Potential Tasks

Your organization may already be using Six Sigma or some other method (e.g., quality operating system [QOS], continuous improvement [CI], TQM, or "your company name" production system). As a process operator, you will be asked by your supervisor or management to help implement improvement of the process or processes you work with. Your challenge will be to look at the process for simple improvements that can be made (preventive maintenance, cleanliness, replacement of worn-out parts, and so on), as well as assist in measuring certain factors of the process in order to find better ways of performing the process.

You may be expected to use the tools in this book, and possibly tools in other books, to study your work and processes for improvement ideas and to implement those ideas. You may already be familiar with some of these tools, and the challenge will be how to use them, possibly in new ways, to make changes that will help your company stay in business in today's fiercely competitive world. We no longer compete against others within just our own country, but against others from countries around the world. How can we compete with our competitors in other countries that can manufacture product or provide service faster, better, and at a lower cost than we can? This is the question that should be on your team's mind.

Ishikawa gave us a road map to follow when first looking at a process that needs to be improved. The words may not make much sense right now, but as you work with process improvement, you will come to understand the importance of what is said here:

1. Determine the assurance unit (what is to be measured)

2. Determine the measuring method (how it will be measured)

3. Determine the relative importance of quality characteristics (is this key to our process?)

4. Arrive at a consensus on defects and flaws (does everyone agree on good and bad quality?)

5. Expose latent defects (look at the process over time)

6. Observe quality statistically (use process behavior charting)

7. Distinguish between "quality of design" and "quality of conformance"

After we know what we can change (quality of conformance) and what we cannot change right now (quality of design—this is left to Design for Six Sigma [DFSS]), we can start working on our processes. Some operators initially view this effort as only more work, but find that doing these studies actually saves them a lot of time and grief in the future as things start to improve and machines start to work better. Questions to ask yourself now are, How often does your process slow down or stop due to something not working the way it should? and Is the output ever scrapped by someone down the line (including at your external customers) because something was missed or processed incorrectly at your operation?

Be willing to experiment with the tools and look for ways of applying them to the work and processes to learn as much as you can about how a process operates. This will allow you to modify it as appropriate and give the customer the best possible output.

The Six Sigma Road Map

As we prepare for the Six Sigma journey, here is a quick view of the suggested map we should follow:

1. Recognize that variation exists in everything that we do; standardize your work.

2. Identify what the customer wants and needs. Reduce variation.

3. Use a problem-solving methodology to plan improvements.

4. Follow the DMAIC model to deploy the improvement.

5. Monitor the process using process behavior charts.

6. Update standard operating procedures and lessons learned.

7. Celebrate successes.

8. Start over for continual improvement.

QUESTIONS

1. Structured problem solving and continual improvement approaches like PDCA have been around since the 1950s. The 1980s and 1990s saw the introduction of many new approaches and methodologies like TQM and business process reengineering. How did an improvement methodology like Six Sigma become the mantra of management and the most widely accepted methodology by organizations?

2. Research the common criticisms of Six Sigma and prepare your position. You may support the criticisms or counterargue with your viewpoint. Ask your audience to weigh in.

Chapter 2
B. Lean Foundations and Principles

Describe the purpose of lean (waste elimination) and its methodologies (just-in-time, poka-yoke, kanban, value-stream mapping). Describe the value of lean to the organization as a whole. (Understand)

Body of Knowledge I.B

PURPOSE OF LEAN

The purpose of lean is to reduce waste in the value stream and provide maximum value to our customers; that is, do more with less. Over the years we have adopted many industry practices that emphasize maximizing output from our investment (like machinery) or from the people we employ. We have not considered whether such outputs are required by our customers at the level of quality and in the quantity they want. We have produced goods that piled up in inventories. Production managers were rewarded for overproduction. Sales managers were pressured to sell the inventories. Gullible customers fell for the marketing ploy and purchased the product only to realize that it was not what they wanted. We ended up with a society that oversupplied products that were undervalued by consumers. There were no winners. Lean concepts address all these weaknesses in the traditional business model and industry practices and provide methodologies that will bring the utmost value to our customers and ensure the organization is economically sustainable.

Value Stream

A *value stream* is the series of activities that an organization performs, such as order, design, produce, and deliver products and services. A value stream often starts from a supplier's supplier and ends at the customer's customer. Wastes are both explicit and hidden along a value stream.

There are three main components of a value stream:

1. **The flow of materials** from receipt of supplier material to delivery of finished goods and services to customers. Examples:

   — Raw material shipped weekly (or at periodic intervals) from supplier to the organization by truck

   — Movement of material from raw material storage to production process through to finished goods warehouse

   — Shipping of the finished goods to overseas customer via customs

2. **The transformation** of raw materials into finished goods, or inputs into outputs. Example:

   — Production steps like cutting, shaping, forging, welding, polishing, and assembly

3. **The flow of information** required to support the flow of materials and transformation of goods and services. Example:

   — Purchase order to supplier, internal work order, shipping notice

This concept is visually illustrated with a lean tool called the value stream map. This map uses simple graphics and icons to illustrate the movement of material, information, inventory, work-in-progress, operators, and so on. Value stream mapping is a simple yet powerful tool. The analysis subsequent to value stream mapping—value stream analysis—can help uncover hidden wastes within the organization. An organization that effectively uses lean thinking and applies lean tools to reduce waste throughout the value stream and offer value to its customers is a *lean enterprise* organization.

Becoming a lean enterprise requires a change in people's attitudes, procedures, processes, and systems. It is necessary to zoom out and look at the flow of information, knowledge, and material throughout the organization. In any organization there are multiple paths through which products, documents, and ideas flow. The process of applying lean thinking to such a path can be divided into the following steps:

1. Walk the process. Go to the gemba (workplace) and produce a value stream map. This is also referred to as a value chain diagram. It has boxes labeled with each step in the process. Information about timing and inventory is provided next to each process box. Figure 2.1 shows some of the symbols used in value stream maps. Figure 2.2 shows an example of a value stream map.

2. Analyze all inventory notes with an eye toward reduction or elimination. Inventory tends to increase costs because:

   — Storage space may be expensive (rubber awaiting use in a tire factory is stored at 120°F; wood inventory may need to be humidity-controlled).

   — Quality may deteriorate (rust, spoilage, etc.).

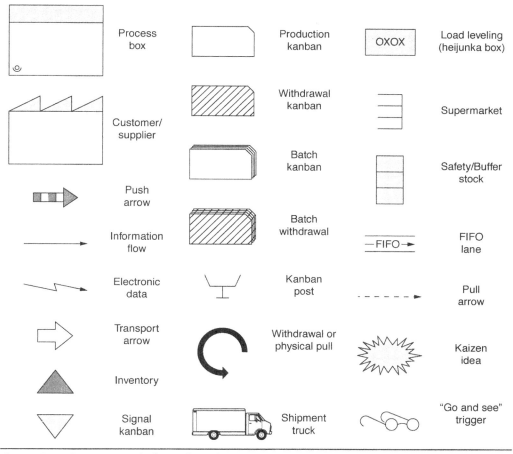

Figure 2.1   Common symbols used in value stream mapping.

— Design changes may be delayed as they work their way through the inventory.

— Money sitting in inventory could be used more productively elsewhere (locked cash).

— Quality problems that are not detected until a later stage in the process will be more expensive to correct if an inventory of defective products has accumulated.

3. Analyze the entire value stream for wasteful steps. These steps are called non-value-added activities and are discussed in detail later in this chapter.

4. Determine how the flow is driven. Strive to move toward value streams in which production decisions are based on the pull of customer demand. In a process where pull-based flow has reached perfection,

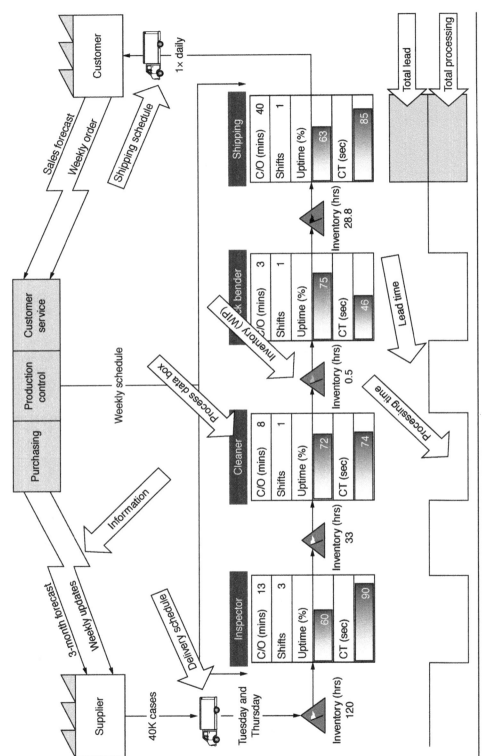

Figure 2.2 Value stream map example.

a customer order for an item will trigger the production of all the component parts for that item.

5. Extend the value stream map upstream into suppliers' plants. When beginning the process, identify a manageable scope with boundaries. The flows of information, material, knowledge, and money are all potential targets for lean improvements.

LEAN METHODOLOGIES

5S

5S is a workplace organization method that can help improve the efficiency and management of operations (see Figure 2.3). 5S is the simplest and most practical improvement that an individual or organization can start with. It requires few or no resources, yet the payback can be impressive from the day of implementation.

A process is impacted by its environment, as is the ability of personnel to visually recognize and respond to process changes. Improvements in the general state of the work area, including access to hand tools, are an aid to process control. Especially critical here are the cleanliness, lighting, and general housekeeping status of any area where measurements are conducted, since process control data are filtered through the measurement system.

A workbench cluttered with tools and accessories wastes the valuable time of skilled workers and causes distraction from work, resulting in poor quality and safety incidents. Similarly, an office table covered with disorganized files and papers can cause clerical errors and delays in processing. 5S is one of the first tools to apply on the path to becoming a lean enterprise organization.

5S and other Toyota Production System methodologies that have helped organizations reduce waste and create value are not limited to manufacturing. The healthcare industry has also taken notice of the lean methodologies and has begun to apply them to improve stakeholder value.[1]

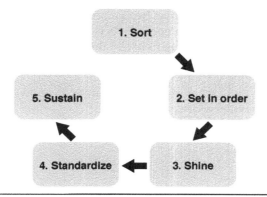

Figure 2.3   The 5S cycle.

The sequence for 5S is as follows:

Sort. Remove unneeded items. Be it in the office or home, we tend to collect items that are very rarely needed or not needed at all. Over a period of time these items accumulate into a mess and make it more difficult to search for needed items, sometimes even causing safety issues. The first step is to sort through the items as required and clean up the work area. Never-used items should be discarded immediately.

Set in order. Arrange the required and rarely required items for ease of accessibility. Items that are required more often, like drawings, instructions, tools, safety goggles, and so on, are placed in designated and marked locations so that they cannot be placed elsewhere—in short, **a place for everything and everything in its place**. Rarely required items, like machine manuals, shop floor layout plans, and so on, can be kept in an out-of-the-way area.

Shine. This involves cleaning the work area and equipment. As simple as this may sound, many quality issues are uncovered through effective cleaning of the work area. For example, cleaning the inspection surface plate provides better measurement results, cleaning the equipment work table provides for better movement, and cleaning the floor helps prevent accidents from oil spills. For some industries, such as semiconductor manufacturing, cleanliness is mandatory and is measured in particle count. Excessive particles in the air beyond the allowable limit could result in poor process yield or, even worse, reliability failure in the field.

Standardize. This involves developing checklists (including a checklist for 5S itself—see Figure 2.4), standards, and work instructions to keep the work area clean and orderly. Standardization involves tools, processes, people skills, materials, and operating environment. Standardization helps reduce variability.

Sustain. This is the most difficult step in 5S. Most organizations are initially successful with the first four steps, but sustaining the efforts requires support from management and empowerment of employees. Management needs to realize that this is time well spent and should be willing to invest the time. The time invested in 5S improves productivity and overall efficiency, and reduces accidents. Management should also empower the employees by allowing them to take ownership of their work areas. Empowered employees take pride in their work.

The 5S methodology can be further improved to include employee and customer safety (Figure 2.5).

Visual Factory

A visual factory provides visual identification of the status of material and information throughout the value stream. Examples of a visual factory include providing the status of material in/out at a raw material warehouse; showing units

Category	Item	Rating level					Remarks
		L0	L1	L2	L3	L4	
Sort (Organization)	Distinguish between what is needed and not needed						
	Unneeded equipment, tools, furniture, and so on, are present						
	Unneeded items are on walls, bulletin boards, and so on						
	Items are present in aisles, stairways, corners, and so on						
	Unneeded inventory, supplies, arts, or materials are present						
	Safety hazards (water, oil, chemical, machines) exist						
Set in Order (Orderliness)	A place for everything and everything in its place						
	Correct places for items are not obvious						
	Items are not in their places						
	Aisles, workstations, equipment locations are not indicated						
	Items are not put away immediately after use						
	Height and quantity limits are not obvious						
Shine (Cleanliness)	Cleaning and looking for ways to keep it clean and organized						
	Floors, walls, stairs, and surfaces are not free of dirt, oil, and grease						
	Equipment is not kept clean and free of dirt, oil, and grease						
	Cleaning materials are not easily accessible						
	Lines, labels, signs, and so on are not clean and unbroken						
	Other cleaning problems of any kind are present						
Standardize (Adherence)	Maintain and monitor the first three categories						
	Necessary information is not visible						
	All standards are not known and visible						
	Checklists don't exist for cleaning and maintenance jobs						
	All quanitities and limits are not easily recognizable						
	How many items can't be located in 30 seconds?						
Sustain (Self-discipline)	Stick to the rules						
	How many workers have not had 5S training?						
	How many times, last week, was daily 5S not performed?						
	Number of times that personal belongings are not neatly stored						
	Number of times job aids are not available or up to date						
	Number of times, last week, daily 5S inspections not performed						
	TOTAL						

Number of problems	3 or more	3–4	2	1	None
Rating level	Level 0 (L0)	Level 1 (L1)	Level 2 (L2)	Level 3 (L3)	Level 4 (L4)

Figure 2.4   5S workplace scan diagnostic checklist.

Source: Jack B. ReVelle, *Quality Essentials: A Reference Guide from A to Z* (Milwaukee, WI: ASQ Quality Press, 2004), 56–58, quoted in ASQ, "Five S (5S) Tutorial," http://asq.org/learn-about-quality/lean/overview/five-s-tutorial.html.

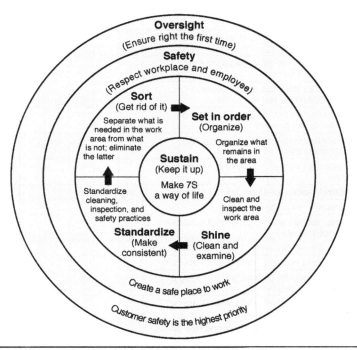

Figure 2.5 The 7S adaptation (Hirano).

Source: H. Hirano, *5 Pillars of the Visual Workplace: The Sourcebook for 5S Implementation* (Portland, OR: Productivity, Inc., 1995).

produced, units needed to complete order, and total produced by shift or day on a production display board; and indicating status with red, yellow, and green lights on the machine (Figure 2.6). Imagine that we need to find out the current status of a work order for a given customer. Often this is achieved by talking to line supervisors, referring to logbooks, conducting internal meetings, and so on. This may take anywhere from several minutes to several hours.

In a visual factory, an employee can walk onto the shop floor and tell which machines are running, what product is being produced, and how many more are to be produced (by customer); follow posted safety instructions; and report to management. This is an effective visual workplace.

Part #	A1308
Model #	1705
Planned for the week	5000
Complete	3800
Balance to reach goal	1200

Figure 2.6 Visual factory.

Kaizen versus Kaizen Event (Kaikaku)

Kaizen is a Japanese term meaning "change for improvement," or improving processes through small, incremental steps. Breakthrough improvement is referred to by another Japanese term, kaikaku.

Kaikaku is referred to in North America as a kaizen event or kaizen blitz. Hence, many practitioners are often confused by the interchangeable usage of "kaizen" and "kaizen event." In lean implementation, kaizen events are used to provide quicker implementation results. Kaizen events are conducted by assembling a cross-functional team for three to five days and reviewing all possible options for improvement in a breakthrough effort. Management support is required for such initiatives. If the employees can't afford to take three to five days to improve a process constraint, then either the problem is unimportant or the organization requires more fundamental cultural adjustment before implementing lean.

Pull System

The pull system is a vital component of the just-in-time (JIT) concept and lean implementation. Traditionally, organizations have produced more than the customer wants and have stored the excess as inventory or work in progress; finished goods tended to be pushed to the next process. This was done with the idea of optimizing the subprocess and not looking at the value stream as a whole. In a pull system, the process produces only when there is a pull from the subsequent process. This is signaled as either an empty bin or a kanban card. The pull system links accurate information with the process to minimize waiting and overproduction.

Just-in-Time

JIT is an inventory strategy that provides for the delivery of material or product at the exact time and place where it will be used. When this material requirements planning system is implemented, there is a reduction of in-process inventory and its related costs (such as inventory carrying cost and warehouse space rental cost), which in turn can dramatically increase the return on investment, quality, and efficiency of an organization.

By implementing JIT, buffer stock is eliminated or reduced, and new stock is ordered when stock reaches the reorder level (facilitated by the use of kanban cards/signals).

Kanban

A system is best controlled when material and information flow into and out of the process in a smooth and rational manner. If process inputs arrive before they are needed, unnecessary confusion, inventory, and costs generally occur. If process outputs are not synchronized with downstream processes, delays and associated costs may occur and customers may be disappointed. A properly administered kanban system will improve system control by ensuring timely movement of products and information. Kanban is implemented using a visual indicator called kanban cards. The card indicates the quantity to be replenished once the minimum level is reached.

An empty bin with a kanban card (can be either a physical card or digital information) is the signal for production to pull material from the previous step. Kanban works with the pull system to deliver customer demand. The kanban quantity is mathematically calculated and fine-tuned during practical implementation. It usually takes a while for the organization to perfect the kanban. Kanban is a more mature concept than the other lean methodologies. It is important that other fundamentals of lean (5S, standard work, total productive maintenance [TPM], and variation reduction) be put in place before venturing into kanban. If not, frequent equipment failure and unstable or inconsistent processes will defeat the purpose of kanban, resulting in huge kanban sizes to shield against these uncertainties.

Poka-Yoke

Poka-yoke, a Japanese term for mistake proofing or error proofing, is a method used to prevent errors. There are a number of examples in daily life that use the mistake-proofing concept, such as electrical outlets that prevent plugging an electrical cord in the wrong way (Figure 2.7), valves that shut once the maximum pressure is reached, and fixtures that prevent loading the component in a wrong orientation. A window envelope is also a mistake-proofing method that allows users to see that the letter has the right address. Similarly, detection-type mistake proofing alerts a user immediately after an error is made (to prevent further errors), for example, an alert that sounds if the driver forgets to turn off a car's headlights, and an automatic gauging machine that sounds an alarm when an oversized or undersized part is produced.

Standard Work

Standard work is a tool that defines the interaction between personnel and machine in producing a part. It has three components: standard time, standard inventory, and standard sequence. Standard work helps in training new operators and reducing the variation in the process.

The basic idea is to make manufacturing methods and/or service processes consistent. Quality management systems like ISO 9001 provide a basic foundation

Instead of a spoon, which can measure too little or too much medicine, a fixed dose packet delivers an exact measurement every time, with the empty packet as evidence of use.

Three-pin design prevents incorrect insertion of plug.

Figure 2.7   Examples of mistake proofing.

for lean implementation by incorporating standard work as part of the controlled documentation. Further, by having standard work, equipment, tools, layout, methods, and materials are standardized and thus reduce variation in processes. A detailed process work instruction with all of the above can be a very useful standard work document. Standard work aligns with the 5S step "standardize."

VALUE OF LEAN TO THE ORGANIZATION

The single most important concept that has been brought to awareness in the business community in recent years is value. Value is defined by the customer based on their perception of the usefulness and necessity of a given product or service.

Once the concept of value is understood, the target cost for the product or service can be determined. According to Womack, Jones, and Roos, the target cost is a mixture of current selling prices of competitors and examination of elimination of waste by lean methods.[2]

Lean experts define a process step as value-added if:

- The customer recognizes the value

- It changes (transforms) the product

- It is done right the first time

Some activities perform functions that do not change the form or function of the product or service, and the customer is not willing to pay for these activities. These activities are labeled non-value-added. A classic example is rework. For example, the customer expects to pay for the printing of a document, but does not want to pay for corrections caused by errors of the supplier. A key step in making an organization lean is the detection and elimination of non-value-added activities.

In searching for non-value-added activities, the operative guideline should be "question everything." Steps that are assumed to be necessary are often ripe with opportunities for improvement. Team members not associated with a process will often provide a fresh perspective. This helps address the response "This is the way we've always done it."

There are, of course, gray areas where the line between value-added and non-value-added is not obvious. One such area is inspection and testing. A process may be so incapable that its output needs to be inspected to prevent defective parts from entering downstream processes. It could be argued that this inspection is a value-added activity because the customer doesn't want defective products. The obvious solution is to work on the process, making it capable and rendering the inspection activity unnecessary. Most authorities would agree that this inspection is non-value-added. On the other hand, an electrical product manufacturer must conduct a safety test for every product in order to comply with regulatory requirements. Customers are willing to pay for the product safety certifications, so this test step is a value-added activity.

Case studies from ASQ's Knowledge Center (http://asq.org/knowledge-center/case-studies) and from the organizations that I have been involved with in value stream mapping have shown that an overwhelming proportion of lead time is non-value-added, much of it spent waiting for the next step. Yet efforts to decrease lead time over the years have often focused on accelerating value-added functions rather than reducing or eliminating non-value-added functions.

Waste (Muda)

Categories of waste, or *muda* as it is referred to in some sources, include overproduction, excess motion, waiting, inventory, excess movement of material, defect correction (rework), excess processing, and lost creativity (underutilization of resource skills).

Overproduction

Overproduction is defined as making more than is needed or making it earlier or faster than is needed by the next process; its principal symptom is excess work-in-progress (WIP). Companies adopt overproduction for various reasons including long setup times, unbalanced workload, and a just-in-case philosophy. One company maintains a six-month supply of a particular small part because the machine that produces it is unreliable. In some cases accounting methods have dictated that machines overproduce to amortize their capital costs. In some organizations, overproduction is attributed to utilization of labor. All WIP should be continuously scrutinized for possible reduction or elimination.

Excess Motion

Excess motion is caused by poor workplace layout, including awkward positioning of supplies and equipment. This results in ergonomic problems, safety incidents, time wasted searching for supplies or equipment, and reduced quality levels. Kaizen events are effectively used to focus a small short-term team on improvements in a particular work area. The team must include employees from the impacted process. In addition, it is essential to include people with the authority to make decisions.

Waiting

Waiting is typically caused by such events as delayed shipments, long setup times, or an insufficient amount of people to provide service. It results in a waste of resources and, perhaps more importantly, demoralization of personnel. Setup time reduction efforts and total productive maintenance are partial answers to this problem. Cross-training of personnel so that they can be effectively moved to other positions is also helpful in some cases. Carefully planned and executed scheduling is key to addressing this waste.

Inventory

When inventories of raw materials, finished goods, or WIP are maintained, costs are incurred for environmental control, record keeping, storage and retrieval, and so on. These functions add no value for the customer. Of course, some inventory may be necessary, but if an organization finds a way to reduce costs by reducing inventory, it may be able to reduce overall cost. One of the most tempting times to let inventory levels rise is when a business cycle is in the economic recovery phase. Instead of increasing inventories based on forecasts, the proper strategy is to synchronize production to increase with actual demand. Similarly, production or administrative functions that use more space or other resources than necessary increase costs without adding value. The common analogy of the sea of inventory, shown in Figure 2.8, illustrates how excess inventory prevents the solution of other problems. As the level of inventory is lowered, some problems will rear their ugly heads and need to be solved before further progress is possible.

Excess Movement of Material

Large conveyor systems, huge fleets of forklifts, and so on, make production costly and complex, and often reduce quality through handling and storing. Poor plant layout is usually to blame. Plants with function-oriented departments (all drilling machines together, all polishing machines together, and so on) require excessive material movement. A better plan is to gather equipment together that is used

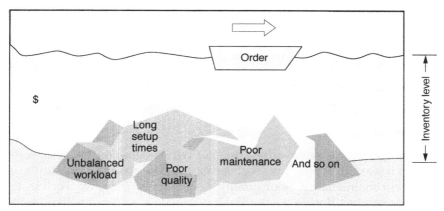

a) The order floats through the system protected from unresolved problems by excess inventory.

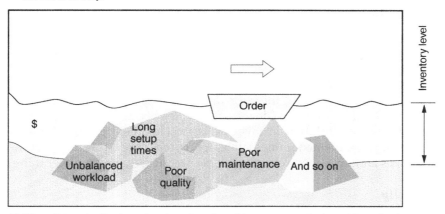

b) When the protective inventory is reduced, problems emerge that must be solved. To reduce costs, we must fix the problems.

Figure 2.8 A sea of inventory often hides unresolved problems.

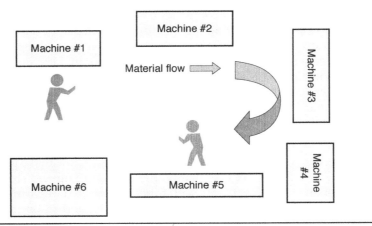

Figure 2.9   C-shaped manufacturing cell.

for one product or product family. This may mean having a manufacturing cell that contains several types of equipment, requiring personnel with multiple skills. Many companies have had success with cells that form a C or U shape, as shown in Figure 2.9, because they can be staffed in several ways. If demand for the cell's output is high, six people could be assigned, one per machine. If demand is very low, one person could move from machine to machine, producing parts one at a time.

Defect Correction

Correcting defects is a non-value-added activity because the effort to fix the defective part is wasted. Typical causes of defects are poor process capability, inadequate equipment maintenance, poor quality system, poor training/work instructions, and poor product design. Lean thinking demands a vigorous look at these and other causes in order to continuously reduce defect levels.

Excess Processing

Extra processing is often difficult to recognize. Sometimes entire steps in the value chain are non-value-added. For example, a steel stamping operation produces a large volume of parts before they are scheduled for painting. This may require the parts to be dipped in an oil solution to prevent rust as they wait to be painted. As the paint schedule permits, the parts are degreased and painted. The customer is unwilling to pay for the dip/degrease activities because they do not enhance the product. The best solution in this case is to schedule the pre-paint activities so that the parts are painted immediately upon production. This may require smaller batch sizes and improved communication procedures, among other things.

Lost Creativity

Lost creativity is perhaps the most unfortunate waste. Most manufacturing employees have ideas that would improve processes if implemented. Standard organizational structures sometimes seem designed to suppress such ideas. Lean thinking recognizes the need to involve employees in teams that welcome and reward their input. These teams must be empowered to make changes in an atmosphere that accepts mistakes as learning experiences. The resulting improved morale and reduced personnel turnover help the bottom line. These are the nontangible benefits of lean thinking.

Once all the different types of wastes are addressed in the process, lean implementation aims for perfection.

Perfection

By now you should understand value-added activities. You also learned about various wastes both hidden and explicit in processes. By optimizing value-added activities and eliminating waste, your organization can aim toward achieving "perfection" in lean. This is not a onetime effort. This is a continual learning process.

QUESTIONS

1. If you were to make a major purchase such as a new home, a solar electric system, or an automobile, how would you, as a consumer, perceive value?

2. Explain why "going to the gemba" is an important step before developing a value stream map.

3. Describe how the 5S tool can be applied in an office setting to improve productivity.

4. Identify examples of everyday poka-yoke that you have come across.

5. Describe how "standard work" plays an important role in lean implementation.

Chapter 3
C. Six Sigma Roles and Responsibilities

> Define and describe the roles and responsibilities of six sigma team members (i.e., individual team members, yellow belt, green belt, black belt, master black belt, process owner, champion, sponsor). (Understand)
>
> **Body of Knowledge I.C**

Six Sigma successes are not just about application of statistical tools. A strong Six Sigma organization is necessary for sustainable success. Without this, there will be no accountability to the investment made in employees in terms of training, resources spent, and a consistent approach of methodologies. Smaller organizations may combine some Six Sigma roles; however, the responsibilities of each role should be maintained. A typical large Six Sigma organization is shown in Figure 3.1.

One factor that has helped Six Sigma be successful is the structure it demands of organizations. Table 3.1 shows typical Six Sigma roles, the organizational members that typically fill the roles, their expected training or background, and the primary responsibilities of each role.

Organizations may employ program managers to assist the Master Black Belts in managing the overall Six Sigma implementation across the organization. The organization's finance department may also play a role by verifying the benefits claimed by the projects before the projects are presented to management.

QUESTIONS

1. You have been assigned to set up a Six Sigma organization for a company with fewer than 100 employees. Understanding that not every organization can afford a structure as identified in Figure 3.1, how would you structure your Six Sigma resources? What roles would you have? What will be their responsibilities?

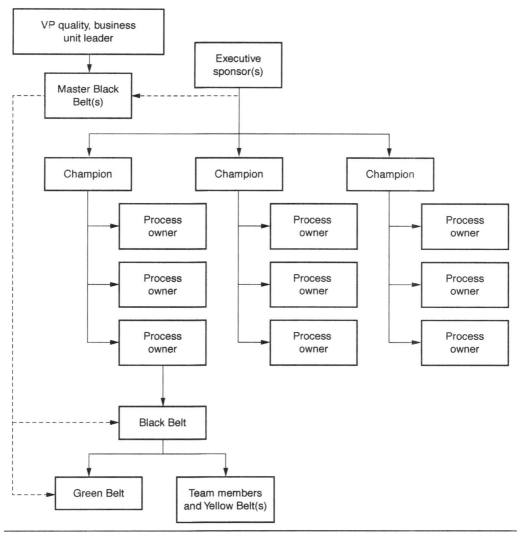

Figure 3.1 Typical large Six Sigma organization.

2. How do you ensure the continuity of the Six Sigma organization? Make recommendations.

3. What are the challenges of sustaining Six Sigma improvement projects without Six Sigma resources?

Table 3.1 Typical Six Sigma roles.

Role	Candidate	Training/background	Primary responsibilities
Executive sponsor	Business unit leader responsible for profit and loss (usually at director level or above)	Six Sigma concepts, strategies, overview, operational definitions.	• Set direction and priorities for the Six Sigma organization • Allocate resources for projects • Set Six Sigma vision and overall objectives for the program • Monitor the progress of the overall program • Initiate incentive programs • Reward successful projects
Champion	Typically upper-level managers	Six Sigma concepts, strategies, tools and methods, operational definitions. Emphasis on management tools. (ASQ Certified Six Sigma Yellow Belt)	• Liaise with senior management • Allocate resources for projects • Determine project selection criteria • Remove barriers hindering the success of the project • Approve completed projects • Implement change
Process owner	An individual responsible and accountable for the execution and results of a given process. The sponsor or champion could also be a process owner.	Six Sigma concepts, strategies, tools and methods, operational definitions. Emphasis on statistical tools. (ASQ Certified Six Sigma Yellow Belt)	• Select team members • Allocate resources for projects • Provide process knowledge • Review process changes • Approve changes/support change management • Implement change • Ensure that improvements are sustained

Table 3.1 Typical Six Sigma roles. *(Continued)*

Role	Candidate	Training/background	Primary responsibilities
Master Black Belt	Individuals trained in Six Sigma methodologies, statistical tools, basic financial tools, change management, risk assessment, project management, executive communication, and well experienced in teaching, coaching, and mentoring Black Belts and Green Belts. This is always a full-time position.	Six Sigma BoK, lean enterprise synergy, finance for nonfinancial managers, risk assessment, project management, change agent skills, Master Black Belt train the trainer, presentation skills, communication skills, leadership skills, facilitation skills. (ASQ Certified Six Sigma Master Black belt)	• Coach Six Sigma Black Belts and Green Belts • Utilize the resources provided by management effectively • Formulate overall business strategy linking to Six Sigma program • Monitor project progress closely • Typically 15–20 projects overseen at a time • Provide coaching, mentoring for new Black Belts and Green Belts • Work with champions and process owners for selection of projects • Address issues of project stagnation • Remove barriers hindering the success of the project • Support as a subject matter expert for the organization • Review and approve completed projects • Share lessons learned with the extended team • Provide inputs to rewards committee
Black Belt	Individuals trained in Six Sigma methodologies, statistical tools, basic financial tools, change management, risk assessment, project management, and well experienced in managing Black Belt projects. This is always a full-time position.	Six Sigma Black Belt Body of Knowledge, lean enterprise synergy, finance for nonfinancial managers, risk assessment, project management, change agent skills, presentation skills, communication skills, leadership and facilitation skills. (ASQ Certified as Six Sigma Black Belt)	• Lead and manage Six Sigma projects • Utilize the resources provided by management effectively • Provide net present value, return on investment (ROI), payback calculations on projects • Work full-time on four to six projects per year • Monitor project progress closely • Follow DMAIC process, apply appropriate statistical methods • Work with champions, Master Black Belts, and process owners for selection of projects • Address issues of project stagnation/consult Master Black Belt • Remove barriers hindering the success of the project • Update and present project progress to management • Review completed projects • Share lessons learned with the extended team

(continued)

Table 3.1 Typical Six Sigma roles. *(Continued)*

Role	Candidate	Training/background	Primary responsibilities
Green Belt	Individuals trained in Six Sigma methodologies, basic statistical tools, and process improvement techniques. This is typically a full-time position. However, some organizations make this part of an existing job responsibility.	Six Sigma Green Belt BoK, lean enterprise synergy, presentation skills, communication skills. (ASQ Certified as Six Sigma Green Belt)	• Support Six Sigma projects with higher ROI • Lead smaller projects with moderate savings and ROI • Follow DMAIC process, apply appropriate statistical methods • Review the approach periodically with the experienced Black Belt and Master Black Belt • Provide inputs to Master Black Belt and Black Belt and process owners during selection of projects • Identify issues of project stagnation/consult Black Belt, Master Black Belt • Identify and report barriers hindering the success of the project • Share lessons learned with the extended team
Yellow Belt	Individuals trained to have awareness in Six Sigma methodologies, and understanding of basic statistical tools, and process improvement techniques. This is not a full-time position. Organizations make this part of an existing job responsibility. Management and Champion are also trained in yellow belt.	Six Sigma methodologies, principles, value, quality tools, process improvement, and teamwork. (ASQ Certified Six Sigma Yellow Belt)	• Support and contribute to Six Sigma projects • Provide inputs during project meeting, brainstorm ideas • Help collect data where responsible • Follow DMAIC process, apply appropriate tools • Review the approach periodically with the Green Belt and experienced Black Belt • Yellow belts may be at a contributor to a project or a champion of a project
Project team member	Selected by process owner and trained in Six Sigma methodologies, quality, basic statistical tools, and process improvement techniques.	Six Sigma methodologies, quality tools, process improvement, teamwork.	• Support and contribute to Six Sigma projects • Participate in charter and scope definition • Provide inputs during project meeting, brainstorm ideas • Help collect data where responsible • Follow DMAIC process, apply appropriate tools • Review the approach periodically with the Green Belt and experienced Black Belt • Provide inputs to Green Belt and Black Belt and process owners during project

Chapter 4
D. Team Basics

Identify the various types of teams that operate within an organization (i.e., continuous improvement, self-managed and cross-functional) and their value. (Understand)

Body of Knowledge I.D.1

1. TYPES OF TEAMS

You are probably familiar with the saying "There is no 'I' in 'team.'" The essence of it is to imply that a team is a collective effort of individuals. To harness the best of each individual, the team members need to understand each other's strengths, roles, and responsibilities and the scope of the task. There are several books that go into detail about how to form a team, organize meetings, manage projects, and accomplish the desired goals. In the context of Six Sigma, we will cover areas important to a Six Sigma Yellow Belt. Protocols such as setting the team agenda, recording the minutes of the meeting with actions, sticking to meeting times, and enforcing meeting attendance need to be followed for an effective team meeting. An initial meeting to kick off the team with introductions and a high-level discussion of the goal, objective, milestones, and so on, will provide an opportunity for the team members to get to know each other and understand the expectations. A team must have an agenda, but it can be flexible.

Some teams have their team goals, objective, and scope/boundaries visibly displayed in every meeting to keep the members on track. Management presence during kickoff and frequently during the project helps enforce the importance of the team objective.

Team Formation

A team usually comprises five to seven members with complementary skills to achieve the goals and objectives of the team. Team composition should be driven by the size and scope of the project; it is possible to have a team of two or three individuals for a smaller project and a large team with subteams for a bigger project. The team includes subject matter experts and stakeholders. Subject matter

33

experts sometimes remain outside the team as resources or extended team members. Stakeholders are always part of the team. The team will not be able to implement its ideas and solutions without having stakeholders or their representation on the team. Teams smaller than five individuals are easier to manage than larger teams, but the opportunity for interaction and ideas is reduced. Teams larger than seven individuals produce a lot of interaction that can be counterproductive to a team's progress. Teams with greater diversity tend to produce better interactions between team members. In some cases, teams bring in individuals who are neither subject matter experts nor stakeholders but outsiders. The outsider helps the team ask questions that were never explored by the team members closest to the process. However, the use of outsiders needs to be moderated, as the outsider might ask too many questions and frustrate the core members by slowing down the progress. Typically, cross-functional Six Sigma teams are formed to address the issues from every angle.

Virtual Teams

Virtual teams are an interesting evolution in the past decade due to the development of technology in communication tools and the Internet, which have led to the ability to meet and share data virtually. Virtual teams enable people from all over the globe to meet via teleconferences, videoconferences, and Internet tools such as shared computers. The virtual team has many benefits, the most prevalent being reduced administrative and logistical costs and real-time data sharing and updating. However, virtual teams also face challenges that include slowing of the progression of normal team-building, inability to get true commitment and buy-in, and the potential for miscommunication—especially with teleconferencing, as the important factor of nonverbal communication is lost. Additionally, technology-related issues can cause distraction and reduce the effectiveness of the meeting. Virtual teaming has its place in every organization and can be very effective, especially if team members are familiar with each other. Hence, it may be beneficial for the team to meet face to face at some period during the project. This relationship can be helpful to project continuity.

Continuous Improvement Teams

Team members are often from the same process with varying responsibilities. The team is given a clear goal by management to improve yield, productivity, safety, and so forth. The team appoints a leader (process owner), meets regularly, applies continual improvement tools, and reaches the goal. Once the goal is achieved, the team goes to work on the next goal.

Self-Managed Teams

A self-managed team is a group of independent team members who plan, direct themselves, and operate with a set of procedures toward a common goal. Team harmony is achieved after the team members have worked with each other on other projects and have appreciation for each other's skill and disposition. Projects and purpose are carefully chosen for self-managed teams. The team members have proven effectiveness.

Cross-Functional Teams

Product development, continual improvement, and problem-solving projects require a cross-functional team to be assembled. Representatives from all the different functions will be required in order to obtain the knowledge and experience needed for a project. Cross-functional team members will be needed in order to implement any solution the team comes up with. Cross-functional teams have several advantages in terms of efficiency and results, but they also have challenges. Priorities for cross-functional members may be different. They may not feel the same sense of urgency and provide the same level of commitment as a team whose members are from one business function. The team leader, with management support from the sponsor of the project, should set the tone for the common purpose.

> Describe the various stages of team evolution: forming, storming, norming, performing, and adjourning. (Understand)
>
> **Body of Knowledge I.D.2**

2. STAGES OF DEVELOPMENT

Team Stages and Dynamics

It is important to understand team dynamics and performance. Many projects have failed miserably because of a lack of teamwork and not understanding the roles and responsibilities of the team members. It is important to note that in those failed projects, the team members were technically competent and had complementary skill sets to succeed in those projects.

According to B. W. Tuckman, teams typically go through the stages of *forming, storming, norming, performing*, and *transitioning* (or adjourning).[1] We will explore each stage and identify the appropriate management approach required for that stage.

Stage 1: Forming

1. Team members getting to know each other

2. Group is immature

3. Sense of belonging to the group

4. Take pride in membership with the group

5. Trying to please each other

6. May tend to agree too much on initial discussion topics

7. Not much work is accomplished

8. Members' orientation on the team goals

9. Members understand the roles and responsibilities

Stage 2: Storming

1. Team members voice their ideas

2. Understanding of the scope and members' roles; responsibilities will be put to test

3. Ideas and understanding start to conflict

4. Disagreements start to slow down the team

5. Not much work is accomplished

6. Necessary evil that every team member has to go through to position themselves on the team

7. Too much disagreement can completely stall team progress

Stage 3: Norming

1. Team members resolve their conflicts

2. Team members agree on mutually acceptable ideas to move forward

3. Some work gets accomplished

4. Start to function as a team

5. Team members start to trust each other and share their ideas and work products without hesitation

Stage 4: Performing

1. Team is effective, skills complement, and synergy is created

2. Team members realize interdependence

3. Develop ability to solve problem as a team

4. Large amount of work gets accomplished

Stage 5: Transitioning (or Adjourning)

1. Team is disbanded

2. Team members go on with other activities of their work

3. If the project is continued with additional scope, team members may be changed

4. Team dynamic changes and tends to go back to one of the earlier stages

5. Major changes can result in going back to forming stage

This is the typical evolution of team stages. Depending on the organization's culture, some stages may be shorter or longer, but the team still goes through them.

It is healthy for the team to go through these stages as it sets ground rules and expectations for team members. Team maturity, complexity of the task (project), and team leadership also have an impact on the stages.

Recognition

Recognition of the team's work is the often forgotten piece of team dynamics or, rather, is taken for granted. Even though team members are compensated monetarily for their time and skill, they should be recognized. Teams can be recognized in many ways, from a simple pat on the back by senior management to thank-you notes, bulletin boards, organization-wide e-mails, newsletters, all-employee meetings, certificates of accomplishment, bonuses, stock options, and so on.

Team Leadership

The team leadership may vary depending on the maturity of the team and the stage the team is at based on the leader's perception. Examples of leadership activities during each of the stages include:

Forming. Appropriate leadership style is *directing*:

— Leader welcomes and encourages the team

— Leader explains the roles, responsibilities, and goals of team members

— Leader instructs the team as to what to do when, where, and how

— Leader provides close supervision, exhibits directive behavior

— Leader listens to team's feedback

— Leader identifies opportunities for developing skills to meet team goals

Storming. Appropriate leadership style is *coaching*:

— Leader continues close supervision, exhibits directive behavior

— Leader also exhibits supportive behavior

— Leader increases the listening level to solicit the team's feedback

— To keep the storming at an acceptable level (not detrimental to the task at hand), the leader may bring in a facilitator or use conflict resolution approaches.

Norming. Appropriate leadership style is *supporting*:

— Leader reduces the level of directive behavior and increases the level of supportive behavior

— Leader encourages the team on decision-making responsibilities

— Leader helps the team move to the performing stage before it can revert to an earlier stage

— Leader emphasizes ground rules, scope, and roles and responsibilities

Performing. Appropriate leadership style is *delegating*:

— Since the team is mature, the leader reduces the levels of directive and supportive behavior in day-to-day functions

— Leader continues to monitor the goals and performance of the team

— Leader watches for any disruption in dynamics due to major changes in the organization

Negative Team Dynamics

If a team has several negative dynamics, this is more a reflection on the organizational culture than on the personalities of the individuals. If something is "acceptable" within the organization as a norm, that becomes the way of running the business. In other words, the organizational culture becomes the "enabler" of the many team problems that organizations face.

Negative dynamics in the team can:

- Have a negative impact on team member motivation
- Hurt a team member's ego and self-esteem
- Intimidate team members
- Reduce the self-confidence of others
- Increase stress and exhaust patience
- Increase feelings of insecurity
- Foster a lack of morale

As a result, unchecked or unaddressed negative team dynamics may cause:

- Goals and objectives of the project/task to not be met
- Targets to be frequently revised to the team's advantage
- The project to be cancelled
- Project milestones and deadlines to be missed
- Poor utilization of project resources
- The project to overrun its cost targets
- Turnover of key project team members

Table 4.1 outlines common negative team dynamics and possible countermeasures. Chapter 1 of *The Team Handbook* discusses additional facilitation tactics.[2]

Table 4.1 Common negative team dynamics and potential countermeasures.

Negative dynamic	Symptoms	Probable causes	Potential countermeasures
Overbearing member(s)	Team interaction is limited to a few individuals. The rest of the team is always in listening mode rather than participating in the discussion.	Team is composed of a few influential members (senior management staff, founders, inventors), members with legitimate authority (investor, major shareholder, owner), subject matter experts, and so on. This may intimidate other team members, who hesitate to voice their opinions.	With the support of the influential team member, the team leader reinforces round-robin voicing of opinions, using methods like nominal group technique, conducting the meeting in a more informal setting, keeping experts and influential members as an extended team, and so on.
Dominant member(s)	Meeting discussion is chaotic and difficult to listen to or understand. Only a few members dominating the entire discussion.	Dominant team members keep interrupting the conversation of other team members.	Structure the agenda to provide equal participation for all team members. Effective moderation by team leader allows other team members to finish their thoughts. Team leader initiates round-robin to provide opportunity for every team member to be heard.
Floundering	Team is currently proceeding or performing in an unsteady, faltering manner.	Lack of team direction. Some teams have high-profile team leaders from the organization, but they hardly ever attend meetings or team discussions. The organization is going through major changes, and no one is clear about the future of the team. Team members are overwhelmed. This can be due to multiple reasons. The organization may be going through major changes: leadership, downsizing, mergers and acquisitions, offshore transfers, and so on. Postponing of team decisions. This is related to lack of direction from the team leadership. If there is no clear direction, decision making gets difficult.	During early stages of the team, more direction is required. Team leadership should be visibly present during the team meetings and decisions. Team leadership should keep the team focused by not getting distracted by events happening within the organization. Team leaders should address the concerns of the team members but not allow the team agenda to be hijacked by other events. Reinforce management support and commitment when team starts to challenge the purpose of the team.

(continued)

Table 4.1 Common negative team dynamics and potential countermeasures. *(Continued)*

Negative dynamic	Symptoms	Probable causes	Potential countermeasures
Reluctant participants	Lack of participation, noncommittal feedback. Basically showing disinterest.	Team member may not have any stake in the team's outcome. Intimidated by other team members or leaders. In the process of moving out of the current job function or organization. Fear of losing job or position by voicing opinions.	Team leaders support the team members' active participation and protect the team members voicing their opinions.
Unquestioned acceptance of opinions as facts	Members present information without backing up data or analysis. Members present unfounded assumptions.	Organizational culture. Lack of management by facts.	Team leader requests supporting data, analysis, and conclusions that are statistically valid. Question the assumptions behind the analysis.
Groupthink	No public disagreements. Doubts expressed in private discussions. There are several other classical symptoms identified by researchers.	Members fear group cohesiveness will be at stake if there are any disagreements. Putting group harmony as paramount.	Bring independent members from outside to participate. Rotate roles and responsibilities of members at milestones. Management by fact.
Feuding	Hostilities resulting in heated arguments, slowed progress, low morale of the team.	Conflict resolution not effectively handled by the team leadership. Lack of mutual respect between team members. Team operating ground rules not enforced.	Confront the adversaries offline and not in the team meeting. Confronting in public can worsen the situation. Enforce discipline and emphasize mutual respect among team members. Restate the objective of the team as main focus.

Table 4.1 Common negative team dynamics and potential countermeasures. *(Continued)*

Negative dynamic	Symptoms	Probable causes	Potential countermeasures
Rush to accomplishment	Incomplete data collection. Inconsistent analysis. Trying to get conclusion faster.	Team under unrealistic deadline. Untrained team members. Looking for short-term gains.	Team leadership asks for data collection, analysis, and statistical significance. Ask for alternate solutions. Revise the deadline to a more realistic one based on resources.
Attribution	Members make casual references. Members don't seek explanations, preferring psychological and emotional judgments.	Similar to "rush to accomplishment" causes.	Team leaders challenge the assumptions made by team members. Use devil's advocate approach. Ask for analysis behind the conclusions drawn.
Discounting	Members' opinions are ignored. Members do not seem to listen to each other. Sarcasm, low team morale.		Encourage mutual respect. Enforce discipline. Ask for clarification from the members providing opinions.
Digressions and tangents	Discussion straying outside meeting agenda. Distractions. Meeting time not properly utilized; little is accomplished.	Organization going through major change. Cultural issues. Lack of focus from leadership.	Enforce compliance with agenda items and time allotment. Restate meeting ground rules. Redirect the discussions.

> Define brainstorming, multivoting, and nominal group technique (NGT), and describe how these tools are used by teams. (Understand)
>
> **Body of Knowledge I.D.3**

3. DECISION-MAKING TOOLS

Brainstorming

Brainstorming is a process where a team develops as many ideas concerning a topic as possible, using various creative methods. Brainstorming is a powerful technique for soliciting ideas, and it is used extensively in many improvement activities at every stage of improvement or problem solving. This tool intentionally encourages divergent thinking through which, hopefully, all possible causes are identified. This is a team exercise and requires a good facilitator to get the ideas flowing. Brainstorming has two phases: the creative phase, in which a large number of ideas are generated, and the evaluation phase, in which the ideas generated are looked at for usefulness or applicability. The two phases should be separated by a time break, as different parts of the brain are used in each phase. At a minimum, a 10-minute break should be taken after the creative phase versus going directly to the evaluation phase.

Criticisms or other distractions are not allowed during the creative phase. Team members should keep their minds open to all the possibilities no matter how wild the idea. The goal is to get as many ideas as possible. Facilitation can be used during the creative phase, but freewheeling also works well. Brainstorming is effectively performed with the help of a trained facilitator. The facilitator's job is to enforce ground rules and encourage ideas. A common tendency of brainstorming teams is to criticize the ideas instantly and discard them during the session. This will discourage team members from contributing for fear of being rejected. Team members must remember that there are no bad ideas. At this stage, quantity of ideas is given priority. A typical brainstorming session can generate between 25 and 40 ideas. If a flip chart is used to record ideas with a large group, two or more individuals should be used to capture all the ideas as they develop. You could also have each person say what they are thinking and then have them or someone else record the idea on a sticky note and put it on the wall. Some basic guidelines that should be followed in the creativity phase of brainstorming include:

- No criticism, compliments, or questions

- Wild ideas are welcome

- Don't wait

- Quantity is important (versus quality)

- Hitchhike—build on previous ideas

During the evaluation phase, it is best to have a facilitator work with the group to look over the ideas in sequence. There are many ways to evaluate the ideas generated. One good starting point is to organize the list of things into like groups or categories (i.e., build an affinity diagram; see Chapter 7, Figure 7.2). The caution here is to not get overly critical, as there may be something in one of those "crazy" ideas that might actually work for the given situation. This is often true because of new technology or different ways of doing things that are not common in our organizations. To get the most out of brainstorming, before starting the activity review, look over the following idea-stopping responses with the team:

- Don't be ridiculous
- Let's shelve it for right now
- It won't work here
- Our business is different
- Let's think about it some more
- We did all right without it
- It's too radical a change
- Management won't like it
- Where did you dig up that idea?
- It's not practical
- It's too expensive
- You can't be serious
- You can't do that
- The technology will not allow that
- Where will you get . . . ?
- We've never done it before
- I have something better
- It's too risky
- Let's be sensible
- We'll never get it approved
- The employees won't like it
- It's good, but . . .
- Let's check on it later
- It's too much work
- Let's get back to reality
- That's been tried before

- That's not my job

- You do not know how we do things around here

- That's too high-tech for us

- It will never work

In practical application, the team identifies the subject or problem at hand and writes it down on a whiteboard. It is important to clearly define the problem. This will keep the ideas on topic. For an issue that is unfamiliar to the team, it is acceptable to keep the scope open so that a wide range of ideas are generated. The team leader explains the problem or subject to the team members.

The following example topics have the scope defined to facilitate the majority of ideas focusing on the defined area:

- Contamination of polished surfaces before optical subassembly

- Low attendance at ASQ section program meetings

- Food menu for Thanksgiving dinner

Following are examples with the scope wide open:

- Global warming

- Unemployment

- Organizational culture

The team is given a few minutes to think about the subject. In structured brainstorming the team leader opens up a round-robin discussion. This way everyone gets the opportunity to contribute. If someone doesn't have an idea at this time, they are allowed to pass and contribute during the next round. Team members are not allowed to criticize each other or evaluate the ideas at this stage. The individual recording the ideas can ask for clarity on an idea and phrases it the same way as the idea contributor. Rephrasing without the consent of the idea owner is not allowed. Everyone is allowed one idea at a time. Some members will have the urge to provide multiple ideas during their turn. The team leader should facilitate such situations. Members are allowed to develop an idea already cited by a fellow member.

Quantity is more important than quality, so the team leader should encourage the team to keep the ideas flowing. All ideas are recorded on a whiteboard or flip chart.

We will now look at an example of defined-scope brainstorming: How can member attendance of ASQ section program meetings be improved? (problem rephrased as a question). Every major city in North America has a local ASQ section run by volunteers. A benefit of this section is the monthly program meeting. Unfortunately, these meetings draw a very low attendance (about 7%–10%) of members from the region, with at least 20% of the members attending once throughout the year.

The program chair (responsible for ASQ section monthly meetings) leads the brainstorming session and the section chair may act as a facilitator. A team has been assembled with other section executives, past section chairs and/or executives, section senior members, and members randomly selected from the membership database.

One of the members volunteered as a recorder, and the team was given three minutes to think about the subject—How can member attendance of ASQ section program meetings be improved?—in a focused manner. The session was started in a round-robin style and ideas began flowing. Team members came up with the following:

1. Bring in reputed speakers

2. Present topics that are current

3. Provide value for time and money

4. Keep program interactive—have a debate, quiz, etc.

5. Survey members for desired topics

6. Rotate program locations based on member concentration

7. Conduct some programs in the organizations with the most members

8. Not charge for meeting

9. Offer refreshments (e.g., pizza, snacks, sandwiches, coffee)

10. Offer time for networking

11. Have section chair and executives mix with members and attendees during break (rather than talking among themselves as a small group)

12. Check weather forecast before planning meetings

13. Inform members of other section events

14. Conduct less frequent but more effective meetings

15. Not waste meeting time with logistics issues—be prepared

16. Offer the meeting virtually—webcast, teleconference

17. Draw name cards from fishbowl and offer a small gift

18. Make the process easier for claiming recertification units for program attendance

19. Present two diverse topics

20. Provide carpool to meeting location for new or potential members

21. Liaise with other professional organizations to offer combined program meeting

22. Post meeting information at universities to attract students

23. Conduct some meetings on the local community college or university campus to attract students

24. Provide "back to basics" programs with applications for students and small business owners

25. Interview a random sample of members who have never attended a meeting and find out why

26. Interview a random sample of members who have attended every meeting and find out why

27. Introduce first-time attendee members/nonmembers in the group to make them feel welcome.

28. Have program chair survey every program for attendee satisfaction and review feedback

29. Appoint a marketing chair to reach a wider member base and potential new members

30. Keep the section website updated and easily accessible

31. Upload archive presentations to the website

32. Communicate at least twice about the monthly program—three weeks before and one week before

33. Announce and recognize newly certified professionals

34. Record and archive the program events and make them available to local libraries and online for free.

Wow, isn't this quite a collection of ideas? The team now reviews the ideas for redundancy and feasibility and then prioritizes them. The selected ideas are categorized under one of the following: personnel (man), machine, material, methods, measurement, environment. Some teams include measurement under methods. Cause and effect diagrams can be tailored to the operation (e.g., software development uses people, processes, products, resources, miscellaneous).

It is not uncommon for the team to continue brainstorming in a second sitting to add more ideas to the existing list. Some teams will break after a few rounds and revisit the list with any additional thoughts. However, a second round of brainstorming should not be prolonged, as the team may get bored and ideas will start to be counterproductive or too critical.

There are other team tools used to take these ideas to the next step:

- *Multivoting*, to short-list the ideas as a group

- *Cause and effect diagram*, to assign each idea to one category, namely, personnel, machine, material, method, measurement, and environment, and further analyze why

Nominal Group Technique

Nominal group technique (NGT) is a type of brainstorming but with limited team vocal interaction—hence the term "nominal." This technique is applied in groups with both very vocal members and less vocal members, to encourage equal participation from all members, or with a controversial or sensitive topic, and so on. This technique helps alleviate peer pressure and reduces the impact of such pressure on the generation of ideas.

As in brainstorming, the facilitator explains the rules, and the team leader presents the topic to the assembled members. The team is given 10–15 minutes to silently sit, think, and generate ideas.

No verbal interactions are allowed during the session. At the end of the session, the member ideas are collected and posted where all can read them. The members may also read the ideas aloud one by one in a round-robin format. At this stage no judgment or criticism is passed. The ideas are simply written down. The members are allowed to expand on existing ideas, provide clarity, and eliminate redundancy during the consolidation. For a controversial or sensitive subject, the team leader may opt to collect the ideas and write them down on the board, maintaining anonymity of the contributors.

Multivoting

Multivoting complements NGT and can also be successfully used with brainstorming results. Even though this tool is typically used in combination with NGT, it can be a technique on its own. The consolidated ideas are numbered or lettered, and the team members are asked to prioritize the top 5 or 10 items that can be of significant influence on the problem. The team members are given 5–10 minutes to prioritize, and the results are tabulated.

Let's return to the example of how to improve attendance at ASQ section program meetings. The members were asked to submit and prioritize ideas. As we saw, the diversified member group provided 34 ideas. Even though many of those ideas are good, the section may not have resources to address them all at one time. The section chair wants to select the five most important ideas to address in the next three years, and implement them in order of priority.

Each team member selects the five most important ideas by placing a check mark by the idea. It is important for the facilitator to restate the objective and refocus the team to select ideas from the ASQ section point of view. If this facilitation is not done, you may end up with multiple ideas with an equal number of check marks. Once this is done and you have the five ideas that most team members have selected as significant for improving the attendance of a section program, the prioritization process has begun. This can be done through either a non-weighted (ranking) or a weighted approach.

The members selected the following ideas, categorized into five themes, as having the most significant impact on improving section attendance:

1. *Value.* Bring in reputed speakers and present topics that are current

2. *Logistics.* Rotate program locations based on member concentration

3. *Affordability.* Do not charge for meeting and offer refreshments (e.g., pizza, snacks, sandwiches, coffee)

4. *Outreach.* Conduct some meetings on the local community college or university campus to attract students

5. *Communication.* E-mails twice per month, updated section calendar event web page

The multivoting ranked approach outcome is shown in Figure 4.1.

Venue: Caribou meeting room
Date: 3-Feb-15
Subject: How can member attendance of ASQ section programs be improved?
Scale: 1 (least important) to 5 (most important)

	Member 1	Member 2	Member 3	Member 4	Member 5	Member 6	Member 7	Member 8	Member 9	Total
A	5	2	4	5	5	2	4	5	5	37
B	2	4	3	3	4	4	3	3	4	30
C	1	5	5	4	3	5	5	4	3	35
D	3	3	1	2	2	3	1	2	2	19
E	4	1	2	1	1	1	2	1	1	14

Figure 4.1   Multivoting ranked approach example.

In the multivoting weighted approach, the team rates rather than ranks the choices. This is like the $100 or 100 points approach, where the team member is asked to split $100 or 100 points among five choices. The multivoting weighted approach outcome is shown in Figure 4.2. As shown in Figure 4.1 and Figure 4.2, the two approaches produce similar rankings in this example. However, this is not always the case, which is why using both approaches can help a team focus on the most critical items. If two items have values that are close to each other, another round of voting can be conducted to select a clear winner.

Note: While this example is not targeted to a specific ASQ section, the problem chosen for this example and the ideas generated are realities for most ASQ sections. The top choices and ranking were created to demonstrate the example rather than to provide solutions to the existing problem.

Venue: Caribou meeting room
Date: 3-Feb-15
Subject: How can member attendance of ASQ section programs be improved?

	Member 1	Member 2	Member 3	Member 4	Member 5	Member 6	Member 7	Member 8	Member 9	Total
A	30	20	25	35	20	25	25	35	30	245
B	15	25	20	20	25	20	20	20	15	180
C	10	30	30	25	30	30	30	25	10	220
D	20	15	10	15	15	10	10	15	20	130
E	25	10	15	5	10	15	15	5	25	125

There is NO ranking scale applicable to this approach. The column total should add up to 100 for all individual columns and the relative importance of A to E to be understood by the points allotted by each member (from that member's point of view). Overall relative importance is understood from reviewing the "Total" column. Based on consolidated input from all members, in this example, A is most important, followed by C, B, D, and E.

Figure 4.2   Multivoting weighted approach example.

> Explain how teams use agendas, meeting minutes, and project status reports, and how they support project success. (Understand)
>
> **Body of Knowledge I.D.4**

4. COMMUNICATION METHODS

Team projects are reviewed through meetings. Effective meetings are key to project success as they provide continual updates of information and action to the team members.

We need to be asking ourselves:

- Are we discussing the right topic?
- Do we have the right audience?
- Do we have actionable discussions?
- Do team members who attend the meeting know what they should do?
- Was the time spent productive and worthwhile?

Why are meetings not productive?

- Overwhelming information
- Too many presentation slides
- Information unrelated to the agenda
- Attendees not well prepared
- Sending delegated attendees on short notice
- Too many side conversations
- Attendees using their smartphones to check e-mail and messages
- Remote attendees calling in through virtual meeting infrastructure may be multitasking
- Preparations are being made for the next meeting while still in the current meeting
- Getting in arguments over "how to" while the meeting is still focused on "what to"
- No actionable discussions—groupthink and philosophical agreements

A worldwide productivity survey conducted by Microsoft revealed the following:

- "People work an average of 45 hours a week; they consider about 17 of those hours to be unproductive (U.S.: 45 hours a week; 16 hours are considered unproductive)."

- "People spend 5.6 hours each week in meetings; 69 percent feel meetings aren't productive (U.S.: 5.5 hours; 71 percent feel meetings aren't productive)."[3]

Ineffective meetings continue to haunt every organization as a major productivity detractor. The organization's culture may contribute a lot to the ineffective meetings. Taking a disciplined approach to meetings will help address many of the issues mentioned earlier. Meetings have to be conducted periodically to ensure continuity.

An effective meeting includes the following:

- *Agenda.* Meetings should not be initiated or attended without a clear agenda. The meeting subject is not the agenda. The agenda should be itemized: meeting subject, items required to be discussed, item presenters, and time allotment. Without a clear agenda and time allotment for agenda items, the meeting can easily get out of control and become unproductive. If it is a project meeting, the scope has to be presented to the team members to ensure that there is no scope creep.

- *Meeting logistics.* This includes meeting room (for face-to-face meetings), virtual call-in infrastructure, and video capability.

- *Meeting minutes.* The meeting minutes are a record of the meeting. Minutes are essential to ensure the key decisions made and the actions agreed on by the team members are formally recorded and keep the team members accountable. The minutes should be well drafted and unambiguous, and they should indicate the date and time of the completed meeting, meeting host, attendees, topics covered, decisions made, actions assigned (what, who, when), minutes reviewed and approved, and scribe name. One might also include "parking lot" items that are pending detailed discussions. Meeting minutes are important to project continuity.

- *Project status report.* This is a periodic status report created by the project manager or team leader and circulated to all team members and management to list the status of the project, upcoming milestones, risks, and mitigation plans. Any unacceptable project variances and risks are addressed early in the project by reviewing the status reports and taking appropriate actions.

QUESTIONS

1. Why is "storming" a necessary evil in the team stages? Discuss your experience in a team that went through the storming stage. Describe any lessons learned.

2. Why is recognition of a team after the successful completion of a project highly recommended? What are your recommendations for recognition for a Six Sigma team?

3. Discuss the effect of "groupthink" in a meeting. How do you ensure due diligence?

4. A team struggling to meet project milestones has repeatedly requested extensions from the management. This is a high-stakes project and the revenue stream is dependent on project success. You have been asked by your Black Belt to conduct a brainstorming session to identify causes of the team's lack of progress. Discuss the issue with your participants and put together a list of plausible causes. Apply the multivoting approach as well.

5. List the major causes of ineffective meetings in your organization. Research best practices for improving meeting effectiveness and share with your participants.

Chapter 5
E. Quality Tools and Six Sigma Metrics

> Select and use these tools throughout the DMAIC process: Pareto charts, cause and effect diagrams, flowcharts, run charts, check sheets, scatter diagram, and histograms. (Apply)
>
> **Body of Knowledge I.E.1**

1. QUALITY TOOLS

Table 5.1 shows several tools that are used across the DMAIC phases. These tools may be a simple check sheet to collect data or a complex multivariate analysis to identify the effect of critical variables. Most improvement projects can be conducted with easy-to-use basic quality and statistical tools.

Let us start with the seven quality tools that are considered to be basic quality tools and are applicable in most improvement or problem-solving projects: Pareto charts, cause and effect diagrams, flowcharts, run charts, check sheets, scatter diagrams, and histograms.

Pareto Charts

The Pareto chart has been so widely used in recent years that "Pareto" is sometimes used as a verb. It is not uncommon to hear from managers to "Pareto" data for presentation. Some people who are not familiar with Pareto charts interchangeably use a bar graph to "Pareto" data. The true Pareto chart, however, is unique. It shows the data arranged in descending order of frequency of occurrence, the "trivial many" data are often pooled together as "miscellaneous" or "other" (represented by the last bar of the Pareto chart), and the chart contains a cumulative percent line with a secondary y axis. These characteristics make the Pareto chart more informative and useful than an ordinary bar graph.

The Pareto chart helps us visualize the items charted as "vital few" and "trivial many" using the famous 80:20 principle of twentieth-century Italian economist Vilfredo Pareto. Joseph Juran is credited with being the first to apply this principle in quality improvement.

Table 5.1 Tools across DMAIC phases.

Define	Measure	Analyze	Improve	Control
Is-is not	Check sheet	Why-why	Mistake proof	SPC
Pareto	MSA	Comparative	Brainstorm	Control plan
Histogram	Process capability indices	DOE	FMEA	Sampling
Timeline	Benchmarking with baseline, best-in-class	Hypothesis test	Flowchart	Gaging
Run chart	COQ/COPQ	ANOVA	Prioritization matrix	Close loop automation
Flowchart	OEE	C & E diagram	Pugh concept selection	5S
SIPOC diagram	Process sigma level (with or without shift)	C & E matrix	Process capability indices	Kanban
Stakeholder analysis	Process audit	Scatter diagram	Single piece flow	Visual management—Andon
Brainstorm	Financial tools such ROI, NPV, IRR, RONA	Stratification	SMED	Process audit
Problem definition (what, where, when, who, and how many)	Dashboard—RYG monitoring	Time series analysis	Pilot study	A3 plan
VOC Table	DPPM/DPMO/DPU/RTY metrics, software defect density, errors per transaction	Regression analysis	Process optimization	Cross training
Kano diagram	Value stream mapping	Power sample size	Horizontal deployment (share improvement across organization)	Standard work
Project charter	Equipment/tool correlation study	Multivariate	Safety and environmental factors	Gemba walk

Note: Some tools are applicable in more than one phase. The intent of this table is to show a variety of tools in various phases.

SIPOC: supplier-input-process-output-customer
VOC: voice of the customer
MSA: measurement system analysis
COQ: cost of quality
COPQ: cost of poor quality
OEE: overall equipment effectiveness
ROI: return on investment
NPV: net present value
IRR: internal rate of return
RONA: return on net assets
RYG: red-yellow-green

DOE: design of experiments
ANOVA: analysis of variance
C & E: cause and effect
SMED: single minute exchange of die
SPC: statistical process control
5S: sort, straighten, shine, standardize, sustain
RTY: rolled throughput yield
DPU: defects per unit
DPPM: defective parts per million
DPMO: defects per million opportunities

In the final assembly inspection example shown in Figure 5.1, the data are presented as a Pareto diagram based on frequency of occurrence. While these data are important, one might want to put their resources into issues that are critical to the customer or that have more financial impact. So the data are assigned weights based on criticality and multiplied by occurrence, and a Pareto diagram is created based on the weighted score. The table in Figure 5.1 shows the reprioritized defects based on criticality. Cost of repair or rework can also be used in place of weight, and the Pareto chart can be expressed in dollars.

Cause and Effect Diagrams

A thorough understanding of process inputs and outputs and their relationships is a key step in process improvement. The cause and effect diagram (also called the

Defect code	Defect description	Occurrences	Criticality	Weight	Weighted score
A	Scratches	15	Minor	10	150
B	Stains	17	Minor	10	170
C	Label smudge	12	Minor	10	120
D	Dent	14	Major	25	350
E	Device nonfunctional	5	Critical	100	500
F	Broken LED	7	Critical	100	700
G	Missing screw	3	Major	25	75

Final assembly inspection (weighted)

Defect code	Broken LED	Device nonfunctional	Dent	Stains	Other
Weighted score	700	500	350	170	345
Percent	33.9	24.2	16.9	8.2	16.7
Cumulative %	33.9	58.1	75.1	83.3	100.0

Figure 5.1 Pareto chart of final assembly inspection defect codes.

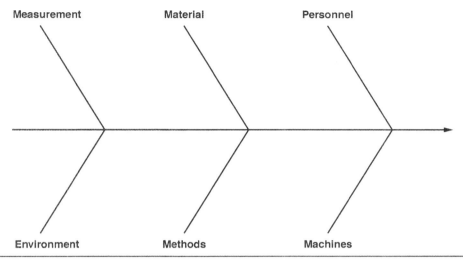

Figure 5.2   Empty cause and effect diagram.

Ishikawa diagram or fishbone diagram) traditionally divides causes into several generic categories. A large empty diagram as shown in Figure 5.2 is often drawn on a whiteboard or flip chart.

This diagram is used as a next step to document the final list of causes from the brainstorming session. The participants in the session should include people with a working knowledge of the process as well as those with a theoretical background. For example, suppose a machining operation is producing surface defects. After a few steps of typical brainstorming, the cause and effect diagram would look like Figure 5.3.

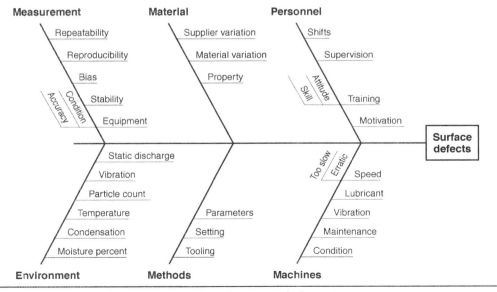

Figure 5.3   Cause and effect diagram after a few steps of a brainstorming session.

CEDAC (cause and effect diagram with addition of cards) is an alternative approach employed by some organizations where the fishbone diagram is displayed on a huge wall or board and employees are encouraged to identify causes by writing on it or using sticky notes. The success of this approach depends on organizational culture and communication.

Flowcharts

A flowchart is a quality tool (and a business process tool) that helps individuals visualize a process in discrete steps arranged in the sequence of events. There are variations of flowcharts that can accommodate complexities in the process, for example, interactions between process steps, ownership, and process measures. Flowcharts can also be used as an improvement tool to understand current complexities, identify opportunities for removing redundancies and waste, and ensure the process is simplified and standardized. Once the process has been simplified and standardized, the flowchart may be used as a training tool and for auditing processes.

Processes

A process is a series of steps for producing products and/or services. A process is often diagrammed with a flowchart depicting inputs, a path that material or information follows, and outputs. An example of a high-level process flowchart is shown in Figure 5.4. Understanding and improving processes is a key part of every Six Sigma project.

Steps in the development of a flowchart are as follows:

1. Determine the scope of the flowchart with boundaries

2. Write down the steps in the process

3. Rearrange where required to reflect the current sequence of steps

4. Draw the flowchart (use appropriate flowcharting symbols for ease of understanding)

5. Walk through the process to test the flowchart

6. Identify opportunities for removal of redundancies, waste reduction, simplification, and standardization

7. Communicate the flowchart to all stakeholders

An example of a flowchart for replacement of a product under warranty is shown in Figure 5.5.

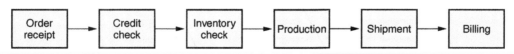

Figure 5.4   High-level flowchart for an order-filling process.

Source: N. R. Tague, *The Quality Toolbox*, 2nd ed. (Milwaukee, WI: ASQ Quality Press, 2005): 257.

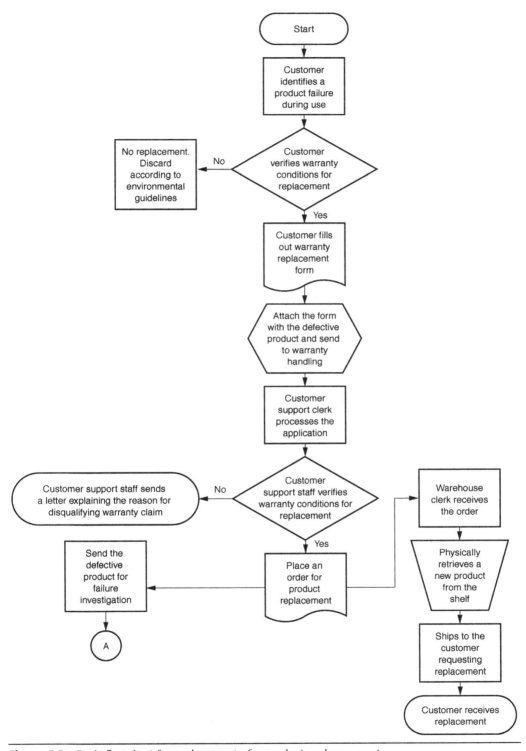

Figure 5.5   Basic flowchart for replacement of a product under warranty.

Run Charts

The run chart is used to identify patterns in process data. All of the individual observations are plotted in a time sequence, and a horizontal reference line is drawn at the median (Figure 5.6). A run chart is typically used when the subgroup size is one. When the subgroup size is greater than one, the subgroup means or medians are calculated and connected with a line, similar to a control chart. However, run charts are different from control charts (e.g., $\overline{X}$ and R charts); run charts do not have statistical control limits to monitor variation. There are also related statistical tests that can be performed to detect any nonrandom behavior.

Run chart tests can detect trends, oscillation, mixtures, and clustering. These are nonrandom patterns and suggest that the variation observed can be attributed to special causes. Lack of steadiness in a process can cause oscillation. In the example shown in Figure 5.6, the *p*-value for oscillation is 0.78, indicating that it is not significant (see Chapter 15 for a discussion of *p*-values). A trend can be either upward or downward due to, for example, tool wear or loosening of a fixture in a piece of equipment.

Check Sheets

Check sheets are used to observe or review a process, usually during execution of the process. Check sheets pre-categorize potential outcomes for data collection using sets of words, tally lists, or graphics. Figure 5.7 is an example of a completed

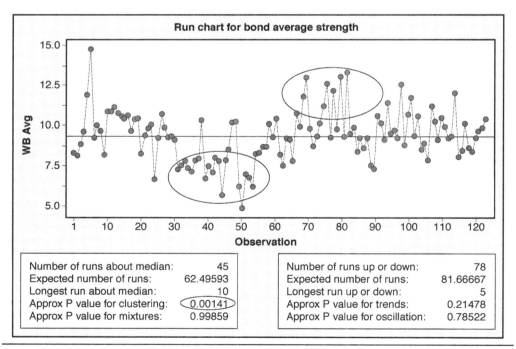

Figure 5.6   Run chart analysis (using statistical software).

Paint color defect causes

Reason	Day of the week							Weekly total
	Mon	Tue	Wed	Thu	Fri	Sat	Sun	
Operator misread instructions	I	I	O	II	₪	₪ II	III	19
Wrong pigment used	III	I	₪	III	IIII	IIII	₪ ₪	30
Wrong color code from customer	II	I	II	O	O	₪	O	10
Outdated base paint	O	O	I	O	III	O	IIII	8
Daily total	6	3	8	5	12	16	17	67

Figure 5.7 Example of a check sheet.

check sheet, in tabular format, used to collect data related to a paint mixing process. This simple tool provides a method of easy data collection. By collecting data on a check sheet, common patterns or trends can be identified.

The basic steps in making a check sheet are as follows:

1. Identify and agree on the causes or conditions that are to be collected.

2. Decide who will collect the data, over what time period(s), and how the data will be collected. (Determine whether any training is required for staff regarding the types of data and the data collection process.)

3. Create a check sheet that will work within the operation where it will be used.

4. Conduct any training or briefing for an effective data collection.

5. Collect the data as designed to ensure consistency and accuracy of the information.

Check sheets can be the basis for other analytical tools and are incorporated into attribute process behavior charts. Creating and using a check sheet helps keep a focus on continual improvement, and the simple act of using a check sheet may foster changes. Data collection is the basis for analysis and subsequent improvement and its importance should not be underestimated.

Scatter Diagrams

A scatter diagram (Figure 5.8) is used to explore the relationship between two sets of variables. This diagram provides a visual display of correlation between the variables. This tool should be used in conjunction with the cause and effect diagram. The scatter diagram is created with the independent variable as the x axis and the dependent variable as the y axis. If one is cause and the other is effect, then effect is the dependent variable and cause is the independent variable. In this diagram, the data are obtained in pairs (X, Y). Once the data pairs are plotted for the range of the axis, the plotted data can be interpreted.

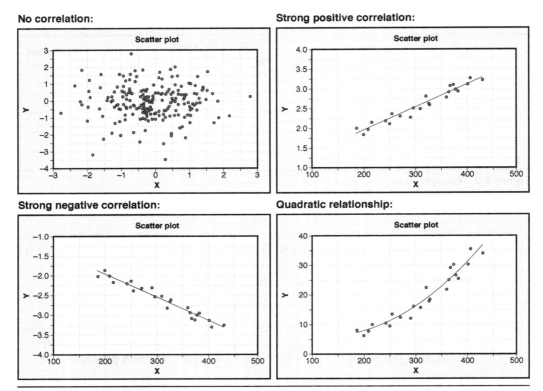

Figure 5.8   Scatter diagrams.

Histograms

The histogram (Figure 5.9) is an easy-to-use tool for graphically summarizing continuous data collected from a process. The frequency of data occurrence is reflected as bars of various heights. Since data can be unique, they are grouped by intervals. The histogram shows the shape of the data, centering of the process, variation, and a rough distribution of the data. The histogram is helpful for comparing "before and after" improvement readily while waiting for a more detailed analysis. An initial indication of process capability may be seen by comparing the center and width of the distribution with the specification limits.

The following are steps for developing a histogram:

1. Identify the process parameter to be analyzed

2. Collect the data to the required precision

3. Divide data into number of intervals (as a guideline, use the square root of number of samples n)

4. Arrange the collected data by interval

5. Draw a histogram based on the frequency of data falling at every interval

We will see some examples of types of distributions and interpretation of process capability in the Measure phase of this book.

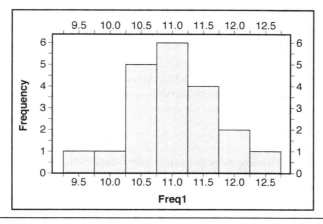

Figure 5.9   Histogram.

Additional Quality Tools

The following quality tools are widely used alongside the seven quality tools.

Control Charts

A control chart (Figure 5.10) is used to monitor process stability and variability. Every process has natural variability from causes like people, equipment, method,

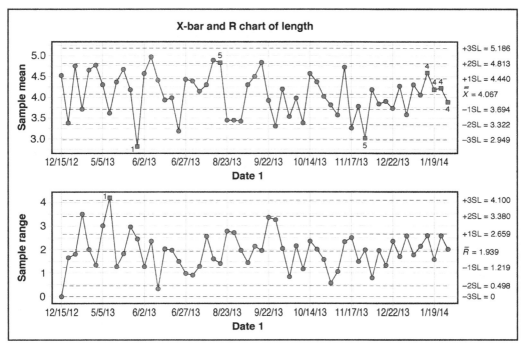

Figure 5.10   Example of $\bar{X}$ and R control chart.

material, and environment. This is "common cause" variation. This variability is measured and drawn as control limits on the chart. A stable process will have process data plotted above and below the central line within the control limits. This is because a stable process has random variation. However, if any "special causes" enter the process, the process tends to go out of control. Examples of special causes include changes in processes, materials, operator skill, or environmental factors like temperature or humidity.

Stratification

In typical manufacturing or service industry data collection, the data have a mixture of multiple variables. As an example, if you are collecting data of process defectives, the data may come from different manufacturing lines, different process steps, different operators, different shifts, different days, different weeks, different factory locations, and so on. In a service example, you are collecting data of customer transaction time. These data may come from different operators, different complexities, different days, different weeks, different service locations, and so on. When you lump all these variables together and analyze the data, it is often difficult to make any interpretation. Hence, stratification is a data mining approach to help dissect data by variables and interpret the patterns and behaviors in the data set.

Select and use these metrics throughout the DMAIC process: defects per unit (DPU), defects per million opportunities (DPMO), rolled throughput yield (RTY), cycle time, and cost of poor quality (COPQ). (Apply)

Body of Knowledge I.E.2

---

2. SIX SIGMA METRICS

Process performance is a measure of how the process is executing against established goals or statistical measures. Metrics can be identified throughout the DMAIC process (Table 5.2). Metrics with operational definitions are required to understand what to improve at the Define stage; the metrics are monitored at the Control stage.

Nonconformance degrades process performance. Nonconformance with requirements or expectations is called a "defect" or "defective." A number of defects can appear in a single unit or service transaction. As an example, a physical product like a painted automotive part could have a scratch, dent, dirt, or nonuniform painted surface. All these are individual defects. In total, the part has four types of defects (four opportunities for defects). Even within the painted part, there could be three scratches, one dent, one area with dirt, and one patch of nonuniform surface, for a total of six defects in the part. If we had 10 such parts and count the average defects per unit, this is the "defects per unit," or DPU.

Table 5.2   Examples of metrics by Six Sigma stage.

Six Sigma stage	Examples of metrics
Define	Describe the problem objectively DPU, DPMO, RTY, COPQ, Cpk, Ppk, RPN, takt time
Measure	P/T, % GRR, % agreement
Analyze	$p \geq 0.05$
Improve	DPU, DPMO, RTY, COPQ, Cpk, Ppk, RPN
Control	DPU, DPMO, RTY, COPQ, takt time

Irrespective of whether the painted automotive part has one or six defects, you would call the part a defective part. The average proportion of defective parts in a production quantity is calculated to measure process capability.

Process performance in terms of defect and defective measures usually includes the following.

Defects (Deficiencies or Nonconformities) per Unit (DPU)

DPU is calculated as the total number of defects divided by the total number of products produced in some time period (e.g., per day). This metric is used when the area under inspection is large in size or volume, for example, the number of defects on a painted chassis or textile.

Defects (Deficiencies) per Million Opportunities (DPMO)[1]

To calculate the number of opportunities, it is necessary to find the number of ways each defect can occur on each item. In a hypothetical product, the product is inspected for the following defects: scratch, dent, broken, and bent. There are four opportunities for defects. If there are 10 units, this totals 40 opportunities. If there are four defects (irrespective of type of defect),

$$DPMO = (\text{Total number of defects} \div \text{Total number of units} \times \text{Number of opportunities per unit}) \times 10^6$$

Manufacturing Example[2]

Process: Painting automotive product

Types of opportunities for defects: Scratch, dent, dirt, nonuniform thickness (bump or base metal visible)

Opportunities = 4

Number of production units = 100

An inspector performed a thorough visual inspection of 100 production units and found the following: 1 scratch in 4 units, 1 dent in 2 units, dirt in 2 units, and non-uniform thickness in 2 units, for a total of 10 defects in 100 units inspected.

$$DPU = 10/100 = 0.1$$

The DPMO is $(10/100 \times 4) \times 10^6 = 25{,}000$

Service Example

Service: Finance department sending invoice to customer

Types of opportunities for defects: incorrect address, incorrect amount, incorrect due date

Opportunities = 3

Number of invoices sampled = 100

An auditor performed a thorough review of 100 invoices and found the following: 2 incorrect address, 3 incorrect amount, and 3 incorrect due date, for a total of 8 defects in 100 invoices sampled.

$$DPU = 8/100 = 0.08$$

The DPMO is $(8/100 \times 3) \times 10^6 = 26{,}667$

Rolled Throughput Yield (RTY)[3]

RTY applies to the yield from a series of processes and is found by multiplying the individual process yields. If a product goes through four process steps whose yields are

Process step #1 = 99.4%,

Process step #2 = 98.7%,

Process step #3 = 95.1%, and

Process step #4 = 99.0%,

then RTY = 99.4% × 98.7% × 95.1% × 99.0% ≈ 92.37%. This means for every 100 products that are started, we end up with 92 good, confirming products. The other 8 products may be able to be reworked, repaired, or regraded. However, they are not fit for shipping to customers without further processing, of which the organization incurs the cost of poor quality.

Throughput yield can also be calculated by knowing $DPU = e^{-DPU}$.

Sigma Levels[4]

A *sigma level* is the quality level of the process—the higher the sigma level, the higher the quality level and the fewer defectives per million units produced or service transactions rendered. There are two types of sigma level calculations: sigma level with Motorola 1.5 sigma shift and without the shift. As an example, 3 sigma level without shift (0 shift) is 2700 defective parts per million (DPPM). However, with 1.5 sigma shift, it is 66,807 DPPM. Six Sigma Quality level without shift is 2 parts per billion (ppb) and with 1.5 sigma shift is 3.4 DPPM.

Cycle Time

Cycle time is the time it takes for a process to be completed, from start to end. As a Six Sigma Yellow Belt, you may occasionally have to also measure *wait time* or *queue time*. This is the time that the material (product or paperwork) sits idle before the transformation is started. *Lead time*—another term used in improvement efforts—is the time it takes for the material to arrive from the time an order is placed at your supplier. Your customer might ask the lead time of your product or service. It is important that you take your supplier's lead time into account when making commitments to your customer. Lead time is a metric that is used interchangeably with cycle time by many practitioners. Every organization may have its own definition. In your organization, you may want to define and document the operational definition to be consistent.

Cost of Poor Quality (COPQ)

COPQ is interchangeably used with cost of quality (COQ). Some organizations choose to distinguish COPQ as the cost of nonconformance and COQ as the cost of conformance (Figure 5.11). However, in some publications, COQ is referred to as the overall cost that includes both the cost of conformance and the cost of nonconformance. The cost of nonconformance is the sum of internal and external failure costs the organization incurs. Examples of internal failure costs are scrap, rework, repair, and retest. Examples of external failure costs are customer return, replacement, investigation, and administration. The cost of conformance is the sum of the

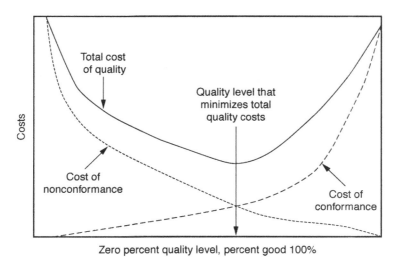

Figure 5.11 Traditional quality cost curves.

appraisal and prevention costs the organization incurs to ensure products and service conform to specifications and customer requirements. Examples of appraisal costs are inspection, administrative costs for quality functions, and supplier surveillance. Examples of prevention costs are training, supplier qualification, risk assessment, and process capability measurement. There are several hidden costs that are not measured by organizations. Examples are lost customers, unused capacity, planning delays, and time spent resolving complaints. Hidden costs are estimated to be as high as three to four times the visible costs.

COPQ and COQ are measured as percent ratio compared with the cost of goods sold or the cost of goods manufactured. Some organizations also compare them with revenue, sales, and so on. It is important to choose the right denominator in order to have a meaningful ratio.

Improvement in COPQ should come from a reduction in failure costs. Improvement in COQ should come from a reduction in appraisal costs and an increase in prevention costs. (See "Cost-Benefit Analysis" in Chapter 16 for more on COPQ.)

QUESTIONS

1. Review Table 5.1 and add tools that you think could be used in DMAIC stages based on your past experience.

2. What is the difference between an affinity diagram (Chapter 7) and a cause and effect diagram? List the applications of each.

3. What differentiates a Pareto chart from a bar graph? Develop a Pareto chart and a bar graph for the data from your business and explain what additional information is provided in the Pareto chart.

4. Measure the height of each class participant and present it in the form of a histogram.

5. Explain the importance of understanding hidden costs in a cost of quality measurement.

Part II
Define Phase

Chapter 6
A. Project Identification

Define the voice of the customer and describe how customer needs are translated into quantifiable, critical-to-quality (CTQ) characteristics. (Understand)

Body of Knowledge II.A.1

1. VOICE OF THE CUSTOMER

One of the key organizational drivers is customer and market knowledge—the ability of an organization to determine the requirements, needs, expectations, and preferences of customers and markets. Also necessary are the relationships with customers and the ability to determine the key factors that lead to customer acquisition, satisfaction, loyalty, and retention, and to business expansion and sustainability. The *voice of the customer* (VOC) is a process for capturing customer-related information. This process is proactive and continuously innovative to capture stated, unstated, and anticipated customer requirements, needs, and desires. The goal is to achieve customer loyalty and to build customer relationships. The VOC might include gathering and integrating survey data, focus group findings, lost customer analysis, lost bids analysis (potential customers), warranty data, complaint logs and field reports, and any other data and information that affect the customer's purchasing and relationship decisions. These days, with the surge in social media, organizations should also be capturing and analyzing data from social networks for the VOC.

Translating customer needs into quantifiable critical to quality (CTQ) characteristics is the execution side of the business. It involves taking customer inputs and designing the product or service, ensuring that the product is manufacturable and the service is consistently delivered to the customer. There are many tools that are used to ensure the customer needs are designed in. Although not commonly used by organizations, quality function deployment (QFD) is one such tool. QFD (Figure 6.1), also known as the house of quality (HOQ), has three stages. Planning house, design house, and manufacturing house (Figure 6.2) cascade explicit and perceived customer needs into a controllable manufacturing or service control

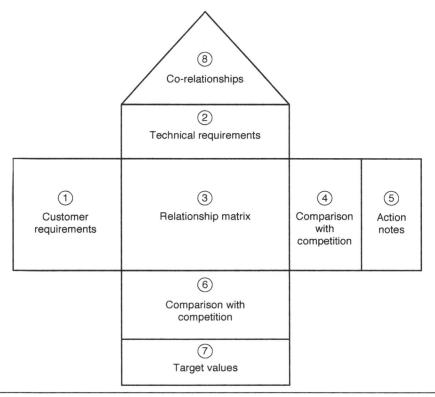

Figure 6.1 Map to the entries for the QFD matrix.

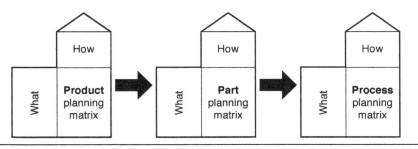

Figure 6.2 Sequence of QFD matrices for product, part, and process planning.

point. Most organizations use a disciplined design and development process that encompasses many tools like the Pugh concept selection matrix, failure mode and effects analysis (FMEA), and the process capability study. These tools, along with a structured approach to product development, help ensure the customer needs are translated into CTQ requirements for the products and services.

> Describe how projects are identified and selected as suitable for a six sigma project using the DMAIC methodology. (Understand)
>
> **Body of Knowledge II.A.2**

2. PROJECT SELECTION

A series of successful Six Sigma projects is likely to lead to more project ideas than it is possible to undertake at one time. Some sort of project proposal format may be needed, along with an associated process for project selection. Project proposals are often required to include a precise statement of the problem definition and some preliminary measures of the magnitude (importance) of the problem, including its impact on the goals of the organization. (An example of a project proposal template is available on the CD-ROM accompanying this book.)

A project selection group, which includes Master Black Belts, Black Belts, organizational champions, and key executive supporters, establishes a set of criteria for project selection and team assignments. In some companies the project selection group assigns some projects to Six Sigma teams and other projects to teams using other methodologies. For example, problems involving extensive data analysis and improvements using designed experiments would likely be assigned to a Six Sigma team, while a process improvement involving waste reduction might be assigned to a lean manufacturing team. New-product design should follow design for Six Sigma (DFSS) guidelines.

The project selection criteria are always a key element of furthering the organization's goals. One key to gauging both the performance and health of an organization and its processes lies with its selection and use of metrics. These are usually converted to financial terms such as return on investment, cost reduction, and increases in sales and/or profit. Other things being approximately equal, the projects with the greatest contributions to the bottom line receive the highest priority. However, some organizations may select and assign projects for Six Sigma Yellow Belts and Green Belts as learning opportunities.

Typical project selection criteria are strategic importance, bottom line improvement, technical complexity, stakeholder risk, and change management.[1] An organization is unlikely to invest resources in projects that do not align with organizational strategy. A good starting point is to look at the A3 Planning sheet. A3 Planning for any organization is the blueprint for strategic goals and objectives. The first step is to ensure alignment with strategic goals and objectives. Equally important is to select projects that will make a positive impact on the bottom line. A more experienced cross-functional Six Sigma team will likely be assigned a project with a high level of technical complexity and stakeholder risk. Projects requiring a high level of change management will be handled by team members with a significant number of project completions under their belts. It takes experience to understand the impact of changes.

In order to avoid Six Sigma members making subjective decisions in selecting projects, it may be beneficial to develop a template to assign scores for various projects. Criteria and weights may be assigned based on consensus. An example of a project selection matrix can be found on the CD-ROM accompanying this book.

Following is an example of a Six Sigma project where a risk analysis and a strengths-weaknesses-opportunities-threats (SWOT) analysis are performed to assess the merit of pursuing the project.

EXAMPLE

A proposed Six Sigma project is aimed at improving quality to a level that will attract one or two new customers. The project will cost $3 million (M). Previous experience indicates that the probability of getting only customer A is between 60% and 70%, and the probability of getting only customer B is between 10% and 20%. The probability of getting both customer A and customer B is between 5% and 10%.

One way to analyze this problem is to make two tables, one for the worst case and one for the best case, as shown in Table 6.1.

Assuming that the data are correct, the project will improve enterprise profits between $1M and $2.5M.

When estimating the values for these tables, the project team should list the SWOT that the proposal implies. A thorough study of this list will help provide the best estimates (see Figure 6.3).

Table 6.1   Risk analysis table.

	Worst-case profit			Best-case profit		
Outcome		Probability	Profit × Probability		Probability	Profit × Probability
A only	$2M	.60	$1.2M	$2M	.70	$1.4M
B only	$2M	.10	$0.2M	$2M	.20	$0.4M
A & B	$7M	.05	$0.35M	$7M	.10	$0.7M
None	–$3M	.25	–$0.75M	–$3M	0	$0M
	Expected profit = $1M			Expected profit = $2.5M		

Strengths:	Weaknesses:
High-quality product Monthly quantity commitment Tooling cost by customer Just-in-time concepts Online interface Product mix	Pricing Union plant High employee turnover Aging equipment—downtime issues
Opportunities:	Threats:
Potential industry leadership More growth Long-term contract	Competition from start-ups Labor force Union plant Unstable market Unstable labor force

Figure 6.3   A format for SWOT analysis.

> Identify end users, subject matter experts, process owners and other people or factors that will be affected by a project, and describe how each of them can influence the project. (Understand)
>
> **Body of Knowledge II.A.3**

3. STAKEHOLDER ANALYSIS

Stakeholders are those who have a vested interest in the process and/or its products and outputs. Generally, stakeholders of an organization include customers, suppliers, employees, investors, and communities. Stakeholder interest and involvement with the process may change over time depending on economic, contractual, and other influences. ISO 9000:2015 has introduced a new term, "interested parties," which is more comprehensive than "stakeholders."

End users are those who eventually consume the product or service. An interim customer for an organization can be a dealer, distributor, or wholesaler. This should not be confused with the end user.

Subject matter experts (SMEs) are those who have demonstrated skill and competency in an area that is important to the existence and sustainability of the business.

Process owners are those who have responsibility for the definition, execution, maintenance, and improvement of a specific process. Process owners are usually formally recognized in this role through related documentation (e.g., procedures, work instructions, documentation approval authority), through their job/position description, or through the organization chart.

In some cases process owners may also be referred to as SMEs. Personnel involved with process design usually have a specific interest in systems, subprocesses, and individual steps within processes.

The most effective methods of process improvement utilize teams representing process owners *and* all stakeholders because:

- Stakeholders have the best knowledge base about the process
- Stakeholders tend to have the best ideas for process improvement
- Stakeholders are often the most aware of unintended consequences of process changes
- Stakeholders' buy-in is usually necessary to implement real process improvement

The stakeholders in a process are:

- Process operators and managers from all shifts
- Process customers, internal and external
- Process suppliers, internal and external

- Process design personnel

- Maintenance personnel

- Others impacted in some way by process changes

A typical stakeholder analysis (Figure 6.4) involves identifying key stakeholders for a given project. A score of –10 to 10 is assigned for attitude, activity, power, and interest. The attitude rating is found by multiplying attitude by activity. The power rating is found by multiplying power by interest. Ideally, the project champion and the leader want people with not only high power but also high interest. Similarly, people with high activity also have high attitude for the success of the project.

Identify Customers

It is important to identify and understand the customers of a product or process. Depending on the maturity of the product or process, the customers may already be known, but it is still a good practice to identify them. Methods used to identify customers include:

- Marketing analysis data

- Brainstorming

- SIPOC

Customers can be internal; for example, one division of an organization may sell a component or service to another division within the same organization. Just because it is the same organization does not mean we can take the customer for granted. The customer may choose to purchase the product or service from a competitive source, making the internal division a likely target for shutdown. In today's globalized market, everything is possible.

The organization may have interim customers, like dealers or distributors. And then there is the end user, who consumes the product or service from the organization.

Knowing your customer is key. Many organizations struggle with the fundamental question, Who is your customer? It may not be very obvious for some organizations. Some level of data collection and analysis is required.

Internal and external customers should be identified when applicable. Customers can be grouped into segments like the following:

- Internal and external

- Age groups, especially for consumer products

- Geographical location, including climate, language, and ethnicity

- Industry type (e.g., construction, agricultural)

Where possible, a listing of customers within a segment should be constructed. When a project team proposes changes of any kind, customers (internal and external) must be consulted or, at a minimum, the customers' concerns must be represented.

Values for **attitude, activity, power,** and **interest** were assigned using the following rating scales:

Attitude	−10 (strongly against)	to	10 (strongly for)
Activity	0 (completely passive)	to	10 (strongly active)
Power	0 (no effective power)	to	10 (powerful influence)
Interest	0 (no interest)	to	10 (very interested)

Stakeholder categories	Relevant stakeholders	Code	Attitude	Activity	Attitude rating	Power	Interest	Power rating
Contract manufacturer	Offshore manufacturing	C	0	4	0.00	5	3	15.00
Management	Your organization	M	10	5	50.00	8	10	80.00
Employees	Trade compliance team	E	5	10	50.00	5	10	50.00
Service providers	Brokers	B	5	3	15.00	5	2	10.00
Government	US Customs	G	0	0	0.00	0	0	0.00

The reference line in the interest/power plot represents the ideal balance for a vital stakeholder. Points above the line represent stakeholders with potentially high influence on the success of the project; they can either be powerful supporters or powerful detractors.

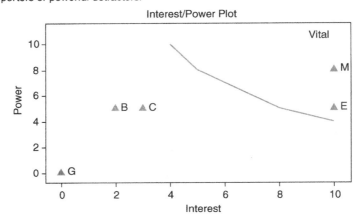

The reference line on the left side of the attitude/activity plot marks the point at which stakeholders are considered potentially adversarial to the project. Points to the left of this line represent stakeholders who could present roadblocks. The reference line on the right marks the point at which stakeholders are considered potentially supportive of the project. Points to the right of this line represent stakeholders who could provide assistance in overcoming roadblocks.

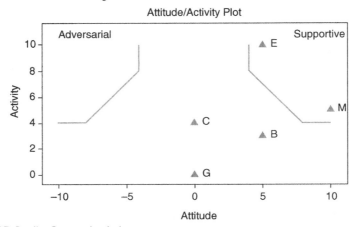

Text from MINITAB Quality Companion help summary.

Figure 6.4 Stakeholder analysis.

Source: Adapted from Janet Jacobsen, "Getting Green with Lean," *Making the Case for Quality,* September 2009, 4.

> Use SIPOC (suppliers, inputs, process, outputs, customers) to identify and define important elements of a process. (Apply)
>
> **Body of Knowledge II.A.4**

4. PROCESS INPUTS AND OUTPUTS

A process is a step or sequence of steps that uses inputs and produces a product or service as an output. Every process has inputs and outputs. Inputs are traditionally categorized as the 5Ms—man (person), material, methods, machines, and Mother Nature. Some organizations also include management, money, and measurement system (as the measurement system may have an impact on the output). Outputs are usually products (hardware, software, systems, etc.) or services. Figure 6.5 depicts the model of a process.

Processes are often made up of subprocesses. For example, a part may be produced through a process that has a machining step. This machining step may be thought of as a process whose steps might include clamping, turning, plunging, facing, and so on. In addition, the plunging step is a process in itself. In a similar manner, a payroll process has subprocesses that include gathering time clock information, making deductions, and so on. The deduction process itself could be thought of as having subprocesses for tax deductions, insurance, and so on.

Process Identification

When planning to study a process or system, it is very important to first identify the boundaries to work within. There are many ways to do this; most are not complex and can be easily implemented with common process knowledge and some investigation.

When defining a process it is important to define its start and end points—its boundaries. If, for example, a team is charged with improving a process, team members need to know these process boundaries. Cross-functional processes may incur subprocess boundaries defined by the organizational structure, geography, and so on.

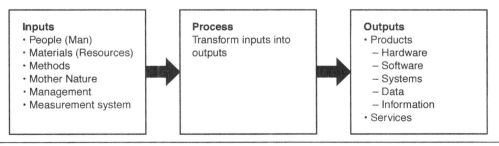

Figure 6.5 Process diagram/model.

The two primary tools used to identify process boundaries are the basic process model identified in Figure 6.5 and the SIPOC diagram in Figure 6.6. The basic process model provides a quick high-level look at the process, but, in some cases, may be too simplistic to provide an improvement team with a clear understanding of the process/problem to work on and the boundaries of where and when to stop.

The SIPOC diagram template in Figure 6.6 can be enhanced by also capturing the requirements of the process and customer.

Understanding the boundaries of the improvement project and/or process does not inhibit outside-the-box thinking; it merely provides clear guidelines on what to deal with as daily activities and improvement activities are performed. Taking the time to actually list or draw the components of the process will assist in visualizing it and being able to find issues more quickly than might have otherwise been possible.

When identifying the process it is important to recognize that processes usually affect multiple departments and organizations. Crossing functional areas (departments) and organizations (suppliers, intercompany) can add challenges to an improvement project. The first step in recognizing the challenges is to understand the organizations and functional areas involved with the process. As noted, the SIPOC diagram can help in identifying these organizations and functional areas as process suppliers and customers. The flowchart (especially the "swim lane" style) and process map are other tools that can be used to help recognize these interactions. Challenges associated with these interactions include, but are not limited to:

- Process ownership (e.g., two or more areas think they own the process and have final decision authority on changes)

- Sharing of information (e.g., proprietary issues, hiding poor performance)

- Commonality of measures (e.g., finance usually measures things in dollars, production uses defects or productivity, engineering considers productivity and design completion)

- Process knowledge or expertise (e.g., manufacturing may not fully understand how the supply chain works or the requirements)

If the challenges identified are significant, they should be included as potential risks for the project so associated mitigation activities can be performed. SIPOC templates for both the basic SIPOC diagram and the SIPOC diagram that captures requirements are provided on the CD-ROM accompanying this book.

QUESTIONS

1. You have been asked to develop a new breakfast menu item for a restaurant chain. Identify your customers (using appropriate tools), capture the voice of the customer using a mock participant group, and determine the product (including packaging) and service requirements.

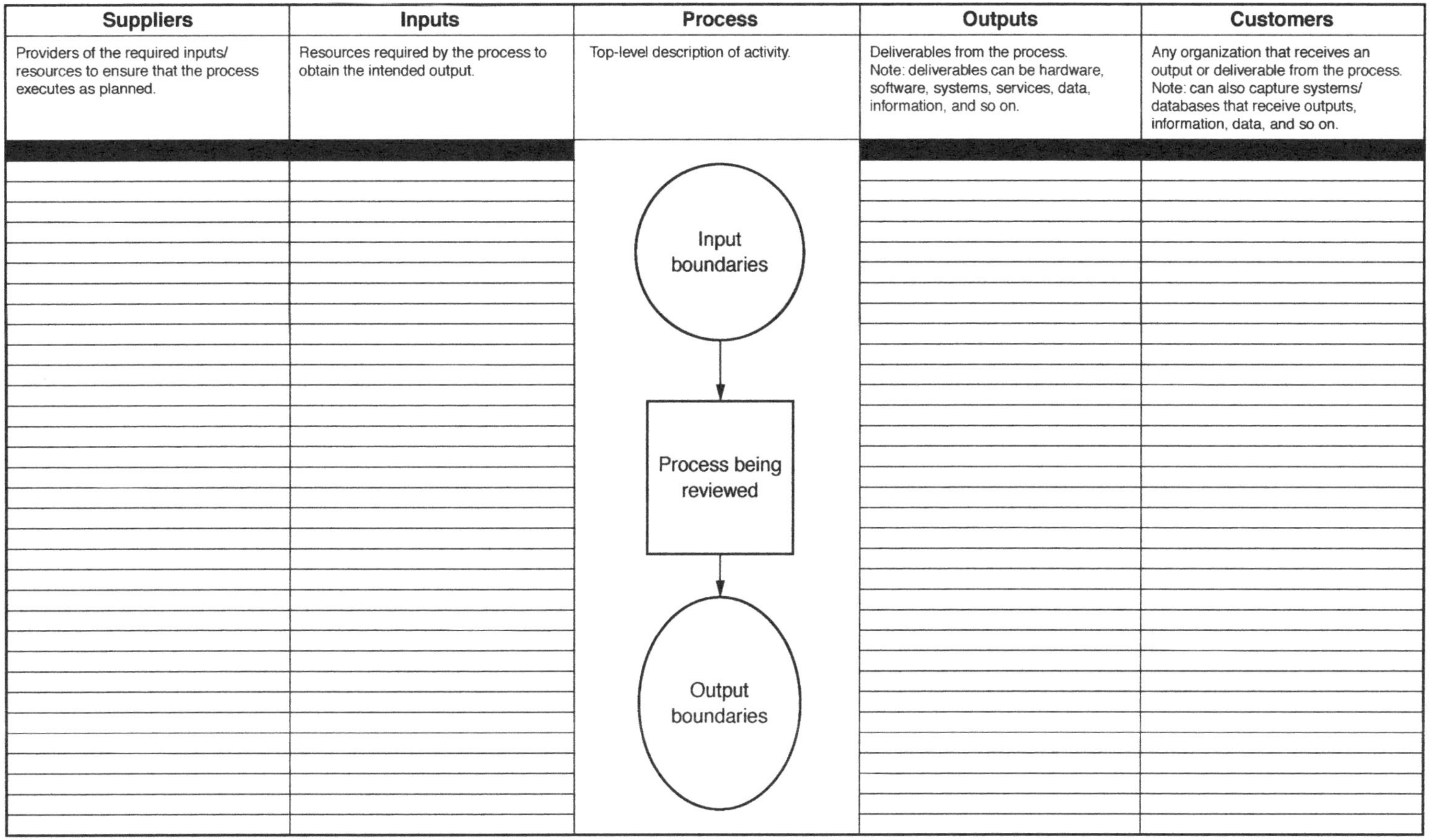

Suppliers	Inputs	Process	Outputs	Customers
Providers of the required inputs/resources to ensure that the process executes as planned.	Resources required by the process to obtain the intended output.	Top-level description of activity.	Deliverables from the process. Note: deliverables can be hardware, software, systems, services, data, information, and so on.	Any organization that receives an output or deliverable from the process. Note: can also capture systems/databases that receive outputs, information, data, and so on.

Process column:

Input boundaries → Process being reviewed → Output boundaries

Figure 6.6   Basic SIPOC diagram.

2. Develop a SIPOC for the example in question #1.

3. Discuss the merits and disadvantages of tools used for customer identification.

4. Identify the criteria used for a Six Sigma project selection. What is the rationale for using these criteria?

Chapter 7
B. Project Management (PM) Basics

Describe the purpose of a charter and its components: problem statement, project scope, baseline
data, and project goal. (Understand)

Body of Knowledge II.B.1

1. PROJECT CHARTER

Project Charter and Problem Statement

A *charter* is a document that states the purpose of a project. It serves as an informal contract that helps the team stay on track with the goals of the organization. A charter should contain the following points:

- *Problem statement.* Identifies what needs to be improved

- *Purpose.* Establishes goals and objectives of the team

- *Benefits.* States how the enterprise will fare better when the project reaches its goals

- *Scope.* Provides project limitations in terms of budget, time, and other resources

- *Results.* Defines the criteria and metrics for project success—including the baseline measures and improvement expectations

The problem statement is a summation of what requires improvement. A problem statement clearly indicates

- Statement of fact (as observed by customer): what, who, where, when, how many

- Project goal of accomplishment (success factors)—described objectively; uses guidance like SMART goals—specific, measurable, achievable, realistic, and time bound

In order to determine project goals, project baseline data are collected. The data can be related to items where improvement is required. Progress is made in comparison with the baseline data.

Examples include:

Eight nonfunctional assemblies manufactured from March 10 to March 20, 2015, were returned by a customer in Fremont, California. Goal is to have *zero* customer returns.

Twenty percent of the calls made by customers from Alameda County in California in 2014 indicate the average permit approval time was 2 weeks against the specified 1 week. Goal is to have 0% complaints.

Project Scope

The purpose of documenting the project scope, or boundaries, is to ensure a common understanding of what the project team, and its associated resources, will work on and what is outside those defined boundaries. The scope is usually defined, at least in part, based on the problem statement, which gives the project its initial focus. Using the problem statement, experience, and tools like SIPOC, brainstorming, and Pareto charts, the scope of the project can be defined and documented.

Project Metrics

Project timelines and activity plans can become little more than paperwork if meaningful performance measurements are not included. These measurements or metrics should link directly to the project goals and through them to the benefits for the enterprise. For example, if a goal is to increase process throughput by 25%, a key metric might be cycle time. The project's intermediate objectives and documentation need to include incremental cycle time reduction measures. Project measures are typically linked to a specific project, usually for the life of just that specific project, and they are often manifested as:

- Percent of work accomplished on time (schedule performance index)

- Percent of work accomplished on budget (cost performance index)

- Other similar measures (e.g., availability of resources, quality of key deliverables)

- Finance metrics like net present value (NPV), return on investment (ROI), payback period, and internal return rate (IRR)

Project Planning Tools

Project planning tools include project charters, project management plans, milestone charts, Gantt charts, project schedules, critical path, and goal and objective statements or bullets. The number of tools used and the depth of data contained in the tools vary based on the project size and scope. Larger projects often have more documentation since they take more time and expend more resources. Project documentation is controlled and maintained (i.e., updated) during the life cycle of the improvement project.

Project Closure

The project charter is an excellent tool to use as a measure of project completion, as it establishes the scope, goals and objectives, and time frame for the project. A review of the charter against documented project results is often sufficient for closing a project. The project sponsor may want an independent review or assessment prior to formal project closure. This is typically done using an audit approach. Another method of proving that the project achieved its intent is analysis of project measures. A postmortem or "lessons learned" session is conducted by the project team to review things that went well and things that could be improved. This summary is used for planning future projects, leveraging any known best practices, and preventing reoccurrence of any past failures. This learning helps strengthen organizational knowledge.

Explain the purpose and benefits of a communication plan and how it can impact the success of the project. (Understand)

Body of Knowledge II.B.2

---

2. COMMUNICATION PLAN

Communication is key to the outcome of a project, be it a simple or complex project. A simple project may require daily or weekly meetings with project members meeting face-to-face or through virtual media to update the status of the project and discuss any new risks encountered.

A complex project, however, may require a formal communication plan. This means setting up a communication protocol (what, who, where, when, how, and how frequently), escalation protocol, escalation threshold (when to escalate), communication effectiveness verification, and so on. Adding to the challenge is a project team that is spread across geographies (distance and time zones), has different cultures, and has a varying level of infrastructure.

There may be a need for high-frequency real-time project updates, as any delay in communication could result in project delay and cost overrun. Having a plan provides structure to communicate the right amount at the right time. While people generally say that there is no such thing as "overcommunication" and that more communication is always good, we need to be cognizant that overcommunication can impact productivity of the team. This may result in team members reading lots of communication rather than being productive. Hence, a communication plan can help with the right amount of communication at the right time.

> Define work breakdown structure (WBS) and Gantt charts and describe how they are used to plan and monitor projects. (Understand)
>
> **Body of Knowledge II.B.3**

3. PROJECT PLANNING

Project planning is a disciplined approach to monitoring how and when a project will be accomplished. You may have heard the quote "Failing to plan is planning to fail." Exactly! Planning for a project involves thinking through the project stages, identifying steps, a timeline, milestones, resources, risks, and so on.

The Gantt chart is a tool used for planning projects. This chart has activities from start to finish, the timeline, the duration, milestones, resources, and interdependence between activities.

Activities identified from start to finish are called the work breakdown structure (WBS). WBS is developed by the project team members by brainstorming. First, high-level activities are identified, and then the team drills down to the subactivities for every high-level activity. By identifying these activities, the project manager can accurately know the progress and delays and can assign or relocate resources to ensure the project stays on schedule. An example of a Gantt chart and template are provided on the CD-ROM accompanying this book.

As with many of the tools and processes listed in this book, there is a lot of information available in various references on project planning and project management. There is even a professional certification available just for project management. In this book, however, only the basics of project planning to assist in daily work are discussed.

Effective project planning requires skills in the following areas:

- Information processing
- Communication
- Resource negotiations
- Securing commitments
- Incremental and modular planning
- Ensuring measurable milestones
- Facilitating top management involvement[1]

> Select and use various PM tools: activity network diagrams, affinity diagrams, matrix charts, relations charts, and tree diagrams. (Understand)
>
> **Body of Knowledge II.B.4**

4. PROJECT MANAGEMENT TOOLS

Activity Network Diagrams

The activity network diagram (AND), also known as the arrow diagram, displays the sequential order in which tasks are carried out in a project (see Figure 7.1). The diagram illustrates the efficiency of the schedule for the entire project. It can also reveal any potential scheduling and resource problems in the sequence planned. A main benefit of the arrow diagram is the calculation of the "critical path" of the project. This is the flow of critical steps in which a delay in any of the steps will affect the duration of the entire project. A project manager looks at the critical path closely to ensure resources are adequately planned to help make up for any delays in the project.

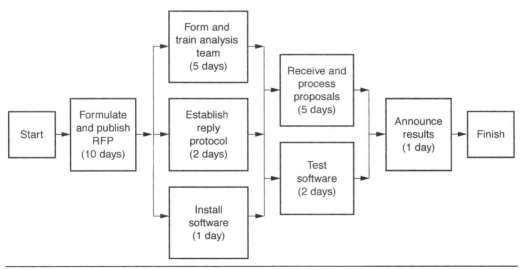

Figure 7.1   Example of an activity network diagram.

Guidelines for Constructing an Activity Network Diagram

Project team members start with brainstorming all the project tasks for every stage. The brainstorming is not sequential; inputs are received at random.

Next, the team members write each task on a card or sticky note. The team must determine the correct sequence of the tasks (this may be an iterative process, as the team may go back and forth on some tasks). The team asks three questions for each task:

1. Which tasks must happen before this one can begin?

2. Which tasks can be done at the same time as this one?

3. Which tasks should happen immediately after this one?

Once the team has agreed on the sequence, the sticky notes are placed on the diagram in sequential order. Time should flow from left to right and concurrent tasks should be vertically aligned (for ease of visualization). Sticky notes are arranged in such a way that circles are drawn between them to depict "events." An event marks the beginning or end of a task. Thus, events are nodes that separate tasks. This is why some practitioners call this useful tool a "node diagram."

The tasks are supplemented with a data box of four grids: earliest start (ES), earliest finish (EF), latest start (LS), and latest finish (LF). Data from the grids are used to calculate slack time for each task.

Slack time is the time a task can be delayed without impacting the overall project duration. Hence, by definition, there is *no* slack time for the tasks that are in the critical path. A step-by-step approach for developing an activity network diagram can be found on ASQ's website (http://asq.org/learn-about-quality/new-management-planning-tools/overview/arrow-diagram.html).

Affinity Diagrams

An affinity diagram (Figure 7.2) is a display of brainstormed ideas, survey results, and any type of inputs arranged by affinity or an overarching theme. The affinity diagram complements brainstorming and organizes a large number of ideas into their natural relationships. When the team is overwhelmed with facts and ideas, issues seem too large and complex to grasp, or group consensus is necessary, the team arranges the ideas in an affinity diagram. This tool is very helpful in analyzing customer qualitative data and feedback. Convergence can also be accomplished by asking brainstorming participants to collect data on the various causes for a future reporting session.

At the outset, it may appear that the data can be interpreted just by eyeballing them. However, grouping them by theme or affinity provides a more effective analysis. There is a definite advantage to using this tool. We are all bombarded with information on a daily basis and receive all kinds of inputs. Our brain is not wired to process information from different categories if they are arranged at random.

Guidelines for Developing an Affinity Diagram

A team related to the subject of discussion is assembled in a physical room or virtual network. The problem statement is clearly written down by the facilitator.

Problem: What are some of the ways to reduce cycle time for process A?

Machine	**Personnel**	**Infrastructure**
• Run machine faster • Get a new machine • Apply new controls • Reduce setup time • Simplify machine operations	• Assign more people • Provide additional training • Let Joe run the process/ machine • Provide help during setup	• Reduce paperwork • Improve forklift uptime • Replace the conveyor • Purchase a new overhead crane • Ensure prompt delivery of route sheets

Vendor	**Maintenance**
• Improve vendor communication • Use cell phone to contact vendor • Have additional sources • Work with vendor to improve quality and delivery • Reduce resupply time	• Better lubricant • Reliability-centered maintenance • More frequent lubrication • More prompt response to maintenance calls

Figure 7.2   Example of an affinity diagram.

Team members clarify the statement in case of any questions. The team is given a specified amount of time to write down their ideas on sticky notes (one idea per note). When time elapses, the facilitator collects the inputs and puts the sticky notes on a sheet of brown paper or butcher paper. Team members work together to group the inputs by theme or common topic. This is affinity. Depending on the number of inputs, the team may create subgroups or merge subgroups to form a super group. Any duplicate inputs are removed.

Users often get confused between the cause and effect diagram and the affinity diagram. Even though the brainstormed inputs are grouped in the cause and effect diagram, there is a cause and subcause relationship among them. In the affinity diagram, the grouping is based on the overarching topic or theme.

A step-by-step approach for developing an affinity diagram can be found on ASQ's website (http://asq.org/learn-about-quality/idea-creation-tools/overview/affinity.html).

Matrix Charts

A matrix diagram is used to display relationships between two or more groups (set or products or entity). There are many types of matrix diagrams depending on the number of groups studied.

Determine the most suitable software package

		Criteria				
		Compatibility 0.25	Cost 0.3	Ease of use 0.40	Training time 0.05	Total
Options	Package A	1.00	0.45	1.20	0.15	2.80
	Package B	0.25	1.20	0.80	0.05	2.30
	Package C	0.75	0.45	1.60	0.20	3.00
	Package D	0.50	0.90	0.40	0.10	1.90

Figure 7.3 Example of a prioritization matrix.

The most popular and commonly used matrix is the L matrix. This provides the interrelationship between two groups. Groups typically have multiple attributes. The relationship is attribute to attribute between the groups. A classical example of this tool is to compare various suppliers on multiple attributes like quality, cost, delivery, and responsiveness (see Figure 7.3).

Other types of matrix diagrams are the T, Y, C, and X diagrams. The most recognizable of the matrix charts is the prioritization matrix.[2]

A step-by-step approach for developing a matrix chart can be found on ASQ's website (http://asq.org/learn-about-quality/new-management-planning-tools/overview/matrix-diagram.html).

Relations Charts

A relation chart (also called a relationship diagram or matrix) provides interrelationships in the form of cause and effect. This easy-to-use tool helps team members explore the causes and effects of each item by pointing the arrow toward the effect. This approach is typically used when the problem or issue at hand is complex and every input from the brainstorm could potentially have multiple causes and effects.

Relationships △ =weak ○ =moderate ⊙ =strong	Pizza not hot enough	Delivered late	Toppings not as per order	Wrong pizza delivered	Burnt crust
Traffic jam	○	⊙			
Oven heater error	○				⊙
Heat insulation quality	⊙				
Difficulty finding address	△	⊙			
Did not understand customer accent			△	△	
Clerical error during order receipt			⊙	⊙	
Order not clearly identified		△	⊙	⊙	
Mix-up on the delivery shelf		△	○	○	○

Figure 7.4 Example of a relationship matrix.

Guidelines for Developing a Relations Chart

A problem statement or the objective of the diagram is documented on a sticky note. The team brainstorms ideas about the issue and writes them on cards or notes. Inputs already presented in an affinity diagram or cause and effect diagram may also be used. The ideas are placed side by side and the team explores whether an idea is a cause or an effect of another idea. The question "Does this idea cause or influence any other idea?" is repeated for every idea. The team draws arrows from each idea to the ones it causes or influences.

Analysis of the diagram:

- Once the cause and effect possibilities are identified for each idea, count the arrows in and out for each idea. Write the counts at the bottom of each box. The ones with the most arrows are the key ideas.

- Note which ideas have primarily outgoing (from) arrows. These are basic causes.

- Note which ideas have primarily incoming (to) arrows. These are final effects that also may be critical to address.

- Also review the ideas with fewer arrows incoming and outgoing from idea. They may be important as well.

A step-by-step approach for developing a relations chart can be found on ASQ's website (http://asq.org/learn-about-quality/new-management-planning-tools/overview/relations-diagram.html).

Tree Diagrams

A tree diagram (also known as a critical to quality tree diagram) is used to analyze and display subtopics and topics branching out from the main topic. This diagram (Figure 7.5) is similar to an organization chart. Sometimes it is flipped

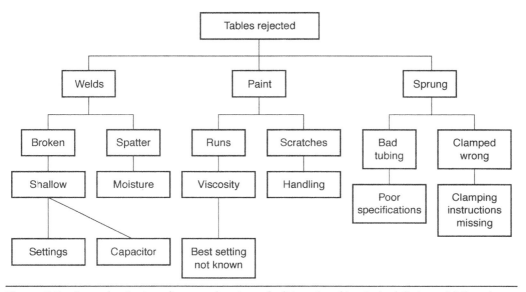

Figure 7.5   Example of a tree diagram showing a fault tree (used to study defects and failures).

counterclockwise from left to right. The head of the organization is your main topic, subordinates and their staff and their organization are subtopics, and so forth.

This diagram can be effectively used in a team setting to solicit inputs and map out the subtopics. An example of this application is root cause analysis of complex topics that can have multiple possibilities.

Guidelines for Developing a Tree Diagram

Identify a key topic and post it on the wall. Ask the team to brainstorm and provide input as to what causes the main topic. The team may not always provide input at the right hierarchy, but this does not mean that the input is useless or that it should be discarded. Collect the input and place it in the diagram. It can always be promoted up in the tree hierarchy or pushed down in the tree. Once all the inputs are arranged with branches and subbranches, the team should review the diagram and verify that the causes and subcauses are in the right hierarchy level.

More details on a step-by-step approach for developing a tree diagram can be found on ASQ's website (http://asq.org/learn-about-quality/new-management-planning-tools/overview/tree-diagram.html).

Explain how tollgate or phase reviews are used throughout the DMAIC lifecycle. (Understand)

Body of Knowledge II.B.5

---

5. PHASE REVIEWS

Tollgate or phase reviews are periodic progress reviews conducted for Six Sigma projects. The project manager and the project team may identify significant milestones at which the project should be reviewed. Milestones may be aligned with the natural stages of the Six Sigma structure (i.e., Define-Measure-Analyze-Improve-Control). Every organization is different. Some organizations set up entry and exit criteria for every stage to ensure all the necessary due diligence is completed before moving to the next stage. There may also be significant milestones between stages. As an example, recognizing the need for a Six Sigma project, building stakeholder consensus, and obtaining sponsor approval may likely be a milestone. Setting up a data collection system could be another milestone. The project manager and the team have to recognize the appropriate stages of the project to plan reviews. The purpose of this periodic review is to ensure that the project follows the necessary structure, deliverables are met, risks are anticipated and mitigated, project cost and time are closely monitored, and customer and other stakeholders are not negatively impacted.

A Six Sigma tollgate review template can be found on the CD-ROM accompanying this book.

QUESTIONS

1. What are the key components of a project charter? Develop a project charter for the examples provided on page 80.

2. Evaluate key challenges of managing a virtual team. Be sure to include complexities like geography and languages.

3. Describe the importance of understanding critical path in a project.

4. Develop a prioritization matrix that you will use in buying a real estate property (residential or commercial). Assign weighting based on relative importance.

5. Suggest examples of questions that you would ask during a tollgate phase review.

Part III
Measure Phase

Chapter 8
A. Basic Statistics

> Define, calculate, and interpret measures of central tendency (mean, median, mode) and measures of dispersion (standard deviation, range, variance). (Apply)
>
> **Body of Knowledge III.A**

Central tendency is one of the key attributes used in our day-to-day expression of measure. Mean, also known as "average," is a frequently used measure. Examples of mean in daily use include the following: the mean weight of a product sold is 100 grams, the mean time between equipment failures is 20,000 hours, and the mean distance to target is 10 meters. Median is another measure of central tendency used extensively in economics (e.g., median household income). Mode is also used in daily context as the most occurring event. For data that are normally distributed, mean, median, and mode are the same. If the distribution is skewed to either the left or the right, the median will be away from the mean.

The average represents a set of observations or data that are added together and divided by the total number of data points. This provides the central value of the observations. This measure is very widely used because of its ease of computing; no advanced knowledge of statistics is required. Although the average is a useful measure for making quick decisions, it is not robust. This measure can be skewed by extreme data.

To find the average of the data set {11, 7, 1, 5, 3, 9, and 13}, first add all the data and then divide by the number of data points.

$$(11 + 7 + 1 + 5 + 3 + 9 + 13)/7 = 7$$

Median is the central value of a set of observations or data arranged in ascending or descending order. If the number of values in the data set is an odd number, then the median is simply the value in the middle of the ordered data set.

To find the median, first arrange the data set {11, 7, 1, 5, 3, 9, and 13} in ascending order.

1 3 5 7 9 11 13

Next, find the middle value of the data set. In this example, 7 is the median; it has three data points before it and three data points after.

In this data set, interestingly, the average (mean) and the median are the same. However, there is no mode. *Mode* is the value in the data set that occurs most frequently. Since the values in this data set appear only once, there is no mode. Mode is easily identified by glancing at the data set; no additional steps are required.

If additional data were added to the data set, it would look as follows:

$$\{11, 7, 7, 1, 5, 3, 9, 7, \text{ and } 13\}$$

Two additional data points of the value 7 have been added. Now the mode is also 7.

If in a data set, mean, median, and mode are equal, the data set tends to be normally distributed. The distribution of the above data set is a small data set, and hence the classical bell shape is not evident. Data sets with more than 30 data points are generally considered large and adequate to make statistical decisions.[1]

Central tendency alone can be misleading without understanding dispersion. Measures of dispersion—range, variance, and standard deviation—are important for knowing how tightly the data are packed or spread around the central value. For a simple measure like range, we use the extreme values' minimum and maximum to describe variability. For standard deviation, an expression of the number of "sigma" is used to describe dispersion.

The spread of the sample is also referred to as dispersion or variation and is usually quantified with either the sample range (defined as the highest value minus the lowest value) or the sample standard deviation. Range is an easy measure of dispersion. This can be done by visually spotting the lowest and highest values in the data set and subtracting them. This approach may be most appropriate for a quick answer and to make a conservative estimate. Variance and standard deviation are more robust measures for dispersion. Range can be easily influenced by extreme outliers in the data set. The sample standard deviation is the more sophisticated metric and is defined as

$$s = \sqrt{\frac{\Sigma(x - \bar{x})^2}{n - 1}}$$

where

$\bar{x}$ = the sample mean or average

n = sample size

This formula produces an estimate of the standard deviation of the population from which the sample was drawn. If data for the entire population are used (rare in practical applications), the population standard deviation is defined as

$$\sigma = \sqrt{\frac{\Sigma(x - \mu)^2}{N}}$$

where

μ = the population mean or average

N = population size

Due to the complexity of these formulas, one could use a calculator with standard deviation capabilities or Microsoft Excel or statistical software.

The shape of the sample refers to a smooth curve that serves as a sort of umbrella covering, approximately, the tops of the bars in the histogram. In this case, it appears that the sample came from a normally distributed population. Other descriptors of shape include kurtosis, symmetry, and skewness.

The following data represent a sample of critical dimensions of a chemical deposition operation. What conclusions can be reached by looking at the data set?

5.551, 5.361, 5.392, 5.479, 5.456, 5.542, 5.423, 5.476, 5.298, 5.499, 5.312, 5.319, 5.317, 5.314, 5.382

The charts in Figure 8.1 reveal information about the sample data that is not obvious from the data list, such as:

- The spread of the sample

- An indication of the shape of the sample

- Center of the sample

- Fitting of normal distribution of the sample (explained later in this chapter)

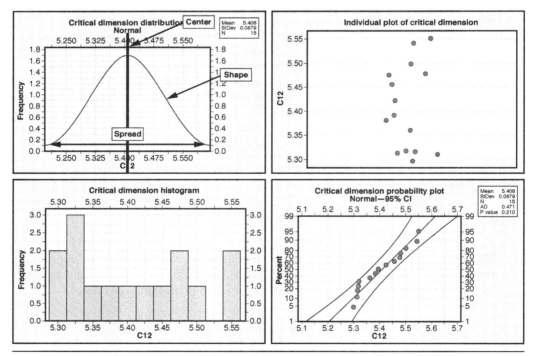

Figure 8.1   Example of a data set as illustrated by a frequency distribution, individual plot, histogram, and probability plot.

Table 8.1   Summary of descriptive measures.

Name	Symbol	Formula/description
Measures of central tendency		
Mean	$\bar{x}$	$\dfrac{\Sigma x}{n}$
Median	$\tilde{x}$	Middle number in sorted list
Mode		Most frequent number
Measure of dispersion		
Range	R	High value – low value
Sample standard deviation	s	$\sqrt{\dfrac{\Sigma(x-\bar{x})^2}{n-1}}$

In the example in Figure 8.1:

- The mean = (sum of the values) ÷ (number of values) = $\Sigma x / n =$ 81.121/15 = 5.408.

- The median of the 15 values would be the eighth value when the sample is sorted in ascending order, in this case 5.392. If there is an even number of values, the median is obtained by averaging the two middle values.

Of the three measures, the mean is the most widely used in quality engineering applications like control charts. The sample mean is often denoted as x with a bar above it and pronounced "x-bar."

A summary of measures for central tendency and dispersion is shown in Table 8.1.

QUESTIONS

1. Calculate the mean, median, and sample standard deviation for the following data set and evaluate whether the data follow a normal distribution.

    8.46, 8.77, 10.16, 10.51, 9.71, 10.89, 8.59, 11.21, 8.78, 9.19, 8.70, 9.33, 11.57, 10.69, 10.75

2. What are the challenges in considering only the average (mean) when making decisions?

3. How do you calculate the median if the data set has an even number of data points?

4. When are sample standard deviation and population standard deviation used? When is it appropriate to use range?

5. If the bell curve is hugging toward the center, would you conclude that the variation is small or large?

6. What are the challenges of using average and range as measures of central tendency and dispersion?

Chapter 9

B. Data Collection

Describe the critical elements of a data collection plan, including an operational definition, data sources, the method to be used for gathering data, and how frequently it will be gathered. Describe why data collection plans are important. (Understand)

Body of Knowledge III.B.1

1. DATA COLLECTION PLANS

Data collection is performed in an organization for various reasons:

- Legal, regulatory, or statutory requirements

- Analysis, improvement, and knowledge management

- Contractual requirements of customers

Irrespective of the reasons, data collection can be very expensive if it is not effectively planned and implemented. Many organizations tend to collect more data than required. Answering some basic questions—such as what, why, where, when, who, and how (5W1H)—before starting to collect the data can help make the data collection more effective. Where possible, real-time data acquisition from equipment is more effective and reduces human errors and data transfer errors.

A typical data collection plan (Table 9.1) includes:

What to measure

    — What do you want to measure?

    — Type of measure

    — Operational definition (e.g., cycle time, lead time, process time; these terms can have different meanings in different organizations)

Table 9.1 Data collection plan.

Define what to measure			Define how to measure			Who will do it?	Sample plan			
Measure	Type of measure	Operational definition	Measurement or test method	Data tags needed to stratify the data	Data collection method	Person(s) assigned	What?	Where?	When?	How many?
Name of parameter or condition to be measured	X or Y attribute or discrete data, product, or process data	Measurement defined in such a way as to achieve repeatable results from multiple observers	Visual inspection or automated test? Test instruments are defined Procedures for data collection are defined	Data tags (e.g., time, date, location, tester, line, customer, buyer, and operator) are defined for the measure	Manual? Spreadsheet? Computer based?	State who has the responsibility	What measure is being collected	Location for data collection	How often the data are collected	The number of data points collected per sample

Measurement systems analysis

How will you know the measures are accurate, linear, stable, repeatable, and reproducible?

Responsibility for measurement system qualification and release? Responsibility for measurement training? Who will measure?

Control plan, FMEA, customer specification, manufacturing work instructions CTQ vs critical to process (CTP) matrix are typical sources of input for "what to measure"

How to measure

— Measurement or test method

— Data tags need to stratify the data

— Data collection method

When? (Frequency)

— Timing and how frequent

Where? (Data collection point)

— Process step or physical location

Who will measure?

— Responsibility to measure (or collect) the data

Sampling plan

— How many? (Number of data points to be statistically valid)

Define and distinguish between these types of data.
(Understand)

Body of Knowledge III.B.2

---

2. QUALITATIVE AND QUANTITATIVE DATA

The term "qualitative data" is derived from "quality" or "attributes." Qualitative data are expressed in words like "tall," "short," "hot," "cold," "long," "wide," and so on. Certain process measures are expressed only in qualitative data. Consumer experience and perceptions are measured qualitatively. With the rise of social media, big-data analytics plays a major role in qualitative data analysis. An example of such analysis can be done using tools like Wordle (http://www.wordle.net), a website where you can construct "word clouds," and trending features in social media software applications.

The term "quantitative data" is derived from "quantity." Quantitative data are expressed through discrete and continuous data. Examples of discrete data are number of defects, number of defectives in a product, or number of errors made in service functions. There are no partial values, like half a defect. Continuous data can be any number of possibilities between two whole numbers; for example, the length of a widget can be 10 mm or 10.1 mm or 10.001 mm and so on. It can go any number of decimals or fractions that the measurement method and technology will practically allow. Examples of continuous data are product dimensions and service quality delivery cycle time. While continuous data are more informative for decision making, data collection can be expensive. Discrete data are easier to measure and collect. The ASQ *Certified Six Sigma Green Belt Handbook* provides statistical methods for analyzing discrete and continuous data.

> Use various data collection techniques, including surveys, interviews, check sheets, and checklists to gather data that contributes to the process being improved. (Apply)
>
> **Body of Knowledge III.B.3**

3. DATA COLLECTION TECHNIQUES

There are several methods for collecting data:

- *Surveys.* This tool is used when a big sample size of data needs to be collected. Inputs are quick and often the first instinct from the input provider. Response rates are usually low, but inexpensive to collect. The quality of the survey feedback can vary significantly based on how the survey was created.

- *Face-to-face interviews.* This method provides highly reliable data, but the data are expensive to collect. The interviewee should be willing to commit time and provide honest feedback. The interviewee's body language and emotions provide additional perspective to data collection, which is not available when soliciting inputs through surveys.

- *Focus groups.* In this method, a group of individuals is assembled to obtain perceptions, thoughts, beliefs, and opinions about a product or service. It is similar to the face-to-face interview in that the interviewer may be able to obtain direct feedback. However, the interactions among the focus group participants may be skewed by dominant participants. Having an experienced moderator will help obtain unbiased feedback.

- *Mystery shopping.* This method is used by organizations to solicit data anonymously by having shoppers try out the organization's products and services. The shoppers are trained to ask certain questions, procure a service, make a complaint, and collect data from their experience. The organization analyzes the inputs provided by mystery shoppers and uses this information to improve its existing products, services, systems, and processes. It may reward employees who personify the organizational value, but it is discouraged from punishing employees who did not perform well during the mystery shopper experience. An advantage of this approach is that the inputs may be similar to how an actual customer would behave.

- *Customer feedback.* Customer feedback may be solicited in many ways: surveys, face-to-face meetings, 1-800 calls, complaints, returned materials due to failures, and so on. Erosion in market share is another indirect customer feedback. All these are lagging indicators. Engaging customers in the early stages of the product and service design, soliciting requirements, and receiving inputs at all stages of development are proactive methods for capturing data.

- *Automatic data capture.* Automatic capture is a real-time data capture. This may be expensive to set up, due to interfacing the hardware and software with the source where the data are generated. This prevents errors in the data and the associated cost of correcting the error, and also prevents wrong decisions made from erroneous data. One of the main advantages of the automatic data capture is the availability of the data to take action. There is no time lag between data collection and availability. This may be important where the risks are high, such as in financial, healthcare, and security management. A classic example is alerting a customer when fraud has been detected on the customer's account.

- *Manual data capture.* In manual data collection, resources go to the source where data are generated and physically collect the data. They either write down the data or capture them electronically. This process is not only slow but may also become expensive depending on the resources required to capture the data.

One-on-one data collection methods, like focus groups and face-to-face interviews, have a high integrity of data and provide an opportunity to clarify answers with the respondents, whereas a data collection method like a survey has a low response rate (approximately 10%–15%). Additionally, improperly constructed surveys can result in misleading conclusions.

Manual data collection includes the use of tools like checklists and check sheets. A checklist has a standard set of items/questions that are required to be verified/answered for a process or product. As an example, an equipment technician uses a maintenance checklist to go over a list of items and confirm each item's fitness for use. In another example, a nurse asks a patient a list of questions and collects data before sending the patient to the doctor. A check sheet is used to tally the occurrence of an event or incident. For example, a process may be producing different types of defects on a product. A tally mark is made on a check sheet to capture the occurrence of each type of defect. See Chapter 5, "Quality Tools and Six Sigma Metrics," for additional information and application.

Where manual data entry is involved, it is more efficient to use data coding to avoid repetitive recording of numbers and errors due to fatigue. Decoding may be applied depending on the analysis to be performed.

EXAMPLE

An inspector is measuring the diameter of a machine part. If the data are expected to fall between the upper and lower specification limits, repetitively typing the measurement data may result in clerical or administrative errors. In this case, the measurement values can be coded in a single-digit number representing the full measurement value. An important aspect of this approach is that we should still be able to arrive at the measurement value after decoding (see Table 9.2).

Table 9.2 Coding–decoding.

Coding		Decoding	
Actual measurements	Coded value	Coded value	Actual measurements
10.120	1	1	10.120
10.121	2	2	10.121
10.122	3	3	10.122
10.123	4	4	10.123

It is important to ensure that the data are collected with accuracy and integrity. Accuracy of the data depends on data collection method, technology used, verification due diligence, and so on. Integrity of the data depends on whether any bias is associated with collecting and reporting the data.

Techniques for Ensuring Data Accuracy and Integrity

Even sophisticated data collection and analysis techniques can be defeated if the data are entered with errors. Common causes of errors include:

- Units of measure not defined (e.g., feet or meters?)
- Closeness of handwritten characters/legibility (e.g., 2 or Z?)
- Inadequate measurement system resolution/discrimination
- Rounding off measurements and losing precision
- Emotional bias resulting in distortion of data
- Inadequate use of validation techniques—using guesswork or personal bias
- Multiple points of data entry—opportunity for inconsistency and errors
- Poor instructions or training causing erroneous data entry
- Ambiguous terminology
- Clerical or typographical errors

To minimize error:

- Have a carefully constructed data collection plan

- Maintain a calibration schedule for data collection equipment

- Conduct repeatability and reproducibility (R&R) studies on measurement system[1]

- Record appropriate auxiliary information regarding units, time of collection, conditions, measurement equipment used, name of data recorder, and so on

- Use appropriate statistical tests to remove outliers

- If data are transmitted or stored digitally, use an appropriate redundant error correction system

- Provide clear and complete instruction and training

QUESTIONS

1. Put together a data collection plan for errors generated at a hospital. (Choose either medical or administrative errors or both based on your experience.)

2. Discuss why an operations definition is important for data collection.

3. Discuss why continuous data are preferred over discrete data, and discuss the pros and cons of each.

4. Provide an example of the type of data collection method you would recommend for a specific scenario.

5. What are the recommendations to reduce or prevent errors for manual data collection?

Chapter 10
C. Measurement System Analysis (MSA)

Define precision, accuracy, bias, linearity, and stability, and describe how these terms are applied in the measurement phase. (Understand)

Body of Knowledge III.C.1

1. MSA TERMS

Measurement system analysis (MSA) is an area of statistical study that explores the variation in measurement data due to:

- *Calibration.* Drift in average measurements of an absolute value.

- *Accuracy.* Closeness of agreement between the average of one or more measured results and a reference value.

- *Precision.* Closeness of repeated readings to each other. Knowing the precision of a measurement and test equipment helps process owners understand the random error during the Measure phase. A random error is a component of the measurement system variation. Precision (P) is used in relation to tolerance (T) to calculate the P/T ratio during the Measure phase.

- *Stability.* Drift in absolute value over time. Drift in equipment explains why the process appears to go out of control at certain intervals. Even though the process might not have shifted, the equipment may indicate that the process is out of control. This is monitored by measuring a controlled sample on a periodic basis and monitoring the control chart from these data.

- *Repeatability.* Variation in measuring equipment when measured by one appraiser in the same setting at the same time. Reviewing repeatability during the Measure phase helps process owners understand the suitability of the equipment.

- *Reproducibility.* Variation in measurement when measured by two or more appraisers multiple times. Reviewing reproducibility during the Measure phase helps process owners understand the variability due to human inability in reproducing same measurement trial after trial.

- *Linearity.* Accuracy of measurement at various points of measuring range in the equipment. Understanding linearity during the Measure phase helps process owners understand why the measurement is inconsistent across the measurement range of the equipment.

- *Bias.* Difference between absolute value and true value with respect to a standard master at various measurement points of the measuring range. (Often in practice accuracy and bias are used interchangeably.) Understanding bias during the Measure phase helps process owners understand why the equipment is not accurate and that there may be a need for calibration and adjustment of bias closer to the true value.

Until the early 1990s MSA was used extensively in measurement laboratories and was less known to the industrial world. After the inception of the QS-9000 (now ISO/TS 16949) standard in the automobile industry, the importance of MSA was well understood by other sectors as well.

An important issue for the Six Sigma Yellow Belt practitioner here is that in the quest to reduce variation, the measurement system should be one of the first things analyzed for two reasons:

- All data from the process are, in effect, filtered through the measurement system

- It often represents the most cost-effective way to reduce variation

Even statistical process control (SPC) experts have begun to write their SPC flows with "conduct an MSA study" as a starting step. MSA is actually that important. It is not uncommon for measurement systems to have an error of 40%–50% of the process specification.

Describe how and why GR&R is used in the measurement phase. (Understand)

Body of Knowledge III.C.2

---

2. GAUGE REPEATABILITY & REPRODUCIBILITY (GR&R)

Repeatability is the equipment measurement variation expressed as standard deviation. Measurements are taken from the same equipment by one appraiser over a short period of time. See Figure 10.1.

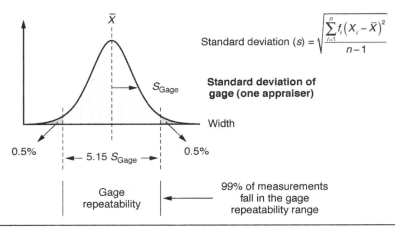

Figure 10.1 Gage repeatability.

Reproducibility is the appraiser measurement variation expressed as standard deviation. Measurements are taken from the same equipment by more than one appraiser. See Figure 10.2.

The repeatability portion of the measurement variation is attributed to the inherent variation of the measurement equipment. One factor that influences this portion of variation is the design of the measurement system itself. In the case of reproducibility, the influential factors are the setting of the work piece (any special loading and unloading), consistency in measurement, and operator training, skill, and knowledge.

Measurement variation is expressed as a ratio of precision to tolerance (P/T). In this case, the value of the divisor "Total variation" is replaced by one-sixth of the tolerance, that is (tolerance) ÷ 6. Most authorities agree that in this situation, %GRR is defined as:

$$(100 \times \text{GRR}) \div (\text{Tolerance}/6)$$

Six is used to cover 99.73% of the variation. Some practitioners use 5.15 to cover 99% of the variation. For information on the theory and constants used in this form, see *MSA Reference Manual.*[1]

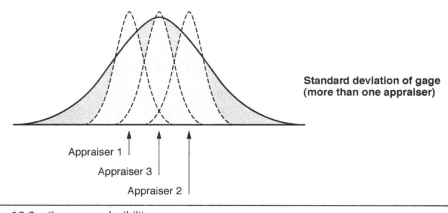

Figure 10.2 Gage reproducibility.

There are also many inexpensive Microsoft Excel–based macro applications available as off-the-shelf software. Figures 10.3 and 10.4 show the same data analyzed using Minitab statistical software.

Sources of measurement variation are shown in Figure 10.5.

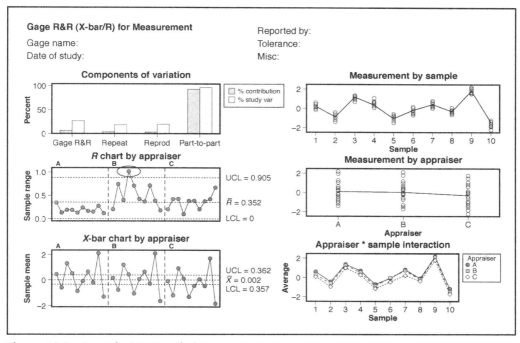

Figure 10.3   Example GR&R analysis.

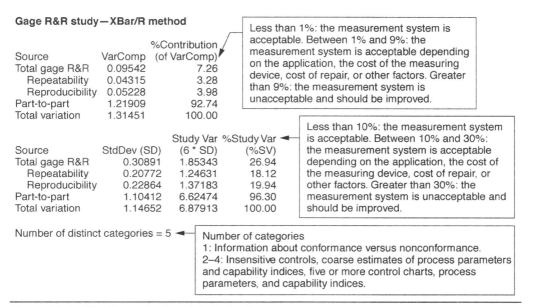

Figure 10.4   GR&R report using statistical software.

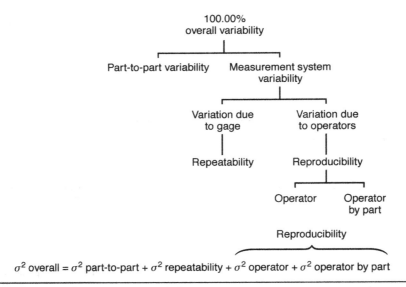

Figure 10.5   Sources of measurement variation.

Measurement system discrimination is the ability to detect changes in the measured characteristic. If a measurement system's discrimination is inadequate, it may not be possible to accurately measure process variation or quantify characteristic values of individual parts.[2]

There are minor differences between the manual method and Minitab software due to rounding errors. The Minitab analysis is more accurate.

As mentioned earlier, the measurement system plays a major role in process capability (C_p) assessment. The higher the GR&R, the higher the error in C_p assessment. This increases even more as the capability increases. For example, with an observed C_p of 1 and a GR&R of 50%, the actual C_p is 1.23. By bringing the GR&R down to 10%, C_p is more reflective of the actual process, that is, 1.01. More details on this table, formula, and graphs are available in *Concepts for R&R Studies*.[3]

More advanced statistics are available for this type of attribute study involving ranking scores. Examples of this application where objectivity is added to subjective measures are as follows:

- Tasting tea, coffee, and wine and assigning a score for taste attributes

- Examiners correcting a paper and assigning a score

- Fabrics or polished surfaces where the score is assigned by feeling the surface

When an independent estimate of process variation is not available, *or* to determine process direction and continued suitability of the measurement system for process control, *the sample parts must be selected from the process and represent the entire production operating range.* The variation in sample parts (PV) selected for MSA study is used to calculate the total variation (TV) of the study. The TV index (i.e., %GR&R to TV) is an indicator of process direction and continued suitability of the measurement system for process control. If the sample parts *do not* represent the production process, TV must be ignored in the assessment. Ignoring TV does not affect assessments using tolerance (product control) or an independent estimate of process variation (process control).

The key point is this: The underlying reason to conduct ongoing MSA of your measurement equipment is to understand the uncertainty of the measurement system; that is, what exactly are you really measuring?

QUESTIONS

1. Compare accuracy and precision. Describe how these measures are used to certify measurement equipment fitness for use.

2. What specific actions would you recommend for higher variation due to (a) repeatability and (b) reproducibility?

3. Explain why it is important to conduct a linearity and bias study for measurement equipment.

4. Identify two or more common misperceptions about MSA study and provide your rationale to counter.

5. What are the applications for variable and attribute GR&R study? Provide examples.

Part IV
Analyze Phase

Chapter 11
A. Process Analysis Tools

Define how 5S and value analysis can be used to identify and eliminate waste. (Understand)

Body of Knowledge IV.A.1

1. LEAN TOOLS

5S concepts and value analysis are explained in detail in Chapter 2, "Lean Foundations and Principles." In this section we will look at how these lean tools can be used to identify and eliminate waste.

Every process that we can think of can be perfected by pursuing a journey of continual improvement. Whether we are paying for a service provided by a government agency or a product provided by a private company, we as consumers are paying for the waste as well. As an example, I recently received a quote from a software company that explicitly provided allowance for additional hours to make corrections to anticipated faulty work. We have been desensitized to accept waste as normal operating procedure. What can be done to challenge this assumption? If every organization identified and eliminated waste, we would be left with just the value-added activities, which are the bare minimum required for the transformation of input to output.

Now, how do you identify waste? Some types are obvious but others are not. Obvious waste in any process is a result of not doing things right the first time (and every time thereafter). In a service industry, wastes include rework, redoing, reinspection of the activity, waiting, delays, and so on. In a manufacturing environment, waste is producing scrap, rework, retest, repair, regrade, reinstall, recall, etc. The manufacturer has to pass the costs of waste on to someone in order to stay in business. This waste is factored into the cost structure and the customer must pay for it. While this is possible for a novel product with minimal or no competition, if the product is a commodity and highly competitive in an open market, the manufacturer cannot always pass on its cost of waste to the customer. The manufacturer will not be competitive. In this case, to reduce operations costs, a few things can happen. The organization can cut the headcount (even letting go those individuals with critical skills), move to low-cost outsourcing locations, use a lower quality of raw materials, or undersell its products to remain afloat. However, all these

Table 11.1 Value-added vs. non-value-added.

	Value-added	Non-value-added
Have control	Customer willing to pay	Eight wastes
No control	Not of interest	Legal, statutory, regulatory requirements. Select customer requirements.

options put the organization at risk. Losing individuals with critical skills and lowering the quality of raw materials will result in manufacturability issues and more field returns. Warranty costs will go up and the organization will soon close down due to a bad reputation for quality. Underselling its product will upset the organization's bottom line and result in closing down the organization. Waste can be identified by walking through the process from start to end and looking for any non-value-added activities. This is where value stream analysis is helpful. By closely reviewing every activity as either value-added or non-value-added, one should be able to identify wastes. There are some items that, even if they fall under non-value-added activity, need to be continued out of necessity. For example, there may be inspection or certain testing that is required by a regulatory body, there may be a process step that the customer is willing to pay for and is considered essential, or there may be a need for additional traceability identification on inner packing, cartons, crates, pallets, and so on. The organization has little or no control over these situations.

Value-added and non-value-added activities can be summarized in a four-quadrant grid (Table 11.1).

Once this simple quadrant is developed, the organization may begin applying lean tools to reduce waste. The first tool to implement is 5S. As explained in Chapter 2, "Lean Foundations and Principles," organizing and standardizing the workplace will help reduce obvious wastes like searching for tools or information, time loss due to accidents, damages during transportation, and so on. Wastes like delays, travel distance, and excess inventory are addressed through tools such as value analysis, one-piece flow, kanbans, problem solving, SPC, and so on.

Define the elements of severity, opportunity, and detection, how they are used to calculate the risk priority number. Describe how FMEA can be used to identify potential failures in a process. (Understand)

Body of Knowledge IV.A.2

---

2. FAILURE MODE AND EFFECTS ANALYSIS (FMEA)

The concept of failure mode and effects analysis (FMEA) has been around a long time. In the past, inventors and product developers thought about possible ways that a product could fail during extreme conditions, handling, and usage. They started to provide countermeasures in the design and manufacturing processes to prevent these failure modes. FMEA thus started to evolve informally. The military standard MIL-STD-1629A (now obsolete) was a formal document used for FMEA by aerospace and defense applications. This is probably the earliest known FMEA document.

The idea behind identifying the failure modes in a system, design, and process started to evolve during the last half century with changes to how risks were weighted, categorized, and calculated. Ford Motor Company used the FMEA approach for design and manufacturing to safeguard against safety- and regulatory-related failure modes. Eventually Ford started to see the benefits of reducing the risks confronting product quality.

In 1993, Chrysler, Ford, and General Motors, with input from several technical professionals, created *Potential Failure Mode and Effects Analysis*, a document that encompasses design and process FMEA. This document became part of the QS-9000 (now ISO/TS 16949) standard's expectations for automotive suppliers. This document, currently in its fourth edition, has been revised with significant input from the SAE J1739 work group and other automotive-product-related organizations.

The Automotive Industry Action Group (AIAG) described FMEA[1] as a systematic group of activities intended to:

- Recognize and evaluate the potential failure of a product/process and the effects of that failure

- Identify actions that could eliminate or reduce the chance of the potential failure occurring

- Document the entire process

The purpose of FMEA is to understand the opportunities for failure and the impact of risks in a product or process design, prioritize the risks, and take actions to eliminate or reduce the impact of these risks. FMEA is a front-end tool. Successful product/process development requires anticipating failure modes and taking actions to eliminate or reduce failures during deployment and the life cycle. FMEA is not a onetime event; the product/process design team needs to periodically review and update the failure modes. During the early stages of product/process development, the team identifies the risks based on existing data from similar processes, knowledge, and experience. As the product/process is deployed, new unforeseen risks and failures may show up. Hence, reviewing the FMEA on a continual basis ensures sustainable success.

It is important to know that the ISO 9001:2015 revision of the standard has multiple references to "risk-based thinking." Annex A indicates that "there is no requirement for formal methods for risk management or a documented risk management process. Organizations can decide whether or not to develop a more extensive risk management methodology than is required by this International Standard, e.g. through the application of other guidance or standards."[2] The standard provides flexibility for implementation for organizations. Not all processes and businesses require a formal risk management methodology. FMEA may be an excellent way to address and provide evidence of risk-based thinking.

FMEA needs to be documented and revision controlled and should be part of the existing quality management system (QMS). In a well-designed QMS, FMEA is linked to quality function deployment in the design and process "houses of quality" and linked to control plans in the production house of quality. FMEA is not just confined to manufacturing applications; it has been successfully used in service/transactional processes, software development, and the medical field.

Although in principle FMEA is conducted to address the potential failures in product design and process design, it is identified separately as design FMEA and process FMEA. (There is also a system FMEA, but this is beyond the scope of this Body of Knowledge.)

Please see the glossary for some of the fundamental terms used in FMEA, such as *failure mode, cause, effect, failure mechanism, severity, occurrence, detection,* and *risk priority number.* Understanding this terminology is key to performing FMEA assessment. Over the years, the author has reviewed a number of FMEAs from internal processes and suppliers. A common mistake is the mixing up of failure mode and cause failure mode and effect. Refer to the ASQ *Quality Progress* article "FMEA Minus the Pain" and the related figures in the online version to understand additional pitfalls.[3]

An evolution of FMEA is FMECA, which includes provisions for assessing and charting the probability of a failure mode occurring versus the severity of the consequences of realizing the failure mode. This is referred to as a criticality analysis—the "C" in FMECA.

Steps in Performing FMEA

The team approach is most effective for conducting an FMEA, so it is discussed here. Assemble a cross-functional team with diverse knowledge about the process, product, or service and customer needs. Functions often included are design, manufacturing, quality, testing, reliability, maintenance, purchasing (and suppliers), sales, marketing (and customers), and customer service. It is important to have process experts' presence in design FMEA and design experts in process FMEA. For effective interaction, the team is typically five to seven people. If additional experts are needed to provide inputs on safety, regulatory, or legal issues, they are included on the team as subject matter experts.

Identify the scope of the FMEA. Is it for concept, system, design, process, or service? What are the boundaries? How detailed should we be? See Table 11.2 for steps in performing an FMEA.

Do's

- Always provide FMEA training to team members before assigning to an FMEA team.

- Always use the team approach.

- Ask for subject matter expertise if required.

- Talk to your customer about how they intend to use the product.

- Take time as a team to standardize the scales (for the nature of the business or organization). This helps when comparing the overall risks between FMEAs and helps set up a cutoff score.

Table 11.2 Steps in performing a design or process FMEA.

	Step	Design FMEA	Process FMEA
1	Review the design/process	Use a schematic diagram and a functional block diagram to identify each of the main components of the design and determine the function or functions of those components and interfaces between them. Make sure you are studying all components defined in the scope of the DFMEA. Some components may have more than one function.	Use flowcharts to identify the scope and to make sure every team member understands it in detail. It is also recommended that the team perform a walk-through of the process and understand the process steps firsthand.
2	Brainstorm potential failure modes	A potential failure mode represents any manner in which the product component could fail to perform its intended function or functions.	A potential failure mode represents any manner in which the process step could fail to perform its intended function or functions.
3	List potential effects of failure	Both the potential interim (local) effects and the end effects are identified. The effect is the ability of the component to perform its intended function due to the failure mode.	Both the potential interim (local) effects and the end effects are identified. The effect is the impact on the process outcome and product quality due to the failure mode.
4	Assign severity rating (S)	The severity rating corresponds to each effect the failure mode can cause. Typically the scale is 1 to 10. Higher severity is rated at the high end of the scale, lower severity at the low end of the scale.	
5	List potential causes	For every failure mode, list possible cause(s). Use team tools like brainstorming, cause and effect charts, nominal group technique, and multivoting. Where applicable, use a pilot experiment, past data, and expert knowledge.	
6	Assign occurrence rating (O)	The occurrence rating corresponds to the likelihood or frequency at which the cause can occur. Typically the scale is 1 to 10. Higher occurrence is rated at the high end of the scale, lower occurrence at the low end of the scale.	
7	Current controls	For each cause, current process controls are identified. Controls can be of different types. They may just detect the failure or prevent the failure from happening. The controls range from work instructions to AQL sampling, SPC, alarms, mistake-proofing fixture, and so on.	
8	Assign detection rating (D)	The detection rating corresponds to the ability to detect the occurrence of the failure mode *after it has happened but before the customer is affected*. Typically the scale is 1 to 10. Higher detectability is rated at the low end of the scale, lower detectability at the high end of the scale.	

Table 11.2 Steps in performing a design or process FMEA. *(Continued)*

	Step	Design FMEA	Process FMEA
9	Calculate RPN	Product of severity (S), occurrence (O), and detection (D) (see Glossary for definitions). S × O × D = risk priority number (RPN). Severity × occurrence = criticality is also important in some industries.	
10	Develop action plan	Action plan may contain tasks to improve the current controls or reduce the frequency of the occurrence of the cause. In order to reduce the severity, the team may have to think of redesigning the product or process. Assign a realistic completion date and responsibility for tasks.	
11	Take action	Many FMEAs fall apart during this step due to lack of management support, conflicting priorities, lack of resources, and lack of team leadership. The actions have to be implemented and results should be validated. Building a prototype, testing the action, and piloting the process in small scale before mass producing are recommended.	
12	Recalculate the RPN	Bring the team back and objectively recalculate the RPN. Use objective evidence like customer feedback, reliability tests, warranty return rate, yield tracking, and so on, to reassess the score.	
13	Periodically review and update new risks	Carefully evaluate customer feedback, warranty analysis, internal nonconformance reports, ongoing reliability test reports, and so on, to explore new risks and update the FMEA. Keep the FMEA as a living document.	

- Brainstorm all possible failure modes (be sure to include those that might happen only occasionally).

- When two risks have the same overall score, the risk with the higher severity rating is escalated.

- Complete the action and reassess the risks as a team.

- Update the FMEA with new learned risks.

Don'ts

- Don't copy the severity-occurrence-detection scales from another industry or organization. The description of the scale levels and impact may be different from that of your organization.

- Don't force-fit risks into a 1–10 scale. If there are not many levels of severity, occurrence, and detection in your industry, try a 1–5 scale.

- Don't create customized scales within the organization unless it is absolutely essential. (Standardization of scales within the organization or product family/technology is helpful when comparing risks.)

- Don't fight over small ratings differences, such as between 4 and 5 or 6 and 7. Analyze the impact thoroughly if the team is divided by two or three ratings points, for example, 4 and 7 or 7 and 10. Don't average scales from participants for team harmony. This may affect the outcome of the risk assessment.

- Don't get hung up on the numbers; the objective is to create a reduced-risk product and/or service.

- Don't perform FMEA just to comply with procedures or standards. FMEA is a business risk management tool. It has to be used with commitment to make it work.

Once the initial risk priority number (RPN) scores are tabulated, the team may decide on a cutoff score. For most organizations, the cutoff score is standardized. The cutoff score of one organization may not be directly applicable to another. Too low a cutoff score can result in spending lots of resources to eliminate or reduce several risks. Too high a cutoff score can result in not addressing important risks. Management needs to review and agree on a score. One of the challenges of RPN prioritization is the risks with high severity and low probability of occurrence. These risks, if they happen, could be disastrous to the organization. It is very common for the team and management to discount risks that are abstract and rare. However, the team should think hard and evaluate a worst-case scenario if indeed these risks do happen.

The Fukushima nuclear disaster is a good example. While the probability of an earthquake triggering a tsunami is rare, it did happen. The nuclear facility reportedly was unprepared for an incident of this magnitude. The effect was known to all of us watching the news from Japan.

Figures 11.1 through 11.3 show various FMEA implementation tools and examples.

Note: FMEA is a powerful tool, but it requires in-depth knowledge to be successfully executed. It is recommended that guidance be sought from others who have performed an FMEA.

Successful FMEA implementation requires leadership and management commitment. FMEA is one of the few tools that can test the patience of team members. Instead of tackling FMEA for multiple process steps for the product in several

Risk ID		Jan 17	Feb 17	Mar 17	Apr 17	May 17	Jun 17
Risk 7	Planned						
	Actual						
Risk 1	Planned						
	Actual						
Risk 3	Planned						
	Actual						
Risk 9	Planned						
	Actual						
Risk 5	Planned						
	Actual						

Figure 11.1 A typical risk action plan Gantt chart.

Before taking action					After taking action				
Risk ID	**S**	**O**	**D**	**Initial RPN**	**Risk ID**	**S**	**O**	**D**	**Recalc RPN**
Risk 7	5	8	7	280	Risk 7	5	5	3	75
Risk 1	8	8	4	256	Risk 1	8	4	3	96
Risk 3	5	5	7	175	Risk 3	5	4	4	80
Risk 9	7	5	4	140	Risk 9	7	3	4	84
Risk 5	8	4	4	128	Risk 5	8	3	3	72
Risk 2	7	4	3	84	Risk 2	7	4	3	84
Risk 4	5	5	3	75	Risk 4	5	5	3	75
Risk 6	3	7	2	42	Risk 6	3	7	2	42
Risk 8	5	3	2	30	Risk 8	5	3	2	30
Risk 10	3	3	3	27	Risk 10	3	3	3	27

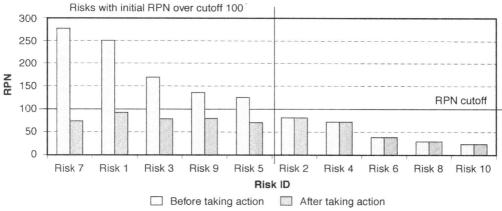

Figure 11.2 Example FMEA reporting and RPN chart.

XYZ Corporation

Management Review Report—FMEA Implementation Progress

No. of FMEA risks over cutoff 100 = 245

Total no. of FMEA risks identified = 550

No. of risks to be reduced below cutoff by end of quarter* = 60

*Organizations review their performance by end of Q1, Q2, Q3, and Q4.

Figure 11.3 A typical top-level management review report for FMEA progress.

meetings, try splitting the process into major process blocks and perform FMEA by block in one sitting. Also, maintaining a good FMEA database will significantly reduce the time spent on successive FMEAs.

QUESTIONS

1. Choose from a bakery shop, bank, car repair shop, or doctor's office and explain how 5S implementation could be beneficial in identifying and eliminating waste.

2. Create a value analysis of the business selected in question #1, and identify the wastes in one of the categories in Table 11.1.

3. What are the main pitfalls to watch for when conducting an FMEA? What are your countermeasures to address these pitfalls at the planning stage of the FMEA?

4. What is the purpose of setting a risk priority number (RPN) cutoff in an FMEA? What is the downside of making risk prioritization decisions based only on the RPN?

5. Develop a process FMEA for every step of either a cake baking or a cooking making process.

Chapter 12

B. Root Cause Analysis

> Describe how the 5-whys, process mapping, force-field analysis and matrix charts can be used to identify the root causes of a problem. (Understand)
>
> **Body of Knowledge IV.B**

Root cause analysis (RCA) is an important step in problem solving. Whether you are following the PDCA approach or DMAIC methodology for problem solving or improvement, RCA is required. Why try to uncover the root cause? Many causes that result in problems that confront us are not obvious. There are apparent causes and root causes. Addressing the apparent causes doesn't eliminate the problem. Problems reoccur, resulting in more time and effort to address the apparent causes every time. Root causes reside deeper. How deep? This depends on the complexity of the problem. There may be more than one cause of the problem experienced. Different causes may have different contributions to the manifestation of the problem.

Apparent causes are those that appear in the first layer of the RCA:

Why didn't the product work?

— Apparent cause: Damage during transport

— Root cause: Packaging not designed to withstand shock and vibration anticipated during the transport

Why does the process have scrap products?

— Apparent cause: Process control (inspection) did not work

— Root cause: Process is not capable

Why did the operator have an accident?

— Apparent cause: Operator did not follow the safety instructions

— Root cause: Safety guard not error proofed to stop equipment

In these cases, it is normal human tendency to jump on the apparent causes and superficially address them. RCA requires knowledge and experience to diagnose the affected process. Resource commitment is required to design a system that will prevent errors (i.e., not allow root cause to enter the process). Problem solving is often underestimated. Performing a comprehensive RCA for problem solving takes time, effort, and resources. Management commitment and patience are required. Patience should not be confused with not having a sense of urgency. Patience is allowing the process to work and not skipping steps to save time.

There are many problem-solving tools available in the quality toolbox; brainstorming, seven quality tools, why-why analysis (5 whys), and is-is not analysis are just a few of the tools.

5 WHYS OR WHY-WHY ANALYSIS

5 whys analysis is an easy-to-use approach for arriving at a root cause. It is widely used because of its simplicity. No special training or skill is required. All you need is the persistence to ask "Why?" every time you get an answer and keep going until you reach the root cause. If you have ever observed a five-year-old child, you know they are very inquisitive. At this age, the child wants to know more by asking "Why?" There are times we as adults run out of answers. So if we all started by asking questions, when did we stop asking? As we age, we are influenced by our experiences and environment. We make up our minds as to the answer for every question and continue to live with assumptions. We hardly ever challenge our assumptions.

The 5 whys tool forces us to keep asking questions. Many quality professionals get hung up on the number 5 in "5 whys" and force themselves to ask why five times. But depending on the complexity of the issue, one might arrive at the root cause at the third or seventh why or even the ninth why. "5" whys is simply a guideline and should not be taken literally. To avoid this misunderstanding, organizations have begun to call this tool "why-why analysis." There is always a question from users as to when to stop asking why. If you stop at the second or third why, the cause may still be shallow. If you keep going to a seventh or eighth why, the cause gets very broad, like "organizational culture" or "business situation." This is not quite actionable by the RCA team. The ideal point at which to stop is where the root cause is specific and actionable and the problem solver or organization has no control to act on the subsequent why.

Let's look at an example from the Toyota website:[1]

1. "Why did the robot stop?" The circuit has overloaded, causing a fuse to blow.

2. "Why is the circuit overloaded?" There was insufficient lubrication on the bearings, so they locked up.

3. "Why was there insufficient lubrication on the bearings?" The oil pump on the robot is not circulating sufficient oil.

4. "Why is the pump not circulating sufficient oil?" The pump intake is clogged with metal shavings.

5. "Why is the intake clogged with metal shavings?" Because there is no filter on the pump.

In this example, if the manufacturing quality practitioner had stopped at the first why, the organization would have thought that the fuse was the root cause and thus would have kept a huge number of fuses as a maintenance spare part inventory. If the practitioner had stopped at the second why, the operator would have been advised to keep pouring more lubrication. This would have resulted in spillage on the floor, which could have led to an accident. In the fifth why, identifying the lack of a filter as the root cause is sufficient because the use of a filter that is periodically replaced during preventive maintenance will prevent the robot from stopping. To understand the system-level root cause, we should continue asking why.

1. "Why wasn't the filter on the pump replaced?" Maintenance technician forgot to replace during the preventive maintenance.

2. "Why did the maintenance technician forget to replace?" There is no process for routine preventive maintenance.

I would stop at this point to ensure that there is a defined, documented, and fully deployed effective maintenance process that not only ensures replacement of the filter but also prevents any errors in the future.

Once a root cause has been identified in the 5 whys/why-why analysis, it is important to verify that the root cause can indeed address the problem symptom. If you have the ability to turn the root cause on and off to verify prevention and re-creation of the problem, this is an effective way to confirm the root cause. However, this is not always practical. Some root causes are not easy to re-create, and even if we could re-create them, it could cause significant undesirable effects on the customer. In these scenarios, practitioners are advised to be creative in verification, for example, using a software simulation or equivalent method. Finally, verify recurrence of the events. Complaints from the customer is a reactive approach for verifying whether the root cause has been correctly identified and the corresponding corrective action is effective.

PROCESS MAPPING

ISO 9000:2015 (*Quality management systems—Fundamentals and vocabulary*) defines a *process* as a set of interrelated or interacting activities that transforms inputs into outputs. A process flowchart is a helpful tool during problem investigation. A process is easily understood by visually presenting the process using common flowcharting shapes and symbols. This method depicts processes, both simple and complex, more effectively than extensive written descriptions. Organizations often send their process information in the form of process map documentation to their suppliers and customers for contractual reasons. In my experience, I have seen process maps and flowcharts used extensively in Japanese organizations. They call it "QC process flow." It is typically an end-to-end process flow starting from contract review and approval through delivery of goods.

Let us clarify upfront that process mapping is a process by itself to map a process, and a flowchart is a tool used to conduct mapping. Practitioners often use process mapping and process flowcharting interchangeably. Some authors try to distinguish a process map as a flowchart with additional process-related information as follows.

Flowcharts show each step in a process, including inputs, decision points, and outputs. Process maps usually contain additional information about the steps, including costs, setup time, cycle time, inventory, types of defects that can occur, probability of defects, and other relevant information that helps in understanding the process better.

The flowchart is typically presented on the left side of the page, continuously running for multiple pages in one column, and the space on the right is used to describe the process, responsibilities, control points, metrics, and so on. Using consistent mapping icons helps different individuals interpret the maps in the same way. International standard ISO 5807:1985 *Information processing—Documentation symbols and conventions for data, program and system flowcharts, program network charts and system resources charts* helps accomplish just that. Process mapping is often the first step in improving a process. Risk analysis tools such as process failure mode and effects analysis (PFMEA) start with process mapping. Value stream mapping (VSM), used in lean enterprise projects, is also a type of process mapping but uses different mapping icons. In addition, VSM focuses more on measurement of the flow of material and information and the utilization of resources.

Process maps and flowcharts enable a broader perspective of potential problems and opportunities for process improvement. Teams using these tools get a better understanding of process steps and sequence of operations. Figure 12.1 shows some of the most frequently used process mapping symbols from the international standard ISO 5807:1985. Figure 12.2 gives a basic flowchart example. There are a number of mapping icons available within most office productivity software applications.

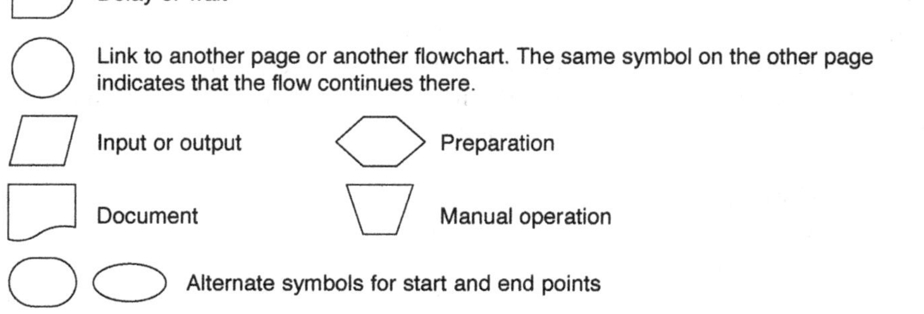

Figure 12.1   Symbols commonly used in flowcharts and process maps.

Source: N. R. Tague, *The Quality Toolbox*, 2nd ed. (Milwaukee, WI: ASQ Quality Press, 2005): 262.

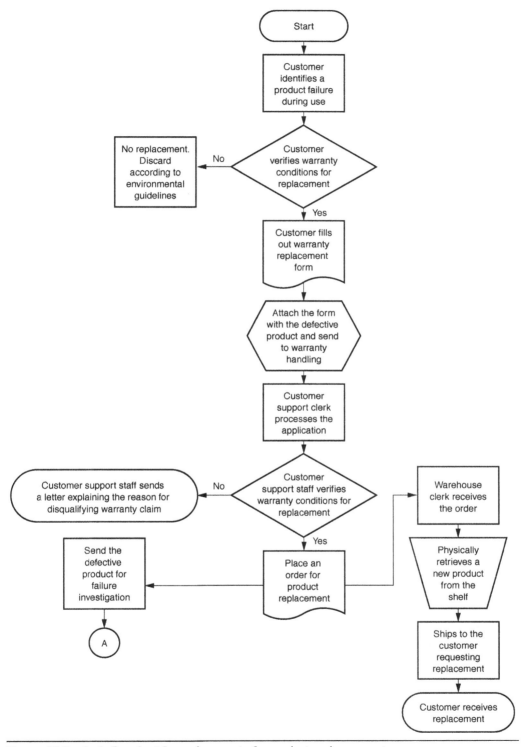

Figure 12.2   Basic flowchart for replacement of a product under warranty.

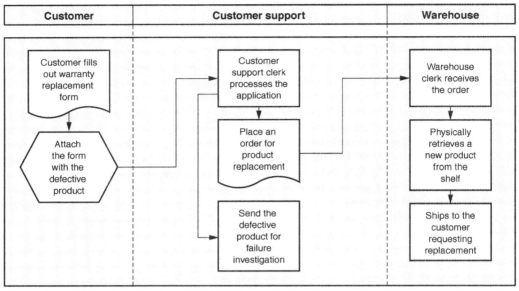

Figure 12.3 Cross-functional or swim lane flowchart.

Process mapping involving multiple departments or functions is more easily understood using "swim lane" mapping. Imagine different departments, functions, or stakeholders involved in a process as being in different swim lanes either horizontally or vertically. A swim lane process map is similar to a typical process map except that the process blocks are aligned with the lane of the department or function that performs a given process step.

Let's re-map the example shown in Figure 12.2 using the swim lane flowchart approach. For simplicity, the decision loops from the previous chart have been taken out. In a real business scenario, the swim lane flowchart in Figure 12.3 contains all the components presented in a basic flowchart. It uses the same flowchart symbols and guidelines shown in Figure 12.1 for creating the chart.

Creating a Flowchart (Process Map or Process Flow Diagram)

When creating a flowchart, we are creating a picture of the actual steps in a process or system as it actually operates or is supposed to operate. Given the old adage that a picture is worth a thousand words, this tool allows us to communicate using standard symbols. The flowchart is very useful when looking at a process we want to improve.

A flowchart should be developed for a new process before the process is implemented. However, there may be situations where you are using a flowchart to document an already-existing process. We can follow some basic steps to create the flowchart:

1. Create the boundaries of the process for which we are creating the flowchart. These might be the inputs and outputs of the process or the suppliers and customers of the process.

2. Determine the various steps in the process through team brainstorming or walking the process (for documenting an already-existing process). At this point, we are not worried about sequence, only collecting all of the steps.

3. Build the sequence of the process, putting everything into the appropriate order. We have to make sure we understand that some process steps happen in parallel, and the chart should reflect this accordingly. There are also alternative paths identified in some charts.

4. Draw the flowchart using the appropriate mapping symbols.

5. Verify that the flowchart is complete and appropriate for the given operation (for a new chart). Verify that the flowchart fully matches with the process (for an already-established process). This is especially important if more than one group is working on a large process. Overlaps or deletions may occur between processes. Hence, this activity is best performed as a team.

Flowcharts are a good graphical tool for both monitoring process changes over time and conducting training of new operators or supervisors. By referencing the flowcharts on a regular basis, we will be able to use them as visual standards to help ensure that things run as they are supposed to. Note that if a change is made to the process, it is important to update the flowchart to reflect the change. Regular audits may be done in a given area for any number of reasons (safety, quality, environmental, and so on), so having the flowcharts readily available helps everyone involved in verifying compliance.

Process mapping can help reveal redundancy in the process, non-value-added steps, and unnecessary complexities. Process mapping can be used to identify and eliminate those process issues and improve the process (see Chapter 2, "Lean Foundations and Principles," for more information). Process maps are helpful in uncovering where the root cause may have originated, where it escaped, and where in the process it was detected. This is important to narrow down root causes. Reviewing flowcharts can reveal missed steps, incorrectly performed steps, and steps not performed in sequence.

Common mistakes in process mapping include the following:

- Team representation for the process is inadequate or inappropriate

- Unclear scope and a lack of coordination with other process-flow mapping teams result in redundant flows

- Team not performing a walk-through of the process (for an existing process) to capture exactly which steps are being followed (team remains in meeting room and tries to complete flowchart using individuals' perceptions of the process)

- Team spending too much time trying to create a "perfect" process flow diagram rather than focusing on the process (turn the focus away from the tool to the process under review)

The biggest mistake of all in process mapping is not doing one!

FORCE FIELD ANALYSIS

Force field analysis is used to offer a counterpoint for every point that favors an issue or a decision. This tool is useful for understanding root causes by reviewing the forces "for" and "against." In their book *Root Cause Analysis and Improvement in the Healthcare Sector*, authors Bjørn Andersen, Tom Fagerhaug, and Marti Beltz explain that "force field analysis is based on the assumption that any situation is the result of forces for and against the current state being in equilibrium. Countering the opposing forces and/or increasing the favorable forces will help induce a change."[2]

Let's evaluate an example of "forces for" and "forces against" for a problem common to many organizations—an employee showing up late for meetings:

For (Driving Forces)

Individuals are professional and respect others' time

Meeting time is used effectively

Meeting is ended on time

Meeting discussion is not repeated for latecomers

All meeting agenda items are covered

Respect for the meeting host

Against (Restraining Forces)

Company culture tolerates tardiness

No reprimand for late attendance

Back-to-back meetings with no break

Get some coffee prior to meeting

Chat with colleagues on the way to meeting

Distraction from colleagues

Lack of preparation for the meeting

Communication on meeting location change ineffective

Large building with no clear directions to the meeting room

Unfamiliar with building logistics

By linking a "for" entry with a corresponding "against" entry, opportunities for improvement emerge. Making sure a 30-minute meeting finishes in 25 minutes and a 1-hour meeting finishes in 50 minutes will allow employees time to take a break, grab a cup of coffee, or walk between meeting room locations, even those that are far apart.

Enforcing a discipline of starting a meeting on time, irrespective of attendance, demonstrates the meeting host's seriousness to stick to the allotted time. Making sure the attendees are aware of meeting venue changes sufficiently ahead of time helps attendees show up at the right place at the right time.

Finally, management's example of being on time for meetings sets the tone for all employees. This is a cultural change.

MATRIX CHARTS

Matrix diagrams and other prioritization tools can be used to prioritize root causes and corrective actions. The cause and effect diagram used to prioritize causes is a type of matrix diagram. During the RCA, 30–50 causes may emerge from brainstorming. Teams often don't have the resources and time to investigate all of them. Prioritization tools can be used to focus on the top causes. Additional details on matrix charts are available in "Project Management Tools" in Chapter 7.

Prioritization Matrix

A prioritization matrix aids in deciding among options.[3] In the example shown in Figure 12.4, the options are four different software packages, A, B, C, and D. The team determines by consensus the criteria against which the options will be measured (e.g., requirements document) and the relative importance of each criterion. In the example, the criteria and their relative importance are compatibility (.25), cost (.30), ease of use (.40), and training time (.05).

Each option is ranked against the criteria, with the larger numbers being desirable. Since there are four options, the highest-ranking option is assigned a value of 4, the second-place item is assigned a 3, and so on. In the case of a tie, each option is assigned the average value for the two places. For example, if two options are tied for third place, the two places are third and fourth, which have values of 2 and 1, respectively, so each of the options would receive a value of 1.5. In the example in Figure 12.4, packages A and C are tied for the most desirable (lowest) cost, so each is assigned 3.5. The package with the next lowest cost is option D and is assigned 2. Option B has the highest cost and is assigned 1.

Once the values are assigned, the next step is to multiply each of the option values by the criteria weights at the top of the column and calculate the row totals. The option with the highest total is the one most favored by the prioritization matrix.

QUESTIONS

1. Research various RCA methods and put together a table listing the advantages and applications of each method. If you see any constraints with the RCA tool, identify these and present to the class.

2. Use appropriate mapping symbols and develop a flowchart for a process of purchasing a gift for a family friend (make creative use of decision loops and alternate paths).

3. List the challenges in developing a flowchart and suggest countermeasures to your class.

Step 1: Each option is scored against the criteria. Larger numbers are desirable, except in the case of cost, where smaller numbers are desirable.

		Criteria			
		Compatibility	Cost	Ease of use	Training time
Option	Package A	1.00	0.45	1.20	0.15
	Package B	0.25	1.20	0.80	0.05
	Package C	0.75	0.45	1.60	0.20
	Package D	0.50	0.90	0.40	0.10

Step 2: Assign ranking on a scale of 1 to 4, where 1 is the least desirable and 4 is the most desirable. Apply averages for a tie. Packages A and C tied for lowest cost.

		Criteria			
		Compatibility	Cost	Ease of use	Training time
Option	Package A	4	3.5	3	3
	Package B	1	1	2	1
	Package C	3	3.5	4	4
	Package D	2	2	1	2

Step 3: Assign weights based on relative importance. Multiply each of the option values by criteria weights at the top of the column and calculate row totals.

		Criteria				
		Compatibility (0.25)	Cost (0.30)	Ease of use (0.40)	Training time (0.05)	Total
Option	Package A	1.00	1.05	1.20	0.15	3.40
	Package B	0.25	0.30	0.80	0.05	1.40
	Package C	0.75	1.05	1.60	0.20	3.60
	Package D	0.50	0.60	0.40	0.10	1.60

The option with the highest total (package C, highlighted) is the one most favored by the prioritization matrix.

Figure 12.4 Prioritization matrix example: determine the most suitable software package.

4. You have recently decided to buy a house. When looking at homes, you will have many criteria to consider. You have a school-age child, and your daily commute to the office is over an hour. Develop a prioritization matrix and select one of the four properties recommended by your real estate agent.

5. Use a force field analysis to explore the common problem of kids not finishing their homework on time. Recommend actions that will improve the situation.

Chapter 13
C. Data Analysis

> Define and distinguish between normal and binomial distributions and describe how their shapes (skewed and bimodal) can affect data interpretation. (Understand)
>
> **Body of Knowledge IV.C.1**

1. BASIC DISTRIBUTION TYPES

Normal Distribution

The normal distribution is a continuous distribution used for variable data like measurement of length, mass, and time, and is the one most frequently used by various professionals. Several statistical analyses make an assumption that data follow a normal distribution.

Central Limit Theorem

It is important to address central limit theorem before explaining normal distribution further. The central limit theorem is the foundation for several statistical procedures. In a nutshell, the distribution of averages tends to be normal, even when the distribution from which the average data are computed is from non-normal distributions. Mathematically, if a random variable X has a mean μ and variance σ^2, as the sample size n increases, the sample mean $\bar{x}$ approaches a normal distribution with mean m and variance $\sigma_{\bar{x}}^2$:

$$\sigma_{\bar{x}}^2 = \frac{\sigma_x^2}{n} \qquad \text{(See number 2 below)}$$

$$\sigma_{\bar{x}} = \frac{\sigma_x}{\sqrt{n}}$$

The central limit theorem consists of three statements:

1. The mean of the sampling distribution of means is equal to the mean of the population from which the samples were drawn.

131

2. The variance of the sampling distribution of means is equal to the variance of the population from which the samples were drawn, divided by the size of the samples.

3. If the original population is distributed normally (i.e., bell shaped), the sampling distribution of means will also be normal.

If the original population is not normally distributed, the sampling distribution of means will increasingly approximate a normal distribution as sample size increases (i.e., when increasingly larger samples are drawn). Non-normal populations will require larger sample sizes for the sampling distribution of the mean to be nearly normal. Statisticians usually consider a sample size of 30 or more to be sufficiently large. See Figure 13.1.

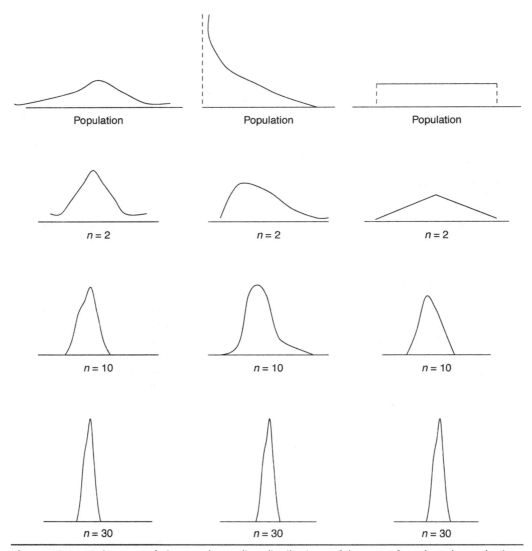

Figure 13.1 Various populations and sampling distributions of the mean for selected sample sizes.

Source: D. W. Benbow and T. M. Kubiak, *The Certified Six Sigma Black Belt Handbook* (Milwaukee, WI: ASQ Quality Press, 2005): 58.

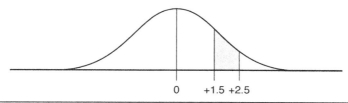

Figure 13.2 Normal distribution (bell) curve.

Since the distribution is in the shape of a bell, it is often referred to as a *bell curve* (Figure 13.2). Mathematically, the formula for the normal distribution probability density function is

$$P(x) = \frac{e^{-\frac{(x-\mu)^2}{2\sigma^2}}}{\sigma\sqrt{2\pi}}$$

See Figure 13.3.

The area under the curve between any two points, expressed in standard deviation units (Z-scores), can be determined from the statistical tables shown in Appendix F. The Z-score is the number of standard deviations that the measurement is from the mean and is calculated by the formula $Z = (x - \mu)/\sigma$. The standard normal distribution has mean = 0 and standard deviation = 1. See details on mean and standard deviation in Table 13.1.

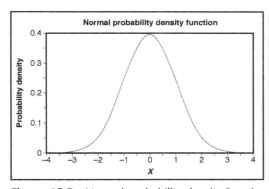
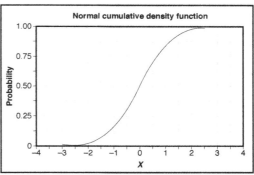

Figure 13.3 Normal probability density function and cumulative density function.

Source: NIST/SEMATECH e-Handbook of Statistical Methods, "1.3.6.6.1. Normal Distribution," http://www.itl.nist.gov/div898/handbook/eda/section3/eda3661.htm.

Table 13.1 Sample versus population notations.

	Sample	Population
Size	n	N
Mean	$\bar{x}$	μ
Standard deviation	s	σ

EXAMPLE

A pizza restaurant's order processing time is normally distributed. A random sample has a mean of 30 minutes and a standard deviation of 5 minutes. Estimate the percentage of orders that are between 35 and 20 minutes.

Solution: Find the Z-score for 20 and 35.

$$Z(20) = (20 - 30)/5 = -2.00$$

$$Z(35) = (35 - 30)/5 = 1$$

Area to the right of −2.00 = 0.97724

Area to the right of +1.00 = 0.15865

Subtracting: 0.8186

Approximately 82% of the orders are processed between 35 minutes and 20 minutes. Put another way, the probability that a randomly selected order will have a processing time between 35 minutes and 20 minutes is approximately 0.82.

Now, let us discuss the distributions that are non-normal. *Skewness* is a measure of the asymmetry of the probability distribution of random variables about its mean. The skewness value can be positive (right skewed) or negative (left skewed) per Figure 13.4.

Skewness may occur in a process due to a gradual change in process settings from tool wear or other factors that cause the process to gradually drift. It may also

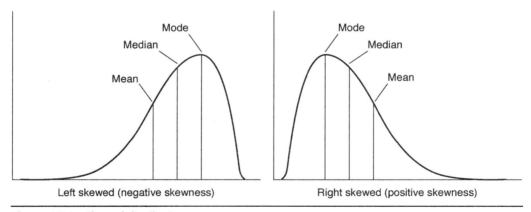

Left skewed (negative skewness)   Right skewed (positive skewness)

Figure 13.4   Skewed distributions.

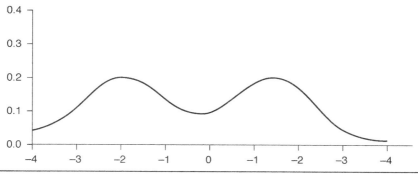

Figure 13.5 Bimodal distribution.

be due to plotting data that are naturally skewed in one direction. Examples are data from one-sided measurements like the maximum breaking strength of glass, minimum pull strength of wire, and flatness of a surface. Six Sigma practitioners have to pay attention to data with a skewed distribution and understand why they are skewed before taking action. If the data are skewed due to changes in a process setting, then the data should be stratified separately before and after the changes to the process setting and analyzed.

Distribution may also be bimodal or multimodal (Figure 13.5). This is often an example of special causes entering a process or lack of homogeneity in a batch of material. Consider a process that is stable and normally distributed. In the next shift there is either a change of operator, a change of raw material from a new supplier, or a tool change that is significantly different from the previous shift; the resulting data from the two shifts of manufacturing may appear as shown in Figure 13.5. It is not always a bimodal; it can be a multimodal if the mix-up of batches has many abrupt changes. If this happens, you will see multiple modes in a frequency distribution.

Formula, mean, and variance are provided for various distributions in Table 13.2.

Binomial Distribution

The "bi-" prefix indicates that a binomial distribution (Figure 13.6) should be applied in situations where each part has just two states, typically:

- Good or bad

- Accept or reject

- Conformance or nonconformance

- Success or failure

Table 13.2 Formula, mean, and variance of certain distributions.

Name	Formula	Mean	Variance
Normal	$P(x) = \dfrac{e^{-\frac{(x-\mu)^2}{2\sigma^2}}}{\sigma\sqrt{2\pi}}$	m	s^2
Exponential	$P(x) = le^{-1x}$	$\dfrac{1}{l}$	$\dfrac{1}{l^2}$
Binomial	$P(x) = \dfrac{n!}{x!(n-x)!}\, p^x(1-p)^{n-x}$	np	$np\,(1-p)$
Poisson	$P(x) = \dfrac{e^{-1}\,l^x}{x!}$	l	l
Hypergeometric	$P(x) = \dfrac{{}_d C_x\left[{}_{(N-d)}C_{(n-x)}\right]}{{}_N C_x}$	$\dfrac{nd}{N}$	$\dfrac{nd(N-d)(N-n)^2}{N^3-N^2}$

The binomial distribution (Figure 13.6) is used to model discrete data. The following are examples of binomial data used in everyday life:

- The number of defectives in a manufacturing lot

- The number of defective quotes sent by an insurance company

- The number of wrong patient prescriptions issued by a healthcare professional

- The number of goods shipped to a wrong address by a forwarding company

The binomial distribution has some conditions. It is applicable when the population denoted by N is greater than 50. In other words, for smaller lots, binomial modeling will not be accurate.

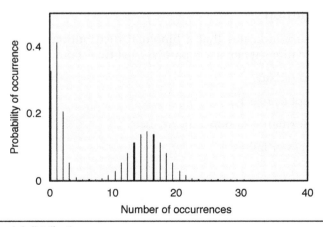

Figure 13.6 Binomial distribution.

Another important condition is the ratio of the sample n to population N. The binomial model best applies when $n < 0.1N$ (i.e., sample size is less than 10% of the population).

In one type of problem that is frequently encountered, the Six Sigma professional needs to determine the probability of obtaining a certain number of defectives in a sample of known size from a population with known percent defective. The symbols are n = sample size, x = number of defectives, and p = defective rate in the population.

The binomial formula is:

$$P(x) = \frac{n!}{x!(n-x)!} p^x (1-p)^{n-x}$$

$x!$ is pronounced "x factorial" and is defined as $x(x-1)(x-2)\ldots(1)$. Most scientific calculators have a factorial key.

EXAMPLE

A sample of size five is randomly selected from a batch with 10% defective. Find the probability that the sample has exactly one defective. Substitute $n = 5$, $x = 1$, $p = .10$ into the binomial formula:

$P(1) = [5!/(1!(5-1)!)](.10)^1(.9)^{5-1} = [120/(1 \times 24)](.10)(.6561) \approx .328$

This is the probability that the sample contains exactly one defective.

The same can be calculated using a simple Microsoft Excel formula (see Figure 13.7):

=BINOMDIST(1,5,0.1,FALSE)

Per Table 13.2, the mean and variance can also be calculated for the binomial distribution.

EXAMPLE

If we toss an unbiased coin (equal probability of heads or tails) 60 times, what is the average and standard deviation of the number of tails?

$$p = (1/2) \text{ or } 0.5$$

$$n = 60$$

$$\mu = np, \mu = (60 \times 0.5) = 30 \text{ tails}$$

$$\sigma = \sqrt{np(1-p)}, \sigma = (30(1-0.5))^{1/2} = 3.872$$

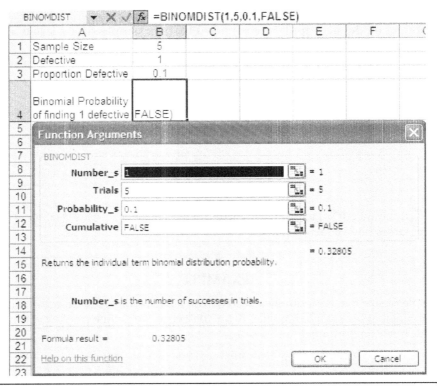

Figure 13.7 Binomial distribution using Microsoft Excel.

Normal Approximation of Binomial

For large values of n, the distributions of the count X and the sample proportion p are approximately normal. This is understood from the central limit theorem. The normal approximation is not accurate for small values of n; a good rule of thumb is to use the normal approximation only if $np \geq 10$ and $np(1 - p) \geq 10$.

> Describe and distinguish between these types of variation. (Understand)
>
> **Body of Knowledge IV.C.2**

2. COMMON AND SPECIAL CAUSE VARIATION

We have so far understood that every process has variability. Variability due to many reasons is inherent in any process. Failure to measure variation in a process with continuous measurements can be due to the following reasons:

- The measurement equipment is broken

- The measurement equipment is not capable of detecting the variability (insensitive)

- The measurement method is not suitable

- The measurement operator is falsifying the data

Process variation has two main categories: special causes and common causes. Variation must be traceable to its sources, making it necessary to distinguish between common and special causes.

Common causes of variation are those that are inherent to the process and generally are not controllable by process operators. Common cause variation is also known as natural variation and refers to the many sources of variation within a process. Common causes reside in processes within statistical control and can be characterized by location (process average), spread (piece-to-piece variability), and shape (distribution) for predictability.

Special causes of variation include unusual events that the operator, when properly alerted, can usually remove or adjust. Special causes are sometimes called assignable causes. Unless all the special causes of variation are identified and mitigated, the process output will be unpredictably influenced with random results.

The principal purpose of control charts is to recognize the presence of special causes so that appropriate action can be taken. While both special and common causes can be detected with statistical techniques, common causes are more difficult to isolate and remove. A process is considered to be in statistical control when special causes have been removed and only common causes remain.

A difficult problem is the separation of special and common causes. If you adjust a process in response to common cause variation, the result is usually more variation rather than less. This is sometimes called overadjustment or overcontrol. Deming warned against tampering with a process that is under statistical control (stable and predictable). If you fail to respond to the presence of a special cause of variation, this cause is likely to produce additional process variation. This is referred to as underadjustment or undercontrol.

Consider timing your daily commute to work or school. Record your times over the next few days, plot them on a chart, and identify what is causing the variation in times. What are the common causes and what are the special causes? You will notice that common cause variations such as stopping at traffic lights are more or less equal from day to day. The occasional spikes in the chart signify special causes such as the unusual traffic jam due to either an accident or a road repair.

Special Cause Examples

Figures 13.8 through 13.10 represent the effects of special causes on a process, resulting in excessive averages and variations.

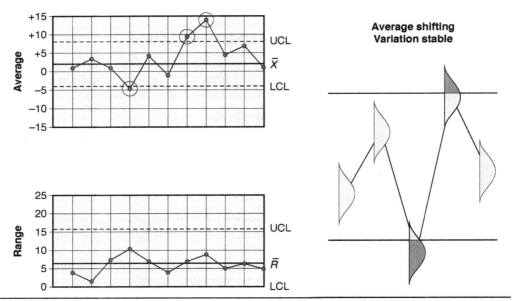

Figure 13.8   Average shifting, variation stable.

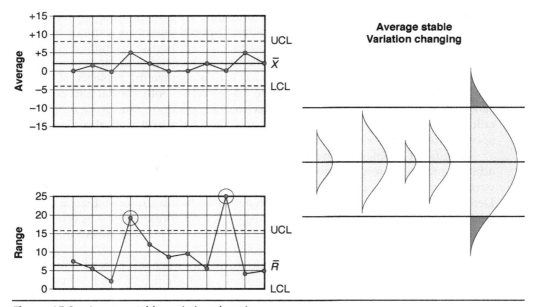

Figure 13.9   Average stable, variation changing.

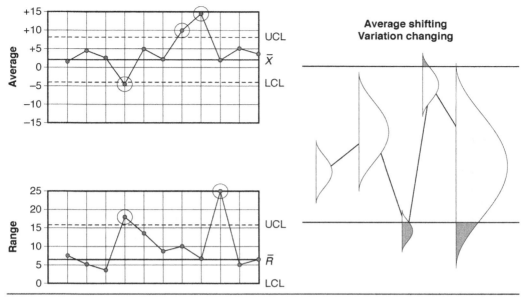

Figure 13.10 Average shifting, variation changing.

Common Cause Example

Figure 13.11 represents the effects of common causes on a process, resulting in changes within the tolerance levels for average and variation.

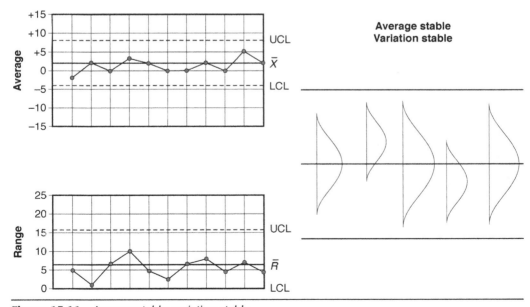

Figure 13.11 Average stable, variation stable.

QUESTIONS

1. Identify the best-fitting distribution for the following practical situations:

   a. Measurement values of widgets with the same setting from a high-volume manufacturing process

   b. Measurement values of widgets with different settings between the day shift and the night shift

   c. Measurement values of widgets with two or more settings from multiple manufacturing lines

2. Differentiate common and special causes in the following:

   a. Variation in operation room temperature and humidity

   b. Measurement method A and measurement method B producing different results

   c. Products manufactured with same supplier material

   d. Variability within trained employees

   e. Measurement values of widgets before and after equipment maintenance

Chapter 14
D. Correlation and Regression

> Describe how correlation is used to identify relationships between variables. (Understand)
>
> **Body of Knowledge IV.D.1**

1. CORRELATION

Correlation is finding a relationship between two or more sets of data. It measures the strength and direction of the relationship between variables. In order to find a correlation, one needs an independent variable (x) that causes an observed variation, dependent variable (y) that is an effect of (x). Table 14.1 lists a few examples of independent and dependent variable pairs.

Correlation versus Causation

A cause that produces an effect or gives rise to any action, phenomenon, or condition is termed *causation*. For example, if a change in X produces a change in Y, X is said to be a cause of Y. One may also observe, however, that there is a W that caused X, a V that caused W, a U that caused V, and so on. Every cause is itself the result of some prior cause or causes. There is no such thing as an absolute cause for an event, the identification of which satisfies and completes all inquiry. The alphabetic example just given implies a "causal chain."

Two variables may be found to be causally associated, depending on how the study was conducted. If the two variables are found to be either associated or correlated, that doesn't mean that a cause-and-effect relationship exists between the

Table 14.1 Examples of dependent and independent variables.

Independent variable (x)	Dependent variable (y)
Hours studied	Exam grade
Hours of exercise	Weight loss
Level of advertising	Volume of sales

two variables. This has to be proved by a well-designed experiment or several different observational studies to show that an association or correlation crosses over into a cause-and-effect relationship.

A scatter plot provides a complete picture of the relationship between two variables. Figure 5.8 in Chapter 5 illustrates the four types of correlations that exist in scatter plots. The convention is to place the *x* variable on the horizontal axis and the *y* variable on the vertical axis.

Caution: Be careful when deciding which variable is independent and which is dependent. Examine the relationship from both directions to see which one makes the most sense. The wrong choice may lead to meaningless results.

Correlation Coefficient

The correlation coefficient *r* provides both the strength and the direction of the relationship between the independent and dependent variables. Values of *r* range between –1.0 and +1.0. When *r* is positive, the relationship between *x* and *y* is positive (Figure 14.1a), and when *r* is negative, the relationship is negative (Figure 14.1b). A correlation coefficient close to zero is evidence that there is no relationship between *x* and *y* (Figure 14.1c). Figure 14.d indicates a nonlinear relationship between variables.

The strength of the relationship between *x* and *y* is measured by how close the correlation coefficient is to +1.0 or –1.0.

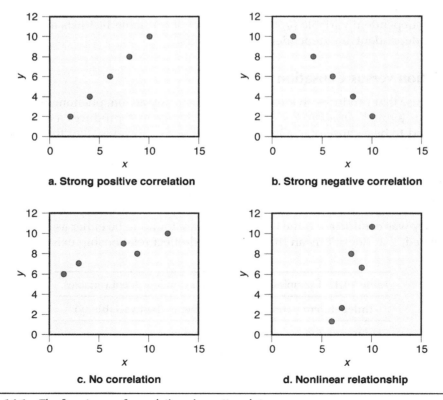

Figure 14.1 The four types of correlations in scatter plots.

We can calculate the correlation coefficient using the following formula:

$$r = \frac{\Sigma xy - \dfrac{\Sigma x \Sigma y}{N}}{\sqrt{\left(\Sigma x^2 - \dfrac{(\Sigma x)^2}{N}\right)\left(\Sigma y^2 - \dfrac{(\Sigma y)^2}{N}\right)}}$$

Using Microsoft Excel to Calculate Correlation Coefficients

You can use Microsoft Excel to calculate correlation coefficients. Use the CORREL function, which has the following characteristics:

CORREL(array1, array2)

where

array1 = the range of data for the first variable

array2 = the range of data for the second variable

Figure 14.2 shows the CORREL function being used to calculate the correlation coefficient for the weight loss example. Cell C8 contains the Microsoft Excel formula

=CORREL(A2:A7,B2:B7) with the result being 0.972717.

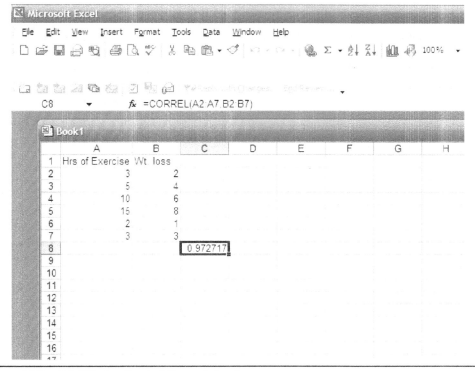

Figure 14.2 CORREL function in Microsoft Excel.

2. REGRESSION

> Describe how regression analysis is used to predict outcomes. (Understand)
>
> **Body of Knowledge IV.D.2**

Simple Regression

Simple regression is used to describe a straight line that best fits a series of ordered pairs (x,y). An equation for a straight line, known as a linear equation, takes the form:

$$\hat{y} = a + bx$$

where

$\hat{y}$ = the predicted value of y, given a value of x

x = the independent variable

a = the y-intercept for the straight line

b = the slope of the straight line

The Least Squares Method

The least squares method is a mathematical procedure to identify the linear equation that best fits a set of ordered pairs by finding values for a (the y-intercept) and b (the slope). The goal of this method is to minimize the total squared error between the values of y and $\hat{y}$.

If we denote the predicted value of y obtained from the fitted line as $\hat{y}$, the predicted equation is:

$$\hat{y} = \hat{a} + \hat{b}x$$

where
$\hat{a}$ and $\hat{b}$ represent estimates of true a and b.

Since we need to choose the best-fitting line, we need to define what we mean by "best." For the purpose of getting the best-fitting criteria, the principle of least squares is employed; that is, one has to choose the best-fitting line, the line that minimizes the sum of squares of the deviations of the observed values of y from those predicted.

Let's look at an example of how the regression statistical method could be used to predict outcomes.

Using Microsoft Excel for Simple Regression

1. Sort the data from Table 14.2 into columns A and B in a blank Microsoft Excel spreadsheet.

2. Under the Tools menu, select Data Analysis. (If Data Analysis does not automatically appear, you may have to go to the Options menu and check Data Analysis.)

3. From the Data Analysis dialog box, select Regression, as shown in Figure 14.3, and click OK.

4. Set up the Regression dialog box as shown in Figure 14.4; enter input x and y range.

5. Click OK, which brings up the results shown in Figure 14.5.

Table 14.2   Temperature viscosity experiment.

Temperature (°C)	Viscosity (centipoise)
10	2
15	3
20	5
15	4

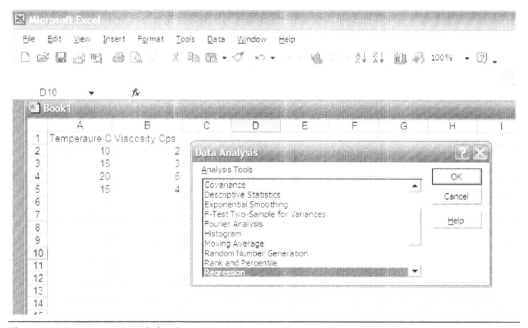

Figure 14.3   Regression dialog box.

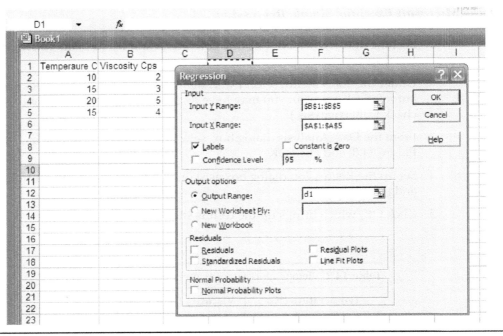

Figure 14.4 Regression data analysis.

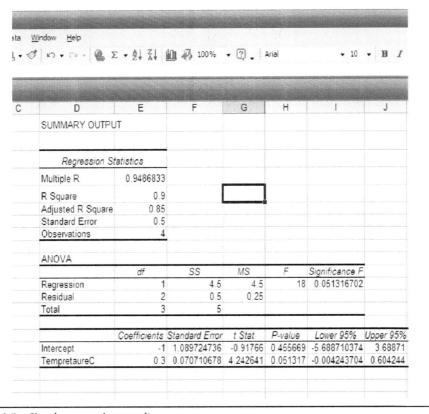

Figure 14.5 Simple regression results.

Six Sigma professionals find the linear regression tool helpful for making an estimate. This analysis can be effectively used during the Measure, Analyze, and Improve phases. In the Measure phase, this tool is used during the MSA-linearity study. In the Analyze phase, this tool is used for exploring relationships between variables. In the Improve phase, this tool can be used to estimate gains after the projected improvement.

QUESTIONS

1. Provide examples of correlation and causation.

2. The data shown in the following table were collected by surveying 100 employees with five years' experience. Find the correlation relationship for the data set using Microsoft Excel. Calculate the correlation coefficient. Identify whether the relationship is positive or negative and whether it is strong.

Years of schooling	Total annual salary
10	$32K
12	$33K
15	$45K
17	$60K

3. Use the regression method to calculate potential revenue in $K if the organization budgets $30K on quality improvement activities.

Money spent on quality improvement ($K)	Revenue ($K)
5	1000
10	1500
15	3000
20	3200

4. Explain your course of action if you find either no correlation or a nonlinear correlation among the data set.

5. Explain the application of the discussed methods in an improvement project or problem solving. At what stage could correlation and regression be used effectively?

Chapter 15
E. Hypothesis Testing

> Define and distinguish between hypothesis terms
> (i.e., null and alternative, type I and type II error,
> p-value and power). (Understand)
>
> **Body of Knowledge IV.E**

A *hypothesis* is an assumption about a population parameter, for example:

The average adult drinks 1.7 cups of coffee per day

No more than 2% of our products are defective

Average transaction time at a call center is 5 minutes

These statements about a population may or may not be true. The purpose of hypothesis testing is to make a statistical conclusion about accepting or not accepting such statements.

The Null and Alternative Hypotheses

All hypothesis tests have both a null hypothesis and an alternative hypothesis. A null hypothesis, denoted by H_0, represents the status quo and involves stating the belief that the mean of the population is $\geq$, $=$, or $\leq$ a specific value. The null hypothesis is believed to be true unless there is overwhelming evidence to the contrary. It is similar to a court trial. The hypothesis is that the defendant is not guilty until proven guilty. However, the term "innocent" does not apply to a null hypothesis. A null hypothesis can only be rejected or fail to be rejected; it cannot be accepted because of a lack of evidence to reject it. If the means of two populations are different, the null hypothesis of equality can be rejected if enough data are collected. When rejecting the null hypothesis, the alternative hypothesis must be considered. For example, the average weight of a component is six grams. The null hypothesis would be stated as:

$$H_0: \mu = 6.0, H_0: \mu \leq 6.0, H_0: \mu \geq 6.0$$

The alternative hypothesis, denoted by H_1, represents the opposite of the null hypothesis and holds true if the null hypothesis is found to be false. The alternative hypothesis always states that the mean of the population is <, ≠, or > a specific value. The alternative hypothesis would be stated as

$$H_1: \mu \neq 6.0, \; H_1: \mu > 6.0, \; H_1: \mu < 6.0$$

In order to test a null hypothesis, a calculation must be made from sample information. This calculated value is called a test statistic and is compared with an appropriate "critical value." A decision can then be made to reject or not reject the null hypothesis. The "critical value" is obtained from the t distribution table in Appendix H against a chosen level of significance. The typical levels of significance are 1%, 5%, and 10% (both tails).

Types of Errors

Two types of errors are possible when formulating a conclusion regarding population based on observations from a small sample:

Type I error: This type of error results when the null hypothesis is rejected when it is actually true. For example, incoming products are good but were labeled defective. This type of error is also called α (alpha) and referred to as the producer's risk (for sampling).

Type II error: This type of error results when the null hypothesis is not rejected when it actually should have been rejected. For example, incoming products are defective but were labeled good. This type of error is also called β (beta) and referred to as the consumer's risk (for sampling).

The types of errors are shown in Table 15.1.

The hypothesis table has four quadrants. Rejecting the null hypothesis when the outcome is false is a "correct" judgment. Similarly, failing to reject the null hypothesis when it is true is also a "correct" judgment. However, judgment error occurs when the null hypothesis is rejected when the outcome is true and when the null hypothesis fails to be rejected when the outcome is false. These are the errors explained as Type I and Type II and presented in the table.

One-Tail Test

Any type of hypothesis test has an associated risk, and it is generally the α risk (Type I error, which rejects the null hypothesis when it is true). The level of this

Table 15.1   Error matrix.

	False	True
Reject H_0	$p = 1 - \beta$, correct outcome	$p = 1 - \alpha$, Type I error
Do not reject H_0	$p = \beta$, Type II error	$p = 1 - \alpha$, correct outcome

Note: $p = 1 - \beta$ is also called power. Higher power is better in a hypothesis test.

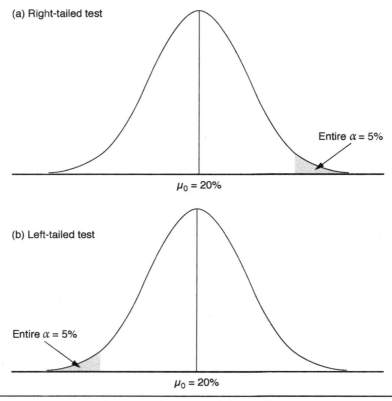

(a) Right-tailed test

Entire $\alpha = 5\%$

$\mu_0 = 20\%$

(b) Left-tailed test

Entire $\alpha = 5\%$

$\mu_0 = 20\%$

Figure 15.1 One–tail test: (a) right–tailed test and (b) left–tailed test.

α risk determines the level of confidence $(1 - \alpha)$ that we have in the conclusion. This risk factor is used to determine the critical value of the test statistic, which is compared with a calculated value.

If a null hypothesis is established to test whether a sample value is smaller or larger than a population value, then the entire α risk is placed on one end of a distribution curve. This constitutes a one-tail test (Figure 15.1).

$$H_0: \text{level} \geq 20\%, H_1: \text{level} < 20\%$$

EXAMPLE

A golf ball manufacturer claims its new golf ball will increase the driving distance off the tee by more than 20 yards. The hypothesis is set up as follows:

$$H_0: \mu \leq 20, H_1: \mu > 20$$

In Figure 15.1, there is only one rejection region, which is the shaded area on the distribution. We follow the same procedure outlined below for the two-tail test and plot the sample mean, which represents the average increase in distance from the tee with the new golf ball. Two possible scenarios exist:

- If the sample mean falls within the white region, we do not reject H_0. That is, we do not have enough evidence to support H_1, the alternative hypothesis, which states that the new golf ball will increase distance off the tee by more than 20 yards.

- If the sample mean falls in the rejection region, we reject H_0. That is, we have enough evidence to support H_1, which confirms the claim that the new golf ball will increase distance off the tee by more than 20 yards.

Note: For a one-tail hypothesis test, the rejection region will always be consistent with the direction of the inequality for H_1. For $H_1: \mu > 20$, the rejection region will be in the right tail of the sampling distribution. For $H_1: \mu < 20$, the rejection region will be in the left tail.

Two-Tail Test

If a null hypothesis is established to test whether a population shift has occurred in either direction, then a two-tail test is required. In other words, a two-tail hypothesis test is used whenever the alternative hypothesis is expressed as ≠. The allowable α error is generally divided into two equal parts (see Figure 15.2).

p-Value

Statistical significance is used to evaluate whether the decision made in a hypothesis test is valid. We often encounter situations like comparing "before and after" improvements, test equipment, service quality level, defects from two processes, and so on. Statistical significance is expressed by a *p*-value. Standard statistical

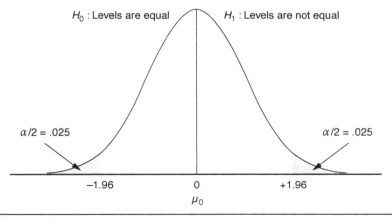

Figure 15.2 Two-tail test.

references define *p*-value as "the probability of obtaining a test statistic result at least as extreme or as close to the one that was actually observed, assuming that the null hypothesis is true."[1] If the calculated *p*-value is greater than the significance level considered (often 1% or 5%), then the *p*-value is not significant enough to conclude that the null hypothesis is true.

As for practical significance, a difference between two data sets may be statistically significant, but the question is, is it practically significant? As an example, the difference between two process defect levels is statistically significant. The difference is 0.5%. The customer is allowing a defect level of 3% for this process since the step is not critical. Similarly, a difference between two pieces of test equipment of up to 50 microns may be practically acceptable, while statistical significance may require a difference of 20 microns to determine that the null hypothesis is true.

It is important to ensure that the sample size calculated for the hypothesis testing is statistically adequate. Without a statistically significant sample size, the analysis may reveal a difference between data sets, but the probability of correctly detecting such a difference may be low due to low power in the experiment. This may lead to making incorrect decisions and taking risks that cost the organization.

By conducting statistical analysis, even if the sample size is inadequate to conclude the difference, we can estimate power in the decision and inform stakeholders of risks involved in the lower-than-desired power.

What Is a Desired Power?

A power of 0.8 and above is typically required for making a conclusion. A power of 0.9 or more may be required in some situations based on the risk to the organization.

A power of 0.8 means an experiment with the current sample size has an 80% likelihood of identifying a significant difference (more than 1% defectives) when one truly exists, and a 20% likelihood it will incorrectly identify a significant difference when the difference does not exist.

When to Calculate a Statistically Significant Sample Size

Statistically significant sample sizes using power and sample size are calculated before you design and run an experiment or improvement or after you perform an experiment or improvement.

How to Calculate a Statistically Significant Sample Size

Inputs for calculating a statistically significant sample size depend on:

σ—The variability in the population (or experimental variability). As σ decreases, power increases.

δ—The size of the effect (difference to detect). As the size of the effect increases, power increases.

α—The probability of a type I error (also called the *level of significance*).

β—When H_0 is false and you fail to reject it, you make a type II error. The probability (p) of making a type II error is called *beta*.

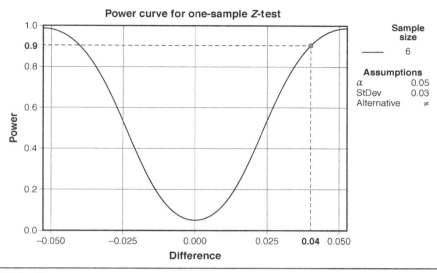

Figure 15.3   Power curve.

From Figure 15.3, a process with standard deviation 0.03 can detect a difference in mean value of 0.04 with 0.9 power if six samples were used.

QUESTIONS

1. The null hypothesis for the average defective rate at the final inspection is less than or equal to 100 DPPM. Write the null and alternative hypotheses statements.

2. The null hypothesis for the waiting time at a popular restaurant during the busy hours is 30 minutes. Write the null and alternative hypotheses statements.

3. If the p-value of a hypothesis test performed is 0.045, would you reject or fail to reject the null hypothesis at a significance level of 5%? For extra credit, explain the risk in this decision and what additional information you might seek to make sure you provide a full picture to your management.

4. When would you provide a high level of protection for producer and consumer risks? Give an example for both scenarios.

5. The power of your experiment performed at the Improve phase is 0.6. Explain to the class what this means.

Part V
Improve and Control Phases

Chapter 16
A. Improvement Techniques

> Define and distinguish between these two methods and describe how they can be used to make improvements to any process in an organization (Understand)
>
> **Body of Knowledge V.A.1**

1. KAIZEN AND KAIZEN BLITZ

Kaizen is a Japanese term meaning "change for improvement," or improving processes through small, incremental steps (Figure 16.1). It is expressed by two characters in Japanese as "change" and "good." This is a key fundamental. Many times organizations make changes with the intention of making something good, but due to either poor conception or poor deployment, the change does not result in something good. Even if the change had a positive outcome, it may not be sustainable or it may create a new problem in another area of business. Kaizen programs are managed at the gemba (workplace), where the process happens. Kaizen improvements are managed by the employees who manage the process. They are empowered to make changes. At the same time, the changes are carefully reviewed by process owners to ensure the changes do not create new issues downstream.

Breakthrough improvement is referred to by another Japanese term, *kaikaku*. Kaikaku is referred to in North America as a kaizen event or kaizen blitz. Hence, many practitioners are often confused by the interchangeable usage of "kaizen" and "kaizen event." In lean implementation, kaizen events are used to provide

Kai   Zen

改 善

Change   Good

Figure 16.1   Meaning of "kaizen."

quicker implementation results. Kaizen events are conducted by assembling a cross-functional team for three to five days and reviewing all possible options for improvement in a breakthrough effort. Management support is required for such initiatives. If the employees can't afford to take three to five days to improve a process constraint, then either the problem is unimportant or the organization requires more fundamental cultural adjustment before implementing lean.

Humans are wired to improve incrementally through continuous improvement. Most industrial development today has evolved over thousands of years of incrementally improving a situation thought to be a constraint in meeting the human needs at that point in time. The evolution of tools, utensils, clothing, and shelter is a great example of such incremental improvements.

If we can exploit the natural skill of humans to think through the constraints, find alternate solutions, and incrementally improve products and processes, we can accomplish improved quality, productivity, safety, cost reduction, customer satisfaction, and overall societal quality of life.

Incremental improvement, or kaizen, is achieved by the people who work on the process every day. By challenging themselves to improve quality and productivity without incurring significant capital investment, employees provide small, steady improvements in their work. Kaizen from day-to-day work is submitted by employees for review and approval. These small, gradual improvements are piloted and implemented across the organization. There needs to be management support and recognition of the efforts for kaizen improvements. Management needs to empower the employees to propose and make incremental changes to the products and processes. If the system bureaucracy gets in the way, employee creativity will be affected and the free flow of ideas will be stopped. If management does not recognize the employees' effort, kaizen initiatives will not succeed.

Kaizen improvements need to be managed through an infrastructure. Improvement implemented ad hoc can cause more harm than good. A process for managing the kaizen improvements needs to be put in place. This process should allow employees to make proposals for kaizen improvements and describe benefits that could be realized. This process should also go through evaluation of the proposed improvements for any undesired or unintended impacts due to implementation of the improvement. This level of due diligence is obviously required to account for the changes and reward the useful improvements. At the same time, the improvements must be visible so that the organization can manage any risks due to changes. Incremental improvements also have limitations. After these improvements are exhausted, the management has to think of breakthrough improvement strategies.

Kaizen improvement management requires the following:

- A documented process

- A form to submit the improvement proposal for review

- Review team

- Approvers

- Implementation and follow-up of the improvement for effectiveness

- Reward and recognition system

- Organization of the changes made by product and process

Additionally, the kaizen improvement infrastructure has to be supported by providing training to employees on continuous improvement methodology, the seven quality tools, and problem solving. Management is also encouraged to create dashboards of the improvements made to products and processes and publicize overall monetary benefits to the organization to motivate employees. Bulletin boards can be used to display pictures of the improvement for additional encouragement. Successful organizations also have dashboard or key process indicator metrics for incremental continuous improvements (e.g., number of improvements/employee/year).

Process owners begin planning for a kaizen event, or kaizen blitz, four weeks ahead of the actual event. The team leader (typically the process owner) starts collecting information related to the process: flowcharts, product specifications, customer requirements, process requirements, equipment information, tools, process performance, dashboards, inventory, and so on. A cross-functional team related to the process is put together. If required, a "sensei" (teacher or mentor) will be hired.

On the first day of the kaizen event, the team is trained on lean enterprise basics and other tools required for the improvement project, like root cause analysis. On the second and third days, the team walks the gemba (workplace), mapping the current value stream or current situation and identifying opportunities for improvement. On days four and five the team creates future value stream maps and starts making improvements. If the process is less complex, the improvements are made during the kaizen event, and sustaining the improved process starts after day five. If the process is rather complex and improvements are likely to take longer than the event duration, the improvements are managed by the kaizen leader. The "before and after" comparison and improvements are presented to the senior management at the end of the event. Team members are formally recognized. Since employees immediately apply their newly learned skills in the improvement project, they retain the skills.

Define and distinguish between the steps in this process improvement tool. (Understand)

Body of Knowledge V.A.2

---

2. PLAN-DO-CHECK-ACT (PDCA) CYCLE

PDCA is an improvement cycle methodology that evolved from 1939 to 1994, from Walter A. Shewhart to W. Edwards Deming and improvisation of the model between Ishikawa and the Japanese Quality Circle movement. Figures 16.2–16.5 show variations of the improvement model.

The model is a simple circle divided into four quadrants, named "plan," "do," "check," and "act." The improvement team brainstorms the activities that the four quadrants should encompass in the context of the problem at hand and populates the quadrant. Quality gurus like Deming and Ishikawa provided the foundation for this model to build on.

Shewhart straight-line process

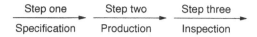

Step one	Step two	Step three
Specification	Production	Inspection

Shewhart cyclical concept

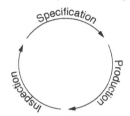

Figure 16.2 Shewhart cycle (1939).

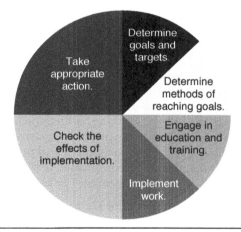

Figure 16.3 Japanese PDCA cycle (1985).

1. Design the product (with appropriate tests).
2. Make the product and test in the production line and in the laboratory.
3. Sell the product.
4. Test the product in service and through market research. Find out what users think about it and why nonusers have not bought it.

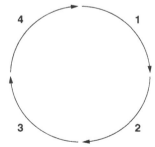

Figure 16.4 Deming wheel (1950).

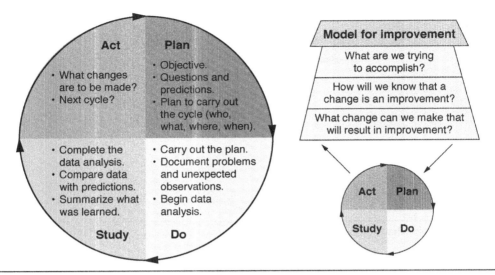

Figure 16.5 PDSA cycle and model for improvement (1991, 1994).

The initial PDCA cycle (Figure 16.2) was created to solve shop floor problems and prevent their recurrence. The seven quality tools were used along with the PDCA model. The model is robust and has many applications, including product design and development, service offering, educational curriculum, and health-care. Regardless of the application, we can map the activities to PDCA. This forces a disciplined approach to program management and provides team members with the big picture of what needs to be accomplished and where they are in the quadrant. The four quadrants of the improvement PDCA are explained as follows:

Plan. Define a problem and hypothesize possible causes and solutions.

Do. Implement a solution.

Check. Evaluate the results.

Act. Return to the Plan step if the results are unsatisfactory or further improvement is required. Standardize the solution if the results are satisfactory.

Ishikawa modified the model by incorporating additions to the Plan and Do steps (Figure 16.3):

Plan. Determine goals and targets; determine methods of reaching goals

Do. Engage in education and training; implement work

Check. Check the effects of implementation

Act. Take appropriate action

At the Plan stage, the process or problem selected for improvement is described. The improvement goals and objectives are defined.

The current process, which is resulting in the problem situation, is described through process mapping. Quality tools are used to analyze the problem and identify the root causes. A cross-functional team is formed to develop a solution and action plan. At the Do stage, the team implements the solution. At the Check stage, the team evaluates the effects of the implementation. At the Act stage, the team takes appropriate actions as to whether to continue the cycle by going back to the Plan stage or to standardize the learning to ensure sustainability of the actions. Deming differentiates his PDSA model (Figure 16.5) from the Japanese PDCA as more of a plan for management. The Study step of the PDSA intends to compare the results with the initial predictions as process learning. The improvement team is encouraged to develop a checklist using the PDCA/PDSA model.

> Explain the importance of this analysis and how it is used in the improve phase. (Understand)
>
> **Body of Knowledge V.A.3**

3. COST-BENEFIT ANALYSIS

Once the Analyze phase is completed, the Six Sigma team starts brainstorming to identify improvement actions. Improvement actions can range from rewriting a procedure to redesigning equipment to retrofitting a factory. Every improvement action will cost money to implement. As the saying goes, in order to make money, first you have to spend money. Unless there are significant benefits, improvement actions will not get resourced by management. How do we objectively evaluate the improvement actions?

Cost of the improvement actions may involve:

Design, development, deployment, sustaining

People, equipment, material, environmental controls, software, communication, transport, security, and so on

These costs are compared with:

Cost prevention or reduction of scrap, errors, defects, failures, accidents, violations (legal and regulatory), nonconformance, and so on

Cost avoidance of repair, regrade, rework, recall, reinstall, rehire, and so on

There are also costs that are difficult to measure, for example, loss of customer confidence and customer dissatisfaction.

A typical cost-benefit analysis involves calculating both the applicable measurable costs that will be incurred and the benefits of the costs avoided. There are financial measures for cost-benefit analysis:

ROI (return on investment): A ratio of net profit to investment expressed in a percentage (for a given period of time); usually the higher the ratio, the better.

Payback period. The time it takes to recoup the investment made in a project; the shorter the period, the better.

NPV (net present value). "The sum of the present values (PVs) of incoming and outgoing cash flows over a period of time. Incoming and outgoing cash flows can also be described as benefit and cost cash flows, respectively."[1] An NPV > 0 is acceptable, but the higher the NPV, the better.

IRR (internal rate of return). The rate of return used in capital budgeting to measure and compare the profitability of investments; the higher the IRR, the better.

Cost of Quality (COQ)

The COQ is a financial tool used to report how quality levels are being sustained on the shop floor within an organization. Improvement actions from the Six Sigma project may impact the COQ. In *Principles of Quality Costs*, Wood explains the COQ as "the difference between the actual cost of a product or service and what the reduced cost would be if there were no possibility of substandard service, product failure, or manufacturing defects."[2]

Many things that are worked on throughout the organization can be classified into either the cost of conformance or the cost of nonconformance. They can be further grouped under one of four categories: prevention costs, appraisal costs, internal failure costs, or external failure costs.

Cost of Conformance

Appraisal costs: Costs associated with measuring, evaluating, and auditing products or services to ensure conformance to quality standards and performance requirements

Prevention costs: Costs of activities specifically designed to prevent poor quality in products or services; quality at the source

Cost of Nonconformance

Internal failure costs: Costs that occur prior to delivery or shipment of products and services to the customer

External failure costs: Costs that occur after shipment of the product to the customer or after servicing

Total cost = Cost of conformance + Cost of nonconformance

Not all expenses of the company are used in the calculations, only those that relate in some way to the products or services shipped to customers. The real power of this tool is not so much that you use the exact or "right" measures for each expense, but that you look at trends over time to see what you are doing. You want to find out what the *total cost* is to provide your customers with products and services (see Figure 5.11 in Chapter 5). It was suggested in the article "Tip of the

Iceberg" that "when added together, the costs of poor quality make up as much as 15 to 30% of all costs."[3]

Traditionally, when an organization first calculates its COQ, a picture such as Figure 5.11 emerges. Part of the reason for this is that many accountants and managers have not been taught about this tool in their formal education, nor does any governmental or professional organization require the reporting of financial data in this format.

On the other hand, organizations that have learned to use the COQ in their cost-benefit analysis are often very surprised at the amount of waste being produced. By focusing on activities that constitute prevention and appraisal costs, failure costs will slowly start to come down. This will not happen overnight and may take years, in stubborn cases, to show improvement as old products work their way out of the customer system.

It is important to note that not all failure costs are visible. There are visible costs and hidden costs (Figure 16.6). Examples of visible costs are customer returns, factory scrap, rework, repair, regrade, and recall. Hidden costs include lost customer revenue, administrative costs in handling complaints, project cost overrun, schedule delays, and expediting costs. Hidden costs could be higher than the visible costs. Reasons for the costs being hidden are that some costs are often difficult to

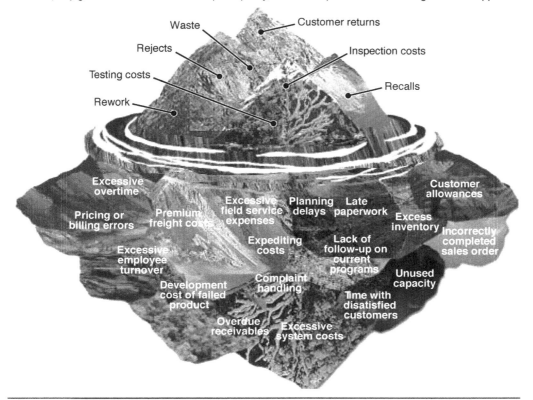

As a company gains a broader definition of poor quality, the hidden portion of the iceberg becomes apparent.

Figure 16.6 Cost of poor quality (COPQ).

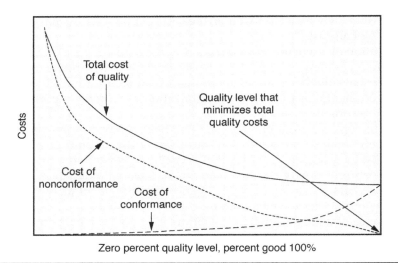

Figure axis labels: Costs (vertical), Zero percent quality level, percent good 100% (horizontal)

Total cost of quality

Quality level that minimizes total quality costs

Cost of nonconformance

Cost of conformance

Figure 16.7 Modern quality cost curves.

measure and monitor and that a sea of inventory hides the problem from surfacing. So people don't pay attention until a problem surfaces. The bigger the inventory, the longer it takes the problem to surface.

No one should be blamed for the poor results of the measurement of the COQ. It is important to look at these numbers as a benchmark from which to measure improvement. The numbers should be made available to everyone so that ideas can be generated as to what can be done and how. Remember the old adage "What gets measured, gets done." Thus, if everyone knows that management is watching the numbers on the COQ, things should start to improve.

In the *Principles of Quality Costs*, Wood offers the following strategy:

1. Take direct focus on failure costs in an attempt to drive them to zero

2. Invest in the right prevention activities to bring about improvement

3. Reduce appraisal costs according to results achieved

4. Continuously evaluate and redirect prevention efforts to gain further improvement[4]

The ultimate goal is to change the overall picture to look like Figure 16.7. As an organization continually improves its products and services, it will see an overall reduction in total cost to manufacture and produce products and services.

QUESTIONS

1. What are the challenges in implementing kaizen? What are your recommendations?

2. Take an improvement project or a problem-solving project and map it to the steps of PDCA. Suggest actions to sustain the improvement and hold the gains.

3. What are the main components of a cost-benefit analysis?

4. Calculate ROI, payback period, and NPV for the project you chose in question #2.

5. Why do visible costs of quality appear to be lower when the organization as a whole is not doing well financially?

Chapter 17

B. Control Tools and Documentation

Describe the importance of a control plan for maintaining improvements. (Understand)

Body of Knowledge V.B.1

1. CONTROL PLAN

A *control plan* is a summarized document of all the key information that an operator needs to know to manage, control, and monitor the process. ASQ defines a control plan as "written descriptions of the systems for controlling part and process quality by addressing the key characteristics and engineering requirements."[1]

A control plan provides information on the following:

- What to measure (product or process characteristics)

- When to measure (after which step or activity)

- How to measure (method, measurement, and monitoring resource)

- How often to measure (frequency of measurement after every nth part or lot or batch)

- What to do and who to contact when something is not right (manufacturing organizations often have an out-of-control action plan or out-of-specification action plan)

The control plan (updated as needed and kept current) explains how to control the workflow in your process. It is closely tied to customer requirements, product requirements, FMEA, SPC, and MSA. Specifically, items of risk with low detection will have a link to a control plan as a recommended action with improved detectability and control. If the control method is SPC, there will be a linkage here. The measurement and test equipment chosen for measurement characteristics would have gone through an MSA prior to being assigned to manufacturing. This will link the control plan with the MSA. When an organization makes any changes to specifications or requirements, the control plan gets updated as well.

A control plan should have, as a minimum, the following basic information:

- A flowchart or other graphical representation of the process with the desired outcomes displayed

- Any special or safety characteristics must be clearly displayed

- A description of the direct relationship between any highlighted characteristics and their controlling process setting or parameters

- Identification of any gages or test equipment needed for the operations

- Identification of appropriate sample sizes and frequencies of all testing

- Any reactions to FMEA conditions should be spelled out to prevent nonconforming products or out-of-control conditions

- Reaction plans that are easily understood by operators

- Verify accuracy with the next operation in the process

The control plan should outline the steps to be followed during each phase of the process to ensure that all process outputs are in a state of control. Operators need to feel comfortable working with the paperwork in their area. A simple plan based on the template in Figure 17.1 should be adequate to track the necessary data on a single page or sheet. Examples are shown as Figures 17.2 and 17.3.

Deming was well known for his constant harping on managers to fix the process, not the people. His 85/15 rule says that 85% of the problems in any operation are within the system and are management's responsibility, while only 15% lie with the worker.[2] Operators need to use data collection tools to demonstrate that they are following the control plan, and so any issue that arises can be shown to be due to system operation.

Control plans provide a structured approach for the design, selection, and implementation of value-added control methods for the total system. The scope of control plans includes dynamic control plans, quality process sheets, and standard operating procedures. In whatever form, control plans are dynamic documents that explain how to control the process workflow.

Dynamic Control Planning

The dynamic control plan (DCP) combines necessary information into one document to help plan, monitor, control, study, and maintain your process. Some of the documents include standard operating procedures (SOPs), control plans, FMEA, gage control plan, and quality planning sheets (QPSs).

The DCP is often called a living document, where operators have the right—and the responsibility—to update it anytime that things change; the documents need to be updated so that others know that something is different in the process.

Plant	Operation	Date control limits calculated	Part number	Specification
Machine	Characteristic	Sample size/ frequency	Part name	Control item
Averages chart				Actions on special causes
Ranges chart				Action instructions
Readings				Subgroup size
Sum of readings				
Process log				
Date/time	Material change	Methods/ equipment change	Operator change	Comments

Figure 17.1 A sample control plan template.

Gage Control Plan

A gage control plan is followed to look at the tools for monitoring and checking the process. Maintaining your tools is important to the safety and quality of your processes. The gage control plan can be a type of FMEA for the tools you use; it should look at maintenance, calibration, and proper handling of the instruments.

The gage control plan, as the control plan, provides for a written method to describe the system that controls the proper usage of the equipment to help ensure that measurement variation is as low as possible given the current set of conditions. The gage control plan is not meant to replace the gage or test equipment instruction sheets, but to guide the operator in what to do if certain circumstances occur.

Soft Start-Up Valve Control Plan

Control plan number: CP714			Control plan revision level: C							Revision date: 12/01/15	
Part/assembly number/rev: 714647-H & 714648-J			Product line: Soft start air dump valve							Originator: J. Hausner	
				Methods							
						Sample				**Reaction plan**	
Sta #	Process description	Machine tools/ equipment	Print no.	Characteristic specification	Evaluation measurement equipment	Size	Freq.	Control method		code	
14	Machine needle bleed port on cover	Drill press	714648	0.060" min diameter	0.60 (minus) gage pin S/N 15-50-2118	1	1 per hour	Check sheet		A	
18	Pressure gage torque	Torque driver	714647 714648	20 +/– 5 IN LB	Torque gage S/N 15-50-2019	5	1 per shift	X̄ chart		B, C	
23	Body-cover screw torque	Torque driver	714647 714648	60 +/– 15 IN LB	Torque gage S/N 15-50-2120	3 per screw	2 per shift	Separate X̄ charts		B, C	
27	Solenoid assembly torque	Torque driver	209647 209648	14 +/– 7 IN LB	Torque gage S/N 15-50-2019	5	1 per shift	X̄ chart		B, C	
29	Final air test	Test tank	209647 209648	Functional test and leak check	Visual: ref. QA spec 203795 Functional: ref. assy instruction	1	100%	Go/no-go		A, B, C, D	
All	All	All	209647 209648	Workmanship	Visual	1	100%	Go/no-go		See note 2	

Note 1: At all times, quarantine one hour's worth of product before releasing to shipping. In the event of a final test failure, the last hour of production should be set aside for possible retest. This should be done on all final test failures with the exception of porosity.

Note 2: Compare suspect unit with visual accept/reject standards. If unit is unacceptable, stop the line and follow standard four-step reaction plan: (A) contain suspect units; (B) diagnose the root cause and implement corrective action; (C) verify that the corrective action is effective; (D) disposition suspect material (sort, scrap, rework, use as-is).

Figure 17.2   An example control plan—first page.

Soft Start-Up Valve Control Plan

Control plan number: CP714	Key contact: J. Hausner	Control plan revision level: C	Revision date: 12/01/15
Part/assembly number/rev: 714647-H & 714648-J	Part name/description: Soft start air dump valve HG & HJ series	Product line: Airlogic control valve series	Originator: J. Hausner

Failure mode	Reaction plan	Code
Valve fails to open	Containment: Segregate nonconforming unit and previous hour of production for MRB. Disposition: Verify that wire leads and power supply are hooked up correctly. Verify needle port diameter > 0.060'. If port diameter is under spec, switch to 100% inspection for the next 50 units and notify the product engineer (PE) if another failure is found. Replace drill bit if hole is not drilled through or burrs are present. Verify that piston ring is installed and free of nicks. Verify that needle valve is open at least one complete turn. Verify that the solenoid port resistor is installed. Try another solenoid. If other tests fail, check diameter of diaphragm. Contact the PE if additional diagnosis is required. Verification: Verify that corrective action eliminates problem. Disposition: Scrap nonconforming components. Rework assemblies as necessary and retest 100% of the previous hour of production.	
Valve fails to close	Containment: Segregate nonconforming product for MRB. Diagnosis: Verify that wire leads and power supply are hooked up correctly. Verify that flow control is open. Verify that diaphragm is installed correctly and check for voids in the seal bead. Verify that the dump hole is drilled completely through bonnet. Check that the fluid resistor is in place. Try another solenoid. If solenoid sticks open, quarantine current batch and switch to a new batch of solenoids. Contact PE if further diagnosis is required to determine cause. Verification: Verify that corrective action eliminates problem. Notify PE if another failure is found on the next 50 units. Disposition: Scrap nonconforming components. Rework assembly and retest.	
Body–bonnet leak	Containment: Segregate nonconforming product for MRB. Diagnosis: Verify torque. For torque adjustments, see Reaction Code "B" below. Ensure that diaphragm is installed correctly and that there are no voids present on the bead. Verify that the bead grooves on the bonnet and body are free of nicks or porosity and that the diameters are within tolerance. Verify that the milled slot on the body is within tolerance. Contact PE if further diagnosis is required. Verification: Verify that corrective action eliminates problem. Disposition: Scrap nonconforming components. Rework assembly and retest. Contact line lead or PE if there are two or more consecutive failures or three failures within one hour.	
Leak at fittings	Containment: Segregate nonconforming product for MRB. Diagnosis: Verify that fittings are installed correctly and have the correct torque applied. Verify that the threads on the fitting and assembly are free of nicks or porosity. Contact PE if further diagnosis is required. Verification: Verify that corrective action eliminates problem. Notify PE if another failure is found on the next 50 units. Disposition: Scrap nonconforming components. Rework assembly and retest.	
Torque out of spec	Containment: Segregate nonconforming product for MRB. Diagnosis: Verify torque using another torque gage. For torque adjustments, take at least 10 samples and adjust torque gun if average is more than one standard deviation away from the nominal. Notify maintenance if average is close to nominal and there are any observations out of spec. Contact PE for further diagnosis. Verification: Measure a minimum of three subgroups and verify that the process is near nominal and in control. Disposition: If undertorqued, retorque assembly. If overtorqued, replace screw(s) and retorque.	
SPC out of control, but parts in spec	Refer to QA/SPC procedure 231573. Comply with SPC procedure requirements. Document the root cause and corrective action in a note on the control chart.	

Figure 17.3 An example control plan—second page.

> Describe how $\bar{X}$–R charts are used for monitoring and sustaining improved processes. (Understand)
>
> **Body of Knowledge V.B.2**

2. CONTROL CHARTS

The foundations for process behavior charts (control charts) were laid by Walter A. Shewhart (called "the father of modern-day quality control") in the late 1920s. Today there are over 30 different charts, but we typically use only six or seven on a regular basis. These charts display the process variation while work is being done. This allows the operator to ensure that the process is stable and continuing to operate within the process boundaries (not necessarily specification limits) established for that process. If something starts to deteriorate or change in the process, the process behavior chart will indicate to the operator that something needs to be adjusted or changed to bring the process back into control.

Process behavior charts (statistical process control charts) can be introduced at a high level with the following descriptions:

- Typically only six or seven types are used on a regular basis

- Create a picture of the process variation while work is being done in real time

- Ensure that the process is stable and continuing to operate within the process boundaries established for that process

- Provide an early warning to adjust or change the process to bring it back into control

- Variable data are continuous (length, mass, time)

- Attribute data are discrete (defect, defectives)

- Ensure that the measurements from the process are recorded, calculated, and plotted appropriately

- Refer to an upper control limit or a lower control limit value from a table

- Being in statistical control refers to being between the upper and lower control limits

Control charts are used to attain a state of statistical control, monitor a process, and determine process capability. Control charts can monitor process stability and achieve parts per million defect levels. Reduction of variation is achieved through other statistical tools like design of experiments (DOE).

A state of statistical control means that only random causes are present in the process (see Chapter 13, "Data Analysis"). It does not mean that products meet specifications. Conversely, a process not in statistical control may still produce product conforming to specifications. Basic steps for setting up control charts are as follows:

- The recommended number of subgroups is 25 (subgroup size of four or five), sampled at equal intervals from the process during data collection; compute trial control limits.

- The data are charted for each subgroup and are reviewed for common and special causes, eliminating special causes resulting in excessive variation and continuing with revised control limits.

- The mean and standard deviation are estimated based on the sample data. Averages are more sensitive to process changes than individual readings. The control chart is fairly robust for non-normal data.

- Control limits based on the statistical variation of the process can be established at ±3 standard deviations from the mean or by using the statistical constants provided in Appendix E.

Rational Subgroup

A rational subgroup is a sample set that is sufficient to determine common-cause scenarios. Normally, the average of a subgroup is used. In rational subgrouping:

- The division of observations into rational subgroups is key

- Success of control charting depends on the selection of subgroups (size and frequency of sampling)

- Selection should result in groups as homogeneous as possible (no mixing between equipment, manufacturing lines, and tools)

Selection of Variables

- Key process input variables (KPIVs) may be analyzed to determine their effect on a process

- Key process output variables (KPOVs) determine process capability and process monitoring using control charting

- DOE and analysis of variance (ANOVA) methods may also identify variables that are significant to process control

Variables that are critical to quality should be selected for control charts based on:

- Importance to customer perception

- Objectivity (counted or measured)

- Clear indicators to suggest whether quality is being achieved

Setting Up Control Charts

- Choose the characteristic to be charted based on what is defective and controlled or adjustable (as mentioned earlier).

- Identify the process variables and conditions contributing to product characteristics.

- Consider attribute data (i.e., percent defective) and variables data (i.e., numerical measurements) to diagnose causes and determine action. Charts for attributes require discrete measurements (i.e., pass/fail, counts) and will be useful provided that the defective rate is high enough to show on a chart with a reasonable subgroup size. Variables charts require measurements on a continuous scale (i.e., length, mass, and time).

- Determine the earliest point in the process where testing can be done to get information on assignable causes. The earlier the cause can be identified, the more likely the consequences can be effectively contained and mitigated.

- Choose the type of control chart used: variable or attribute, individual or averages, range or standard deviation.

- Decide on the central line and the basis for calculating control limits.

- Choose the rational subgroup and the appropriate strategy (subgroup frequency, size, etc.).

- Provide the system for collecting data.

- Calculate the control limits and provide specific instructions on the interpretation of results and actions to be taken.

By identifying and resolving the special causes, the Six Sigma practitioner can facilitate bringing the process into statistical control. At this point, the process results are predictable and the suitability of the process to achieve customer specifications is revealed. From here on out, continual improvement can be realized.

An example of a variable control chart is presented in Figure 17.4. An example of an attribute control chart is presented in Figure 17.5.

Control charts can be used for maintaining statistical control. After the expected process level and dispersion are attained, the expected range of variation will become the standard against which subsequent samples are compared to detect the presence of significant causes of variation. Use of the expected range of variation (sometimes referred to as "natural control limits") as a standard will help detect significant changes in the process.

Control charts maintain statistical control and provide traceable evidence through three key actions:

- *Collection.* Run the process and collect the data for plotting on a graph or chart

- *Control.* Calculate control limits, establish process variability and control limits, and monitor stability

- *Capability.* Establish the ability of the process to meet customer specifications without producing or shipping nonconforming units

X̄ and R Control Chart   Machine_____   Process_____

Product/part name and number: *mp plate w239*   Gage: *64e*   Specification limits: 7.125+.010

Date/operator: *3/17 G. Turner*

Time		7am	8	9	10	11	Noon	1pm	2	3	4		
	1	7.127	7.125	7.123	7.127	7.128	7.125	7.126	7.126	7.127	7.128		
	2	7.123	7.126	7.129	7.127	7.125	7.125	7.123	7.126	7.129	7.123		
	3	7.123	7.121	7.129	7.124	7.126	7.127	7.123	7.127	7.128	7.122		
	4	7.126	7.122	7.124	7.125	7.127	7.128	7.125	7.128	7.129	7.124		
	5												
Ave, X̄		7.125	7.124	7.126	7.126	7.127	7.126	7.124	7.127	7.128	7.124		
Range, R		.004	.005	.006	.003	.003	.003	.003	.002	.002	.006		

Notes:

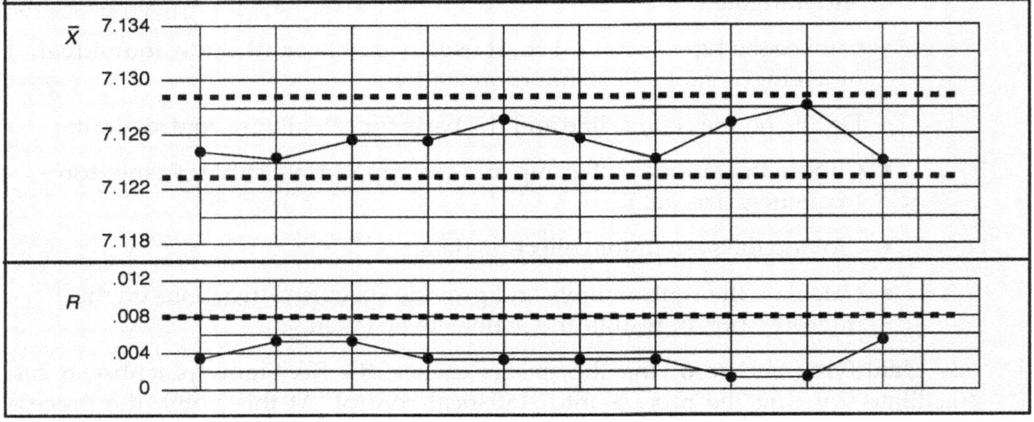

Figure 17.4 X̄ and R control chart example with data plotted.

Advantages of Control Charts

- Allow operators to collect data at the process
- Increase yield by revealing and containing problems at the stage the problem is identified
- Provide consistency between operators, shifts, and facilities
- Determine whether problems require local or management action

Monitoring the Process

Monitoring the control chart requires periodic review of variability in the process and review of, or possible revisions to, control limits.

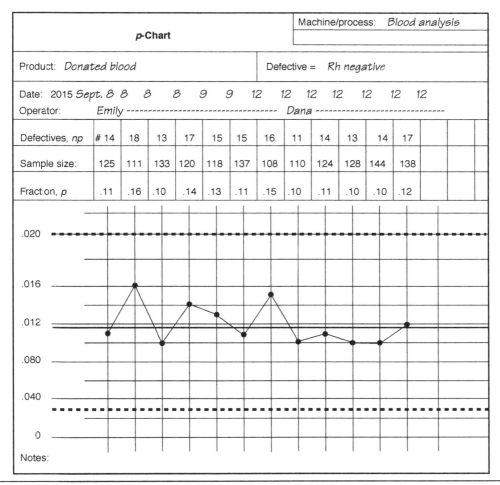

Figure 17.5 Example of a *p*-chart.

Sustaining the Process

Control charts are relatively easy to set up but difficult to sustain. There are many factors that affect continued implementation:

- Not making effective use of SPC (data are ceremoniously plotted with no analysis or review to take actions)

- Production and productivity seen as more important than time allocation for plotting and monitoring process health

- Lack of training of people who plot charts and managers who are required to interpret and take actions

Management commitment to resources and to set expectations is key to the success of any quality initiative.

> Describe the importance of documenting changes to a process and communicating those changes to stakeholders. (Understand)
>
> **Body of Knowledge V.B.3**

3. DOCUMENT CONTROL

Standard Operating Procedures

When the process is developed or updated, SOPs should be developed to ensure consistency in the process (whether manufacturing or service). This is one of the methodology under Lean enterprise organization approach to standard work. An SOP is a step-by-step description of how to complete a task.

Documented evidence will go a long way in preventing finger-pointing or faultfinding and the operator being blamed for something out of their control. SOPs create consistency and establish the proper methods for completing a process.

Standardization is the process of locking in the gains made during the improvement process. Following the SDCA (Standardize-Do-Check-Adjust) process, standardization is done after control plans and process documentation have been updated.

Many different terms are used for SOPs, such as "work instructions," "level three ISO 9001 documentation," "operating guides," "job aids," and "standard job practices." SOPs should give the details and address questions such as What is the job? Where does the SOP apply? When does the SOP apply? and Who is responsible?

Operators are responsible for following the SOPs as written. If at any time the operator deviates from the SOP, the operator needs to document what was done and why. This will be a big help if at a later date a problem arises and an investigation is done.

The SOP should be a living document; if something changes in the system, the operator should ensure that the SOP is updated. When something changes in the process and a new desirable level is achieved, the operator should update all documents relating to that process.

Changes to documents have to be made in a disciplined manner. Most mature organizations have a process for change management. Changes are reviewed by a designated cross-functional team, approved, and piloted on a small scale through a temporary change notice. Once the results of the pilot are analyzed and the team is convinced of the benefits (no negative impacts elsewhere), the change is formally approved in the system for implementation across the organization or multiple geographical locations.

In my experience, organizations and functions that primarily perform research development usually show resistance to documenting changes. There is a misperception that documentation and communication of change is non-value-added administrative work and does not quite fit a creative organization. We as

Six Sigma professionals have responsibility to explain the importance of documentation and communication. Documenting changes in a disciplined manner helps the organization trace back and reassess a risk, evaluate customer-reported issues, and so forth.

Organizations with ISO 9001 or equivalent management systems implemented have a process to control document changes and communication to stakeholders. It is important to identify the appropriate stakeholders for change review, approval, and communication. Sometimes the stakeholders may be outside the organization, for example, customers, suppliers, and the regulating body. Those with authority to make changes in the organization should also pay attention to retrieve obsolete communications and discard them. It is very easy in an organization to leave old information at various process locations if there is no system for controlled distribution and retrieval. This may cause major confusion and inconsistency in operations where one area is following the old process and another area is using the newly implemented changes. Change management also involves training personnel and mistake proofing the system so that employees do not regress to the old ways.

In a typical manufacturing organization, a change in a manufacturing document could result in stakeholder communication as shown in Table 17.1.

For a service organization, a change in a process document could result in stakeholder communication as shown in Table 17.2.

The list of plausible stakeholders can vary case by case. It is recommended that the individual who performs or initiates a change conduct a brainstorming with team members to identify stakeholders affected by the change. Some stakeholders may need to take action based on the change. For example, the change might involve setting up a vendor managed inventory at the organization; the organization's purchasing function should discuss this with the supplier and agree to

Table 17.1 Change communication (manufacturing).

Function (as an example)	Nature of impact
Manufacturing	Change to related process documentation linked to the affected document
Engineering	Changes to tools, jigs, fixtures, and gauges; change to equipment maintenance documents
Purchasing	Changes to purchasing specifications, communication to supplier, assess impact on inventory at supplier location, disposition of affected materials
Quality	Change to FMEA, quality plan, SPC, MSA, control plan
Training	Change to training documentation
IT	Changes to application software, testing software
Customer support	Communication to customer on nature of change and impact (typically informed prior to making change)

Table 17.2 Change communication (service).

Function (as an example)	Nature of impact
Service delivery	Change to related process documentation linked to the affected document
Service design	Changes to design, service infrastructure
Purchasing	Changes to purchasing specifications, communication to supplier, assess impact on outsourced service provider
Service quality	Change to FMEA, service quality plan, SPC, control plan
Training	Change to training documentation
IT	Changes to process management software, testing software
Customer support	Communication to customer on nature of change and impact (typically informed prior to making change)

make this a contract condition. Others are communicated as an information of change. Typical change communication documents have check boxes to identify who is impacted by the change and what actions they need to take. Customers often require a written submission of a change proposal for approval before the change is introduced. From the organization's perspective, the change might be small and inconsequential or it could be a change that improves the process. However, the customer might see the change as a risk to product reliability. Functions like environmental health and safety, human resources, and legal may also need to be involved in process changes; for example, a change of chemicals in a cleaning process could violate environmental regulations.

If the communication to stakeholders is not well managed, change will not be effectively rolled out. This may result in manufacturing nonconforming products or delivery of services that do not meet customer requirements, product recall, violation notices from regulatory bodies, and unfavorable public relations perceptions. This may also result in a negative impact on the cost of quality metrics, along with a market share that defeats the very purpose of the Six Sigma program. Six Sigma professionals are required to ensure that the proposed changes in the Improve phase are assessed for risk and adequately managed in the Control phase.

QUESTIONS

1. Develop a control plan for a cake-baking process. Identify whether the requirement is customer-facing or from the process.

2. As a Six Sigma Yellow Belt, you have been asked to identify an appropriate type of control chart for measuring the volume of liquid in a soda can. The manufacturing is a high-volume filling station. You are to select four consecutive soda cans every hour and measure the actual filled volume and record the data. Explain your selection rationale.

3. As a Six Sigma Yellow Belt, you have been asked to identify an appropriate type of control chart for a car-painting process. You are to inspect a car every shift and record all the defects found on the painted surface. Explain your selection rationale. (For extra credit, look up in an earlier chapter what type of recording method is ideal for this type of defect capture.)

4. Discuss the key challenges of sustaining process control through control chart monitoring. Brainstorm additional factors that you know from your experience and share with the class. Recommend solutions.

5. Why is documenting and communicating change important to reducing risk to the organization? Discuss with examples.

Part VI
Appendices

Appendix A
ASQ Code of Ethics

FUNDAMENTAL PRINCIPLES

ASQ requires its members and certification holders to conduct themselves ethically by:

1. Being honest and impartial in serving the public, their employers, customers, and clients.

2. Striving to increase the competence and prestige of the quality profession, and

3. Using their knowledge and skill for the enhancement of human welfare.

Members and certification holders are required to observe the tenets set forth below:

RELATIONS WITH THE PUBLIC

Article 1—Hold paramount the safety, health, and welfare of the public in the performance of their professional duties.

RELATIONS WITH EMPLOYERS, CUSTOMERS, AND CLIENTS

Article 2—Perform services only in their areas of competence.

Article 3—Continue their professional development throughout their careers and provide opportunities for the professional and ethical development of others.

Article 4—Act in a professional manner in dealings with ASQ staff and each employer, customer or client.

Article 5—Act as faithful agents or trustees and avoid conflict of interest and the appearance of conflicts of interest.

RELATIONS WITH PEERS

Article 6—Build their professional reputation on the merit of their services and not compete unfairly with others.

Article 7—Assure that credit for the work of others is given to those to whom it is due.

Source: http://asq.org/about-asq/who-we-are/ethics.html

Appendix B
ASQ Certified Six Sigma Yellow Belt (CSSYB) Body of Knowledge (2014)

The topics in this Body of Knowledge include additional detail in the form of sub-text explanations and the cognitive level at which test questions will be written. This information will provide guidance for the candidate preparing to take the exam. The subtext is not intended to limit the subject matter or be all-inclusive of what might be covered in an exam. It is meant to clarify the type of content to be included in the exam. The descriptor in parentheses at the end of each entry refers to the maximum cognitive level at which the topic will be tested. A complete description of cognitive levels is provided at the end of this document.

I. *Six Sigma Fundamentals* (21 Questions)

    A. *Six sigma foundations and principles.* Describe the purpose of six sigma (reducing variation), its methodology (DMAIC) and its evolution from quality. Describe the value of six sigma to the organization as a whole. (Understand)

    B. *Lean foundations and principles.* Describe the purpose of lean (waste elimination) and its methodologies (just-in-time, poka-yoke, kanban, value-stream mapping). Describe the value of lean to the organization as a whole. (Understand)

    C. *Six sigma roles and responsibilities.* Define and describe the roles and responsibilities of six sigma team members (i.e., individual team members, yellow belt, green belt, black belt, master black belt, process owner, champion, sponsor). (Understand)

    D. *Team basics*

        1. *Types of teams.* Identify the various types of teams that operate within an organization (i.e., continuous improvement, self-managed and cross-functional) and their value. (Understand)

        2. *Stages of development.* Describe the various stages of team evolution: forming, storming, norming, performing, and adjourning. (Understand)

        3. *Decision-making tools.* Define brainstorming, multivoting, and nominal group technique (NGT), and describe how these tools are used by teams. (Understand)

4. *Communication methods.* Explain how teams use agendas, meeting minutes, and project status reports, and how they support project success. (Understand)

E. *Quality tools and six sigma metrics*

1. *Quality tools.* Select and use these tools throughout the DMAIC process: Pareto charts, cause and effect diagrams, flowcharts, run charts, check sheets, scatter diagram, and histograms. (Apply)

2. *Six sigma metrics.* Select and use these metrics throughout the DMAIC process: defects per unit (DPU), defects per million opportunities (DPMO), rolled throughput yield (RTY), cycle time, and cost of poor quality (COPQ). (Apply)

II. *Define Phase* (12 Questions)

A. *Project identification*

1. *Voice of the customer.* Define the voice of the customer and describe how customer needs are translated into quantifiable, critical-to-quality (CTQ) characteristics. (Understand)

2. *Project selection.* Describe how projects are identified and selected as suitable for a six sigma project using the DMAIC methodology. (Understand)

3. *Stakeholder analysis.* Identify end users, subject matter experts, process owners and other people or factors that will be affected by a project, and describe how each of them can influence the project. (Understand)

4. *Process inputs and outputs.* Use SIPOC (suppliers, inputs, process, outputs, customers) to identify and define important elements of a process. (Apply)

B. *Project management (PM) basics*

1. *Project charter.* Describe the purpose of a charter and its components: problem statement, project scope, baseline data, and project goal. (Understand)

2. *Communication plan.* Explain the purpose and benefits of a communication plan and how it can impact the success of the project. (Understand)

3. *Project planning.* Define work breakdown structure (WBS) and Gantt charts and describe how they are used to plan and monitor projects. (Understand)

4. *Project management tools.* Select and use various PM tools: activity network diagrams, affinity diagrams, matrix charts, relations charts, and tree diagrams. (Understand)

5. *Phase reviews.* Explain how tollgate or phase reviews are used throughout the DMAIC lifecycle. (Understand)

III. *Measure Phase* (15 Questions)

A. *Basic statistics.* Define, calculate, and interpret measures of central tendency (mean, median, mode) and measures of dispersion (standard deviation, range, variance). (Apply)

B. *Data collection*

1. *Data collection plans.* Describe the critical elements of a data collection plan, including an operational definition, data sources, the method to be used for gathering data, and how frequently it will be gathered. Describe why data collection plans are important. (Understand)

2. *Qualitative and quantitative data.* Define and distinguish between these types of data. (Understand)

3. *Data collection techniques.* Use various data collection techniques, including surveys, interviews, check sheets, and checklists to gather data that contributes to the process being improved. (Apply)

C. *Measurement system analysis (MSA)*

1. *MSA terms.* Define precision, accuracy, bias, linearity, and stability, and describe how these terms are applied in the measurement phase. (Understand)

2. *Gauge repeatability & reproducibility (GR&R).* Describe how and why GR&R is used in the measurement phase. (Understand)

IV. *Analyze Phase* (15 Questions)

A. *Process analysis tools*

1. *Lean tools.* Define how 5S and value analysis can be used to identify and eliminate waste. (Understand)

2. *Failure mode and effect analysis (FMEA).* Define the elements of severity, opportunity, and detection, how they are used to calculate the risk priority number. Describe how FMEA can be used to identify potential failures in a process. (Understand)

B. *Root cause analysis.* Describe how the 5-whys, process mapping, force-field analysis and matrix charts can be used to identify the root causes of a problem. (Understand)

C. *Data analysis*

1. *Basic distribution types.* Define and distinguish between normal and binomial distributions and describe how their shapes (skewed and bimodal) can affect data interpretation. (Understand)

2. *Common and special cause variation.* Describe and distinguish between these types of variation. (Understand)

D. *Correlation and regression*

1. *Correlation.* Describe how correlation is used to identify relationships between variables. (Understand)

2. *Regression.* Describe how regression analysis is used to predict outcomes. (Understand)

E. *Hypothesis testing.* Define and distinguish between hypothesis terms (i.e., null and alternative, type I and type II error, p-value and power). (Understand)

V. *Improve and Control Phases* (12 Questions)

A. *Improvement techniques*

1. *Kaizen and kaizen blitz.* Define and distinguish between these two methods and describe how they can be used to make improvements to any process in an organization. (Understand)

2. *Plan-do-check-act (PDCA) cycle.* Define and distinguish between the steps in this process improvement tool. (Understand)

3. *Cost–benefit analysis.* Explain the importance of this analysis and how it is used in the improve phase. (Understand)

B. *Control tools and documentation*

1. *Control plan.* Describe the importance of a control plan for maintaining improvements. (Understand)

2. *Control charts.* Describe how $\bar{X}$–R charts are used for monitoring and sustaining improved processes. (Understand)

3. *Document control.* Describe the importance of documenting changes to a process and communicating those changes to stakeholders. (Understand)

LEVELS OF COGNITION BASED ON BLOOM'S TAXONOMY (REVISED 2001)

In addition to *content* specifics, the subtext for each topic in this BoK also indicates the intended *complexity level* of the test questions for that topic. These levels are based on "Levels of Cognition" (from Bloom's Taxonomy—Revised, 2001) and are presented below in rank order, from least complex to most complex.

Remember

Recall or recognize terms, definitions, facts, ideas, materials, patterns, sequences, methods, principles, etc.

Understand

Read and understand descriptions, communications, reports, tables, diagrams, directions, regulations, etc.

Apply

Know when and how to use ideas, procedures, methods, formulas, principles, theories, etc.

Analyze

Break down information into its constituent parts and recognize their relationship to one another and how they are organized; identify sublevel factors or salient data from a complex scenario.

Evaluate

Make judgments about the value of proposed ideas, solutions, etc., by comparing the proposal to specific criteria or standards.

Create

Put parts or elements together in such a way as to reveal a pattern or structure not clearly there before; identify which data or information from a complex set is appropriate to examine further or from which supported conclusions can be drawn.

Appendix C
ASQ BoK Comparison

CSSYB BoK reference	CCSYB BoK	CSSGB Bok reference
	I. Six Sigma fundamentals (21 questions)	
	A. Six Sigma foundations and principles	
I.A	Describe the purpose of six sigma (reducing variation), its methodology (DMAIC) and its evolution from quality. Describe the value of six sigma to the organization as a whole. (Understand)	I.A
	B. Lean foundations and principles	
I.B	Describe the purpose of lean (waste elimination) and its methodologies (just-in-time, poka-yoke, kanban, value-stream mapping). Describe the value of lean to the organization as a whole. (Understand)	I.B.1
	C. Six Sigma roles and responsibilities	
I.C	Define and describe the roles and responsibilities of six sigma team members (i.e., individual team members, yellow belt, green belt, black belt, master black belt, process owner, champion, sponsor). (Understand)	II.F.2
	D. Team basics	
I.D.1	1. Types of teams: Identify the various types of teams that operate within an organization (i.e., continuous improvement, self-managed and cross-functional) and their value. (Understand)	II.F.1
I.D.2	2. Stages of development Describe the various stages of team evolution: forming, storming, norming, performing, and adjourning. (Understand)	II.F.1
I.D.3	3. Decision-making tools Define brainstorming, multivoting, and nominal group technique (NGT), and describe how these tools are used by teams. (Understand)	II.F.3
I.D.4	4. Communication methods Explain how teams use agendas, meeting minutes, and project status reports, and how they support project success. (Understand)	II.F.4

CSSYB BoK reference	CCSYB BoK	CSSGB Bok reference
	E. Quality tools and Six Sigma metrics	
I.E.1	1. Quality tools Select and use these tools throughout the DMAIC process: Pareto charts, cause and effect diagrams, flowcharts, run charts, check sheets, scatter diagram, and histograms. (Apply)	III.D.4
I.E.2	2. Six Sigma metrics Select and use these metrics throughout the DMAIC process: defects per unit (DPU), defects per million opportunities (DPMO), rolled throughput yield (RTY), cycle time, and cost of poor quality (COPQ). (Apply)	II.E.1
	II. Define phase (12 questions)	
	A. Project identification	
II.A.1	1. Voice of the customer Define the voice of the customer and describe how customer needs are translated into quantifiable, critical-to-quality (CTQ) characteristics. (Understand)	I.A.2, II.A.1
II.A.2	2. Project selection Describe how projects are identified and selected as suitable for a six sigma project using the DMAIC methodology. (Understand)	I.A.2, II.A.1
II.A.3	3. Stakeholder analysis Identify end users, subject matter experts, process owners and other people or factors that will be affected by a project, and describe how each of them can influence the project. (Understand)	I.A.2, II.A.5
II.A.4	4. Process inputs and outputs Use SIPOC (suppliers, inputs, process, outputs, customers) to identify and define important elements of a process. (Apply)	II.A.4
	B. Project management (PM) basics	
II.B.1	1. Project charter Describe the purpose of a charter and its components: problem statement, project scope, baseline data, and project goal. (Understand)	II.C.1, II.C.2
II.B.2	2. Communication plan Explain the purpose and benefits of a communication plan and how it can impact the success of the project. (Understand)	I.E.2
II.B.3	3. Project planning Define work breakdown structure (WBS) and Gantt charts and describe how they are used to plan and monitor projects. (Understand)	II.C.4
II.B.4	4. Project management tools Select and use various PM tools: activity network diagrams, affinity diagrams, matrix charts, relations charts, and tree diagrams. (Understand)	II.D
II.B.5	5. Phase reviews Explain how tollgate or phase reviews are used throughout the DMAIC lifecycle. (Understand)	II.C.7

CSSYB BoK reference	CCSYB BoK	CSSGB BoK reference
	III. Measure phase (15 questions)	
	A. Basic statistics	
III.A	Define, calculate, and interpret measures of central tendency (mean, median, mode) and measures of dispersion (standard deviation, range, variance). (Apply)	III.B.2, III.D.3
	B. Data collection	
III.B.1	1. Data collection plans Describe the critical elements of a data collection plan, including an operational definition, data sources, the method to be used for gathering data, and how frequently it will be gathered. Describe why data collection plans are important. (Understand)	III.D.2
III.B.2	2. Qualitative and quantitative data Define and distinguish between these types of data. (Understand)	III.D.1
III.B.3	3. Data collection techniques Use various data collection techniques, including surveys, interviews, check sheets, and checklists to gather data that contributes to the process being improved. (Apply)	III.D.2
	C. Measurement system analysis (MSA)	
III.C.1	1. MSA terms Define precision, accuracy, bias, linearity, and stability, and describe how these terms are applied in the measurement phase. (Understand)	III.E
III.C.2	2. Gauge repeatability & reproducibility (GR&R) Describe how and why GR&R is used in the measurement phase. (Understand)	III.E
	IV. Analyze phase (15 questions)	
	A. Process analysis tools	
IV.A.1	1. Lean tools Define how 5S and value analysis can be used to identify and eliminate waste. (Understand)	V.C.1
IV.A.2	2. Failure mode and effect analysis (FMEA) Define the elements of severity, opportunity, and detection, how they are used to calculate the risk priority number. Describe how FMEA can be used to identify potential failures in a process. (Understand)	I.C.2, I.C.3
	B. Root cause analysis	
IV.B	Describe how the 5-whys, process mapping, force-field analysis and matrix charts can be used to identify the root causes of a problem. (Understand)	V.B

CSSYB BoK reference	CCSYB BoK	CSSGB BoK reference
	C. Data analysis	
IV.C.1	1. Basic distribution types Define and distinguish between normal and binomial distributions and describe how their shapes (skewed and bimodal) can affect data interpretation. (Understand)	III.C
IV.C.2	2. Common and special cause variation Describe and distinguish between these types of variation. (Understand)	VI.A.1
	D. Correlation and regression	
IV.D.1	1. Correlation Describe how correlation is used to identify relationships between variables. (Understand)	IV.A.2
IV.D.2	2. Regression Describe how regression analysis is used to predict outcomes. (Understand)	IV.A.2
IV.E	E. Hypothesis testing Define and distinguish between hypothesis terms (i.e., null and alternative, type I and type II error, p-value and power). (Understand)	IV.B.1, IV.B.2
	V. Improve and control phases (12 questions)	
	A. Improvement techniques	
V.A.1	1. Kaizen and kaizen blitz Define and distinguish between these two methods and describe how they can be used to make improvements to any process in an organization (Understand)	V.C.3
V.A.2	2. Plan-do-check-act (PDCA) cycle Define and distinguish between the steps in this process improvement tool. (Understand)	I.A.1
V.A.3	3. Cost-benefit analysis Explain the importance of this analysis and how it is used in the improve phase. (Understand)	II.C.6
	B. Control tools and documentation	
V.B.1	1. Control plan Describe the importance of a control plan for maintaining improvements. (Understand)	VI.B
V.B.2	2. Control charts Describe how $\bar{X}$–R charts are used for monitoring and sustaining improved processes. (Understand)	VI.A.3
V.B.3	3. Document control Describe the importance of documenting changes to a process and communicating those changes to stakeholders. (Understand)	II.C.5, II.E.2

Appendix D
Control Limit Formulas

VARIABLES CHARTS

$\bar{x}$ and R chart:

    Averages chart : $\bar{\bar{x}} \pm A_2 \bar{R}$ *Range chart* : $LCL = D_3 \bar{R}$ $UCL = D_4 \bar{R}$

$\bar{x}$ and s chart:

    Averages chart : $\bar{\bar{x}} \pm A_3 \bar{s}$ *Standard deviation chart* : $LCL = B_3 \bar{s}$ $UCL = B_4 \bar{s}$

Individuals and moving range chart (two-value moving window):

    Individuals chart : $\bar{x} \pm 2.66 \bar{R}$ *Moving range* : $UCL = 3.267 \bar{R}$

Moving average and moving range (two-value moving window):

    Moving average : $\bar{\bar{x}} \pm 1.88 \bar{R}$ *Moving range* : $UCL = 3.267 \bar{R}$

Median chart:

    Median chart : $\bar{x}' \pm A_2' \bar{R}$ *Range chart* : $LCL = D_3 \bar{R}$ $UCL = D_4 \bar{R}$

ATTRIBUTES CHARTS

    Variable sample size: Constant sample size:

p chart: $\bar{p} \pm 3 \sqrt{\dfrac{\bar{p}(1-\bar{p})}{\bar{n}}}$ np chart: $n\bar{p} \pm 3 \sqrt{n\bar{p}(1-\bar{p})}$

u chart: $\bar{u} \pm 3 \sqrt{\dfrac{\bar{u}}{\bar{n}}}$ c chart: $\bar{c} \pm 3 \sqrt{\bar{c}}$

D chart: $\bar{D} \pm 3 \sigma_D$ U chart: $\bar{U} \pm 3 \sigma_U$

Appendix E
Constants for Control Charts

Subgroup size										A_2 for median charts	
N	A_2	d_2	D_3	D_4	A_3	c_4	B_3	B_4	E_2		A_4
2	1.880	1.128	–	3.267	2.659	0.798	–	3.267	2.660	1.880	2.224
3	1.023	1.693	–	2.574	1.954	0.886	–	2.568	1.772	1.187	1.091
4	0.729	2.059	–	2.282	1.628	0.921	–	2.266	1.457	0.796	0.758
5	0.577	2.326	–	2.114	1.427	0.940	–	2.089	1.290	0.691	0.594
6	0.483	2.534	–	2.004	1.287	0.952	0.030	1.970	1.184	0.548	0.495
7	0.419	2.704	0.076	1.924	1.182	0.959	0.118	1.882	1.109	0.508	0.429
8	0.373	2.847	0.136	1.864	1.099	0.965	0.185	1.815	1.054	0.433	0.380
9	0.337	2.970	0.184	1.816	1.032	0.969	0.239	1.761	1.010	0.412	0.343
10	0.308	3.078	0.223	1.777	0.975	0.973	0.284	1.716	0.975	0.362	0.314

Appendix F
Areas under Standard Normal Curve

z	0.00	0.01	0.02	0.03	0.04
0.0	0.50000000000	0.49601064369	0.49202168628	0.48803352659	0.48404656315
0.1	0.46017216272	0.45620468746	0.45224157398	0.44828321335	0.44432999519
0.2	0.42074029056	0.41683383652	0.41293557735	0.40904588486	0.40516512830
0.3	0.38208857781	0.37828047818	0.37448416528	0.37069998106	0.36692826396
0.4	0.34457825839	0.34090297377	0.33724272685	0.33359782060	0.32996855366
0.5	0.30853753873	0.30502573090	0.30153178755	0.29805596539	0.29459851622
0.6	0.27425311775	0.27093090378	0.26762889347	0.26434729212	0.26108629969
0.7	0.24196365222	0.23885206809	0.23576249778	0.23269509230	0.22964999716
0.8	0.21185539858	0.20897008787	0.20610805359	0.20326939183	0.20045419326
0.9	0.18406012535	0.18141125489	0.17878637961	0.17618554225	0.17360878034
1.0	0.15865525393	0.15624764502	0.15386423037	0.15150500279	0.14916995033
1.1	0.13566606095	0.13349951324	0.13135688104	0.12923811224	0.12714315056
1.2	0.11506967022	0.11313944644	0.11123243745	0.10934855243	0.10748769707
1.3	0.09680048459	0.09509791780	0.09341750899	0.09175913565	0.09012267246
1.4	0.08075665923	0.07926984145	0.07780384053	0.07635850954	0.07493369953
1.5	0.06680720127	0.06552171209	0.06425548782	0.06300836446	0.06178017671
1.6	0.05479929170	0.05369892815	0.05261613845	0.05155074849	0.05050258347
1.7	0.04456546276	0.04363293652	0.04271622079	0.04181513761	0.04092950898
1.8	0.03593031911	0.03514789358	0.03437950245	0.03362496942	0.03288411866
1.9	0.02871655982	0.02806660666	0.02742894970	0.02680341888	0.02618984494
2.0	0.02275013195	0.02221559443	0.02169169377	0.02117826964	0.02067516287
2.1	0.01786442056	0.01742917794	0.01700302265	0.01658580668	0.01617738337
2.2	0.01390344751	0.01355258115	0.01320938381	0.01287372144	0.01254546144
2.3	0.01072411002	0.01044407706	0.01017043867	0.00990307556	0.00964186995
2.4	0.00819753592	0.00797626026	0.00776025355	0.00754941142	0.00734363096
2.5	0.00620966533	0.00603655808	0.00586774172	0.00570312633	0.00554262344
2.6	0.00466118802	0.00452711113	0.00439648835	0.00426924341	0.00414530136
2.7	0.00346697380	0.00336416041	0.00326409582	0.00316671628	0.00307195922
2.8	0.00255513033	0.00247707500	0.00240118247	0.00232740021	0.00225567669
2.9	0.00186581330	0.00180714378	0.00175015693	0.00169481002	0.00164106123

(continued)

z	0.00	0.01	0.02	0.03	0.04
3.0	0.00134989803	0.00130623845	0.00126387343	0.00122276869	0.00118289074
3.1	0.00096760321	0.00093543672	0.00090425520	0.00087403152	0.00084473917
3.2	0.00068713794	0.00066367486	0.00064095298	0.00061895109	0.00059764850
3.3	0.00048342414	0.00046647986	0.00045008724	0.00043422992	0.00041889195
3.4	0.00033692927	0.00032481440	0.00031310568	0.00030179062	0.00029085709
3.5	0.00023262908	0.00022405335	0.00021577340	0.00020777983	0.00020006352
3.6	0.00015910859	0.00015309850	0.00014730151	0.00014171061	0.00013631902
3.7	0.00010779973	0.00010362962	0.00009961139	0.00009573989	0.00009201013
3.8	0.00007234804	0.00006948340	0.00006672584	0.00006407163	0.00006151716
3.9	0.00004809634	0.00004614806	0.00004427448	0.00004247293	0.00004074080
4.0	0.00003167124	0.00003035937	0.00002909907	0.00002788843	0.00002672560
4.1	0.00002065751	0.00001978296	0.00001894362	0.00001813816	0.00001736529
4.2	0.00001334575	0.00001276853	0.00001221512	0.00001168457	0.00001117599
4.3	0.00000853991	0.00000816273	0.00000780146	0.00000745547	0.00000712414
4.4	0.00000541254	0.00000516853	0.00000493505	0.00000471165	0.00000449794
4.5	0.00000339767	0.00000324138	0.00000309198	0.00000294918	0.00000281271
4.6	0.00000211245	0.00000201334	0.00000191870	0.00000182833	0.00000174205
4.7	0.00000130081	0.00000123858	0.00000117922	0.00000112260	0.00000106859
4.8	0.00000079333	0.00000075465	0.00000071779	0.00000068267	0.00000064920
4.9	0.00000047918	0.00000045538	0.00000043272	0.00000041115	0.00000039061
5.0	0.00000028665	0.00000027215	0.00000025836	0.00000024524	0.00000023277
5.1	0.00000016983	0.00000016108	0.00000015277	0.00000014487	0.00000013737
5.2	0.00000009964	0.00000009442	0.00000008946	0.00000008476	0.00000008029
5.3	0.00000005790	0.00000005481	0.00000005188	0.00000004911	0.00000004647
5.4	0.00000003332	0.00000003151	0.00000002980	0.00000002818	0.00000002664
5.5	0.00000001899	0.00000001794	0.00000001695	0.00000001601	0.00000001512
5.6	0.00000001072	0.00000001012	0.00000000955	0.00000000901	0.00000000850
5.7	0.00000000599	0.00000000565	0.00000000533	0.00000000502	0.00000000473
5.8	0.00000000332	0.00000000312	0.00000000294	0.00000000277	0.00000000261
5.9	0.00000000182	0.00000000171	0.00000000161	0.00000000151	0.00000000143
6.0	0.00000000099	0.00000000093	0.00000000087	0.00000000082	0.00000000077

(continued)

z	0.05	0.06	0.07	0.08	0.09
0.0	0.48006119416	0.47607781735	0.47209682982	0.46811862799	0.46414360741
0.1	0.44038230763	0.43644053711	0.43250506832	0.42857628410	0.42465456527
0.2	0.40129367432	0.39743188680	0.39358012680	0.38973875244	0.38590811880
0.3	0.36316934882	0.35942356678	0.35569124520	0.35197270758	0.34826827346
0.4	0.32635522029	0.32275811025	0.31917750878	0.31561369652	0.31206694942
0.5	0.29115968679	0.28773971885	0.28433884905	0.28095730890	0.27759532475
0.6	0.25784611081	0.25462691467	0.25142889510	0.24825223045	0.24509709367
0.7	0.22662735238	0.22362729244	0.22064994634	0.21769543759	0.21476388416
0.8	0.19766254312	0.19489452125	0.19215020210	0.18942965478	0.18673294304
0.9	0.17105612631	0.16852760747	0.16602324606	0.16354305933	0.16108705951
1.0	0.14685905638	0.14457229966	0.14230965436	0.14007109009	0.13785657203
1.1	0.12507193564	0.12302440305	0.12100048442	0.11900010746	0.11702319602
1.2	0.10564977367	0.10383468112	0.10204231507	0.10027256795	0.09852532905
1.3	0.08850799144	0.08691496195	0.08534345082	0.08379332242	0.08226443868
1.4	0.07352925961	0.07214503697	0.07078087699	0.06943662333	0.06811211797
1.5	0.06057075800	0.05937994059	0.05820755564	0.05705343324	0.05591740252
1.6	0.04947146803	0.04845722627	0.04745968180	0.04647865786	0.04551397732
1.7	0.04005915686	0.03920390329	0.03836357036	0.03753798035	0.03672695570
1.8	0.03215677480	0.03144276298	0.03074190893	0.03005403896	0.02937898004
1.9	0.02558805952	0.02499789515	0.02441918528	0.02385176434	0.02329546775
2.0	0.02018221541	0.01969927041	0.01922617223	0.01876276643	0.01830889985
2.1	0.01577760739	0.01538633478	0.01500342297	0.01462873078	0.01426211841
2.2	0.01222447266	0.01191062542	0.01160379152	0.01130384424	0.01101065832
2.3	0.00938670553	0.00913746753	0.00889404263	0.00865631903	0.00842418640
2.4	0.00714281074	0.00694685079	0.00675565261	0.00656911914	0.00638715476
2.5	0.00538614595	0.00523360816	0.00508492575	0.00494001576	0.00479879660
2.6	0.00402458854	0.00390703257	0.00379256235	0.00368110801	0.00357260095
2.7	0.00297976324	0.00289006808	0.00280281463	0.00271794492	0.00263540208
2.8	0.00218596145	0.00211820504	0.00205235899	0.00198837585	0.00192620913
2.9	0.00158886965	0.00153819521	0.00148899875	0.00144124192	0.00139488724

(continued)

z	0.05	0.06	0.07	0.08	0.09
3.0	0.00114420683	0.00110668496	0.00107029385	0.00103500297	0.00100078248
3.1	0.00081635231	0.00078884569	0.00076219469	0.00073637526	0.00071136397
3.2	0.00057702504	0.00055706107	0.00053773742	0.00051903543	0.00050093691
3.3	0.00040405780	0.00038971236	0.00037584092	0.00036242915	0.00034946312
3.4	0.00028029328	0.00027008769	0.00026022918	0.00025070689	0.00024151027
3.5	0.00019261558	0.00018542740	0.00017849061	0.00017179710	0.00016533898
3.6	0.00013112015	0.00012610762	0.00012127523	0.00011661698	0.00011212703
3.7	0.00008841729	0.00008495668	0.00008162377	0.00007841418	0.00007532364
3.8	0.00005905891	0.00005669351	0.00005441768	0.00005222823	0.00005012211
3.9	0.00003907560	0.00003747488	0.00003593632	0.00003445763	0.00003303665
4.0	0.00002560882	0.00002453636	0.00002350657	0.00002251785	0.00002156866
4.1	0.00001662376	0.00001591238	0.00001522998	0.00001457545	0.00001394772
4.2	0.00001068853	0.00001022135	0.00000977365	0.00000934467	0.00000893366
4.3	0.00000680688	0.00000650312	0.00000621233	0.00000593397	0.00000566753
4.4	0.00000429351	0.00000409798	0.00000391098	0.00000373215	0.00000356116
4.5	0.00000268230	0.00000255768	0.00000243862	0.00000232488	0.00000221623
4.6	0.00000165968	0.00000158105	0.00000150600	0.00000143437	0.00000136603
4.7	0.00000101708	0.00000096796	0.00000092113	0.00000087648	0.00000083391
4.8	0.00000061731	0.00000058693	0.00000055799	0.00000053043	0.00000050418
4.9	0.00000037107	0.00000035247	0.00000033476	0.00000031792	0.00000030190
5.0	0.00000022091	0.00000020963	0.00000019891	0.00000018872	0.00000017903
5.1	0.00000013024	0.00000012347	0.00000011705	0.00000011094	0.00000010515
5.2	0.00000007605	0.00000007203	0.00000006821	0.00000006459	0.00000006116
5.3	0.00000004398	0.00000004161	0.00000003937	0.00000003724	0.00000003523
5.4	0.00000002518	0.00000002381	0.00000002250	0.00000002127	0.00000002010
5.5	0.00000001428	0.00000001349	0.00000001274	0.00000001203	0.00000001135
5.6	0.00000000802	0.00000000757	0.00000000714	0.00000000673	0.00000000635
5.7	0.00000000446	0.00000000421	0.00000000396	0.00000000374	0.00000000352
5.8	0.00000000246	0.00000000231	0.00000000218	0.00000000205	0.00000000193
5.9	0.00000000134	0.00000000126	0.00000000119	0.00000000112	0.00000000105
6.0	0.00000000072	0.00000000068	0.00000000064	0.00000000060	0.00000000056

Appendix G
Binomial Distribution

Probability of x or fewer occurrences in a sample of size n

Binomial distribution

n	x	0.01	0.02	0.03	0.04	0.05	0.06	0.07	0.08	0.09	0.10	0.15	0.20	0.25	0.30	0.35	0.40	0.45	0.50
2	0	0.980	0.960	0.941	0.922	0.903	0.884	0.865	0.846	0.828	0.810	0.723	0.640	0.563	0.490	0.423	0.360	0.303	0.250
2	1	1.000	1.000	0.999	0.998	0.998	0.996	0.995	0.994	0.992	0.990	0.978	0.960	0.938	0.910	0.878	0.840	0.798	0.750
3	0	0.970	0.941	0.913	0.885	0.857	0.831	0.804	0.779	0.754	0.729	0.614	0.512	0.422	0.343	0.275	0.216	0.166	0.125
3	1	1.000	0.999	0.997	0.995	0.993	0.990	0.986	0.982	0.977	0.972	0.939	0.896	0.844	0.784	0.718	0.648	0.575	0.500
3	2	1.000	1.000	1.000	1.000	1.000	1.000	1.000	0.999	0.999	0.999	0.997	0.992	0.984	0.973	0.957	0.936	0.909	0.875
4	0	0.961	0.922	0.885	0.849	0.815	0.781	0.748	0.716	0.686	0.656	0.522	0.410	0.316	0.240	0.179	0.130	0.092	0.063
4	1	0.999	0.998	0.995	0.991	0.986	0.980	0.973	0.966	0.957	0.948	0.890	0.819	0.738	0.652	0.563	0.475	0.391	0.313
4	2	1.000	1.000	1.000	1.000	1.000	0.999	0.999	0.998	0.997	0.996	0.988	0.973	0.949	0.916	0.874	0.821	0.759	0.688
4	3	1.000	1.000	1.000	1.000	1.000	1.000	1.000	1.000	1.000	1.000	0.999	0.998	0.996	0.992	0.985	0.974	0.959	0.938
5	0	0.951	0.904	0.859	0.815	0.774	0.734	0.696	0.659	0.624	0.590	0.444	0.328	0.237	0.168	0.116	0.078	0.050	0.031
5	1	0.999	0.996	0.992	0.985	0.977	0.968	0.958	0.946	0.933	0.919	0.835	0.737	0.633	0.528	0.428	0.337	0.256	0.188
5	2	1.000	1.000	1.000	0.999	0.999	0.998	0.997	0.995	0.994	0.991	0.973	0.942	0.896	0.837	0.765	0.683	0.593	0.500
5	3	1.000	1.000	1.000	1.000	1.000	1.000	1.000	1.000	1.000	1.000	0.998	0.993	0.984	0.969	0.946	0.913	0.869	0.813
5	4	1.000	1.000	1.000	1.000	1.000	1.000	1.000	1.000	1.000	1.000	1.000	1.000	0.999	0.998	0.995	0.990	0.982	0.969
6	0	0.941	0.886	0.833	0.783	0.735	0.690	0.647	0.606	0.568	0.531	0.377	0.262	0.178	0.118	0.075	0.047	0.028	0.016
6	1	0.999	0.994	0.988	0.978	0.967	0.954	0.939	0.923	0.905	0.886	0.776	0.655	0.534	0.420	0.319	0.233	0.164	0.109
6	2	1.000	1.000	0.999	0.999	0.998	0.996	0.994	0.991	0.988	0.984	0.953	0.901	0.831	0.744	0.647	0.544	0.442	0.344
6	3	1.000	1.000	1.000	1.000	1.000	1.000	1.000	0.999	0.999	0.999	0.994	0.983	0.962	0.930	0.883	0.821	0.745	0.656
6	4	1.000	1.000	1.000	1.000	1.000	1.000	1.000	1.000	1.000	1.000	1.000	0.998	0.995	0.989	0.978	0.959	0.931	0.891
6	5	1.000	1.000	1.000	1.000	1.000	1.000	1.000	1.000	1.000	1.000	1.000	1.000	1.000	0.999	0.998	0.996	0.992	0.984
7	0	0.932	0.868	0.808	0.751	0.698	0.648	0.602	0.558	0.517	0.478	0.321	0.210	0.133	0.082	0.049	0.028	0.015	0.008
7	1	0.998	0.992	0.983	0.971	0.956	0.938	0.919	0.897	0.875	0.850	0.717	0.577	0.445	0.329	0.234	0.159	0.102	0.063
7	2	1.000	1.000	0.999	0.998	0.996	0.994	0.990	0.986	0.981	0.974	0.926	0.852	0.756	0.647	0.532	0.420	0.316	0.227
7	3	1.000	1.000	1.000	1.000	1.000	1.000	0.999	0.999	0.998	0.997	0.988	0.967	0.929	0.874	0.800	0.710	0.608	0.500
7	4	1.000	1.000	1.000	1.000	1.000	1.000	1.000	1.000	1.000	1.000	0.999	0.995	0.987	0.971	0.944	0.904	0.847	0.773
7	5	1.000	1.000	1.000	1.000	1.000	1.000	1.000	1.000	1.000	1.000	1.000	1.000	0.999	0.996	0.991	0.981	0.964	0.938
7	6	1.000	1.000	1.000	1.000	1.000	1.000	1.000	1.000	1.000	1.000	1.000	1.000	1.000	0.999	0.998	0.996	0.992	0.992

(continued)

Binomial distribution *(Continued)*

n	x	0.01	0.02	0.03	0.04	0.05	0.06	0.07	0.08	0.09	0.10	0.15	0.20	0.25	0.30	0.35	0.40	0.45	0.50
8	0	0.923	0.851	0.784	0.721	0.663	0.610	0.560	0.513	0.470	0.430	0.272	0.168	0.100	0.058	0.032	0.017	0.008	0.004
8	1	0.997	0.990	0.978	0.962	0.943	0.921	0.897	0.870	0.842	0.813	0.657	0.503	0.367	0.255	0.169	0.106	0.063	0.035
8	2	1.000	1.000	0.999	0.997	0.994	0.990	0.985	0.979	0.971	0.962	0.895	0.797	0.679	0.552	0.428	0.315	0.220	0.145
8	3	1.000	1.000	1.000	1.000	1.000	0.999	0.999	0.998	0.997	0.995	0.979	0.944	0.886	0.806	0.706	0.594	0.477	0.363
8	4	1.000	1.000	1.000	1.000	1.000	1.000	1.000	1.000	1.000	1.000	0.997	0.990	0.973	0.942	0.894	0.826	0.740	0.637
8	5	1.000	1.000	1.000	1.000	1.000	1.000	1.000	1.000	1.000	1.000	1.000	0.999	0.996	0.989	0.975	0.950	0.912	0.855
8	6	1.000	1.000	1.000	1.000	1.000	1.000	1.000	1.000	1.000	1.000	1.000	1.000	1.000	0.999	0.996	0.991	0.982	0.965
8	7	1.000	1.000	1.000	1.000	1.000	1.000	1.000	1.000	1.000	1.000	1.000	1.000	1.000	1.000	0.999	0.998	0.996
9	0	0.914	0.834	0.760	0.693	0.630	0.573	0.520	0.472	0.428	0.387	0.232	0.134	0.075	0.040	0.021	0.010	0.005	0.002
9	1	0.997	0.987	0.972	0.952	0.929	0.902	0.873	0.842	0.809	0.775	0.599	0.436	0.300	0.196	0.121	0.071	0.039	0.020
9	2	1.000	0.999	0.998	0.996	0.992	0.986	0.979	0.970	0.960	0.947	0.859	0.738	0.601	0.463	0.337	0.232	0.150	0.090
9	3	1.000	1.000	1.000	1.000	0.999	0.999	0.998	0.996	0.994	0.992	0.966	0.914	0.834	0.730	0.609	0.483	0.361	0.254
9	4	1.000	1.000	1.000	1.000	1.000	1.000	1.000	1.000	0.999	0.999	0.994	0.980	0.951	0.901	0.828	0.733	0.621	0.500
9	5	1.000	1.000	1.000	1.000	1.000	1.000	1.000	1.000	1.000	1.000	0.999	0.997	0.990	0.975	0.946	0.901	0.834	0.746
9	6	1.000	1.000	1.000	1.000	1.000	1.000	1.000	1.000	1.000	1.000	1.000	1.000	0.999	0.996	0.989	0.975	0.950	0.910
9	7	1.000	1.000	1.000	1.000	1.000	1.000	1.000	1.000	1.000	1.000	1.000	1.000	1.000	1.000	0.999	0.996	0.991	0.980
9	8	1.000	1.000	1.000	1.000	1.000	1.000	1.000	1.000	1.000	1.000	1.000	1.000	1.000	1.000	1.000	1.000	0.999	0.998
10	0	0.904	0.817	0.737	0.665	0.599	0.539	0.484	0.434	0.389	0.349	0.197	0.107	0.056	0.028	0.013	0.006	0.003	0.001
10	1	0.996	0.984	0.965	0.942	0.914	0.882	0.848	0.812	0.775	0.736	0.544	0.376	0.244	0.149	0.086	0.046	0.023	0.011
10	2	1.000	0.999	0.997	0.994	0.988	0.981	0.972	0.960	0.946	0.930	0.820	0.678	0.526	0.383	0.262	0.167	0.100	0.055
10	3	1.000	1.000	1.000	1.000	0.999	0.998	0.996	0.994	0.991	0.987	0.950	0.879	0.776	0.650	0.514	0.382	0.266	0.172
10	4	1.000	1.000	1.000	1.000	1.000	1.000	1.000	0.999	0.999	0.998	0.990	0.967	0.922	0.850	0.751	0.633	0.504	0.377
10	5	1.000	1.000	1.000	1.000	1.000	1.000	1.000	1.000	1.000	1.000	0.999	0.994	0.980	0.953	0.905	0.834	0.738	0.623

Appendix H
Values of the *t*-Distribution

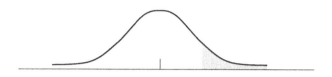

Values of *t* distribution

ν	$t_{0.100}$	$t_{0.050}$	$t_{0.025}$	$t_{0.010}$	$t_{0.005}$	ν
1	3.078	6.314	12.706	31.821	63.656	1
2	1.886	2.920	4.303	6.965	9.925	2
3	1.638	2.353	3.182	4.541	5.841	3
4	1.533	2.132	2.776	3.747	4.604	4
5	1.476	2.015	2.571	3.365	4.032	5
6	1.440	1.943	2.447	3.143	3.707	6
7	1.415	1.895	2.365	2.998	3.499	7
8	1.397	1.860	2.306	2.896	3.355	8
9	1.383	1.833	2.262	2.821	3.250	9
10	1.372	1.812	2.228	2.764	3.169	10
11	1.363	1.796	2.201	2.718	3.106	11
12	1.356	1.782	2.179	2.681	3.055	12
13	1.350	1.771	2.160	2.650	3.012	13
14	1.345	1.761	2.145	2.624	2.977	14
15	1.341	1.753	2.131	2.602	2.947	15
16	1.337	1.746	2.120	2.583	2.921	16
17	1.333	1.740	2.110	2.567	2.898	17
18	1.330	1.734	2.101	2.552	2.878	18
19	1.328	1.729	2.093	2.539	2.861	19
20	1.325	1.725	2.086	2.528	2.845	20
21	1.323	1.721	2.080	2.518	2.831	21
22	1.321	1.717	2.074	2.508	2.819	22
23	1.319	1.714	2.069	2.500	2.807	23
24	1.318	1.711	2.064	2.492	2.797	24
25	1.316	1.708	2.060	2.485	2.787	25
26	1.315	1.706	2.056	2.479	2.779	26
27	1.314	1.703	2.052	2.473	2.771	27
28	1.313	1.701	2.048	2.467	2.763	28

(continued)

Values of *t* distribution *(Continued)*

v	$t_{0.10}$	$t_{0.05}$	$t_{0.025}$	$t_{0.01}$	$t_{0.005}$	v
29	1.311	1.699	2.045	2.462	2.756	29
30	1.310	1.697	2.042	2.457	2.750	30
31	1.309	1.696	2.040	2.453	2.744	31
32	1.309	1.694	2.037	2.449	2.738	32
33	1.308	1.692	2.035	2.445	2.733	33
34	1.307	1.691	2.032	2.441	2.728	34
35	1.306	1.690	2.030	2.438	2.724	35
40	1.303	1.684	2.021	2.423	2.704	40
45	1.301	1.679	2.014	2.412	2.690	45
50	1.299	1.676	2.009	2.403	2.678	50
55	1.297	1.673	2.004	2.396	2.668	55
60	1.296	1.671	2.000	2.390	2.660	60
70	1.294	1.667	1.994	2.381	2.648	70
80	1.292	1.664	1.990	2.374	2.639	80
90	1.291	1.662	1.987	2.368	2.632	90
100	1.290	1.660	1.984	2.364	2.626	100
200	1.286	1.653	1.972	2.345	2.601	200
400	1.284	1.649	1.966	2.336	2.588	400
600	1.283	1.647	1.964	2.333	2.584	600
800	1.283	1.647	1.963	2.331	2.582	800
999	1.282	1.646	1.962	2.330	2.581	999

Appendix I
Acronym List

14 Points—Doctor Deming's 14 management practices

3C—cognition, comprehension, commitment

3D—dirty, dangerous, difficult

3P—people, planet, profit

3P—people, product, process

3P—production preparation process

5M&P—materials, methods, machines, measurement, Mother Nature, and people

5P—Honda problem solving approach

5S—sort (seiri), straighten (seiton), shine (seiso), standardize (seiketsu), sustain (shitsuke)

5W1H—what, where, when, why, who, and how

6S—**5S** with *safety* added

7P—proper prior planning prevents piss poor performance

7S—**6S** with *oversight* added

8D—eight disciplines of problem solving

8M—man (people), machine (equipment), methods (operating procedures), materials, measurement, Mother Nature (environment), management, and money

A2LA—American Association for Laboratory Accreditation

A3—executive report on one page

ABET—ABET, Inc. (formerly the Accreditation Board of Education and Training)

AD—Anderson-Darling test

AHP—analytic hierarchy process

AHT—average handling time

AIAG—Automotive Industry Action Group

AMA—American Management Association

ANAB—American National Accreditation Board

AND—activity network diagram

ANOM—analysis of means

ANOVA—analysis of variance

ANSI—American National Standards Institute

AOQ—average outgoing quality

AOQL—average outgoing quality limit

APQP—advanced product quality planning

AQL—acceptable quality level

AQP—advanced quality planning

AQP—Association for Quality and Participation

AQS—advanced quality system

AQT—acceptable quality test

ARL—average run length

AS—aerospace standards

ASA—American Statistical Association

ASCII—American standard code for information interchange

ASEE—American Society for Engineering Education

ASI—American Supplier Institute

ASME—American Society of Mechanical Engineers

ASN—average sample number

ASNT—American Society for Nondestructive Testing

ASQ—American Society for Quality

ASQC—American Society for Quality Control (ASQ name before 1997)

ASSE—American Society for Safety Engineers

ASTD—American Society for Training and Development

ASTM—ASTM International—formerly American Society for Testing and Materials

AV—appraiser varation

B2C—business to customer

BB—Black Belt

BBS—behavior based safety

BIA—business impact analysis

BIB—balanced incomplete block design

BIC—best in class

BIC—business improvement coach

BIT—built-in test

BITE—built-in test equipment

BOB—best of the best

BoK—body of knowledge

BOM—bill of materials

BOS—business operating system

BPR—business process reengineering

BSI—British Standards Institute

BTW—by the way

C&E—cause and effect

C/N—change notice

C/O—changeover time

C/T—cycle time

CAD—computer-aided design

CADQAD—computer-aided development of quality assurance data

CAE—computer-aided engineering

CAFÉ—corporate average fuel economy

CAM—computer-aided manufacturing

CANDO—clean up, arranging, neatness, discipline, ongoing improvement

CAP—change acceleration process

CAP—corrective action plan

CAPA—corrective and preventive action

CAQ—computer-aided quality assurance

CAR—corrective action recommendation

CAR—corrective action report

CASE—computer-aided software engineering

CASE—coordinated aerospace supplier evaluation

CBA—ASQ Certified Biomedical Auditor

CBP—customer benefits package

CBT—computer-based training

CC—critical characteristic

CCR—capacity constraint resource

CCR—critical customer requirement

CCT—ASQ Certified Calibration Technician

CE—cause and effect (for example, CE matrix)

CE—concurrent engineering

CEDAC—cause-and-effect diagram with additional cards

CEO—chief executive officer

CEPT—Centre (for) Environmental Planning (and) Technology [India]

CFO—chief financial officer

CFR—USA Code of Federal Regulations

CGMP—current good manufacturing practice

CHA—ASQ Certified HACCP Auditor

CI—continual improvement

CIM—change-in-mean-effect

CIO—chief information officer

CIT—critical items list

CLCA—closed-loop corrective action

Cm—capability machine

CM—condition monitoring

CMI—ASQ Certified Mechanical Inspector

Cmk—machine capability index

CMM—capability maturity model for software (also known as SW-CMM)

CMM—coordinate measuring machine

CMQ/OE—ASQ Certified Manager of Quality and Operational Excellence

CMQOE—ASQ Certified Manager of Quality Organizational Excellence

CNC—computer numerical control

COA—certificate of analysis

COB—chairman of board

COB—close of business

COC—certificate of conformance

COC—cost of conformance

COCQ—cost of current quality

CONC—cost of nonconformance

COO—chief operating officer

COP—code of practice

COP—customer oriented process

COPIS—customer, output, process, input, supplier

COPQ—cost of poor quality—measure of waste in operation

COQ—cost of quality (*see* COPQ)

COQC—certificate of quality compliance

CP—control plan

CPR—corrective preventive report

C_p—Process capability measurement—compares engineering specification divided by process six standard deviations

C_{pk}—Process capability measurement—compares engineering specification to process mean divided by three standard deviations

CPM—critical path method

CPN—critical path network

CPU—cost per unit

CQA—ASQ Certified Quality Auditor

CQA—contract quality assurance

CQE—ASQ Certified Quality Engineer

CQIA—ASQ Certified Quality Improvement Associate

CQM—Center for Quality of Management

CQMP—clinical quality management program

CQP—corporate quality policies

CQPA—ASQ Certified Quality Process Analyst

CQR—contract quality requirement

CQT—ASQ Certified Quality Technician

CR—conditionally required

Cr—ratio of process variation

CR/CR—concern report/change request

CRE—ASQ Certified Reliability Engineer

CRM—certified reference material

CRM—corporate records management

CRM—customer relationship management

CS—customer satisfaction

CSA—compliance safety accountability

CSF—critical success factors

CSM—customer–supplier model

CSP—continuous sampling plan

CSQE—ASQ Certified Software Quality Engineer

CSSBB—ASQ Certified Six Sigma Black Belt

CSSGB—ASQ Certified Six Sigma Green Belt

CSSMBB—ASQ Certified Six Sigma Master Black Belt

CSSYB—ASQ Certified Six Sigma Yellow Belt

CTC—critical to customer

CTQ—critical to quality

CTS—critical to satisfaction

CUSUM—cumulative sum control chart

CVEP—continuous value enhancement process

CWAP—Clean Water Action Plan

CWQC—company-wide quality control

D—detection

DAX—desire, attitude, execution

DBR—discounted cash flow

DCCDI—define–customer–concept–design–implement

DCF—discounted cash flow

DCOV—define–characterize–optimize–verify

DCP—dynamic control plan

DDW—drill deep and wide

DE—directed evolution

DER—designated engineering representative

df—degrees of freedom

DFA—design for assembly

DFD—design for disassembly

DFE—design for ergonomics

DFM—design for manufacturing

DFMA—design for manufacturing and assembly

DFMEA—design failure mode and effects analysis

DFSS—design for Six Sigma

DFX—design for X

DMADOV—define–measure–analyze–design–optimize–verify

DMADV—define–measure–analyze–design–verify

DMAIC—define, measure, analyze, improve, and control

DMEDI—define–measure–explore–develop–implement

DOE—design of experiment(s)

DOT—United States Department of Transportation

DPM—deficiencies (defects) per million units

DPMO—deficiencies (defects) per million opportunities

DPO—deficiencies (defects) per opportunity

DPPM—defective parts per million

DPU—deficien

DPU—deficiencies (defects) per unit

DQC—data quality control

DRBFM—design review based on failure mode (Toyota version of FMEA)

DSL—digital subscriber line

DSU—digital service unit

DTD—dock to delivery

DV&PR—design verification and product reliability

DVP—design verification plan

DVP&PV—design verification, production and process validation

DVR—design verification report

DVT—design verification test

EARA—Environmental Auditors Registration Association

EC—European Community

ECC—estimated cost to complete

ECDF—empirical cumulative distribution function

ECN—engineering change notice

ECO—engineer change order

ECR—engineering change request

EDA—exploratory data analysis

EDI—electronic data interchange

EI—employee involvement

EIO—engineering or installation caused outage

ELT—extract load transfer

EMI—electromagnetic interference

EMS—environmental management system

EOQ—economic order quantity

EPSS—electronic performance support system

ER—engineering requirements

ERI—early return indicator

ERP—enterprise resource planning

ES—engineering specification

ESC—extreme service conditions

ESER—engineering sample evaluation report

ET—educational technology

ETA—event tree analysis

EU—European Union

EV—equipment variation

EVOP—evolutionary operation

EWMA—exponentially weighted moving average

FAHQMT—fully automatic high-quality machine translation

FAI—first article inspection

FAIR—first article inspection report

FAR—Federal Acquisition Regulation

FAST—function analysis system technique

FCE—frequently committed errors

FEA—finite element analysis

FEA—front-end analysis

FIFO—first in, first out

FISH—first in still here

FMA—failure mode analysis

FMEA—failure mode and effects analysis

FMECA—failure mode effects and criticality analysis

FMEDA—failure modes, effects, and diagnostic analysis

FMEM—failure mode effects management

FPA—first party audit

FPS—Ford Production System

FQ&P—flight, quality, and performance

FQI—Federal Quality Institute (*see* OPM)

FR—field replaceable unit returns

FRT—fix response time

FSL—flow synchronization leveling

FSS—full service supplier

FTA—fault tree analysis

FTPM—Ford Total Productive Maintenance

FTQ—first time quality

FTT—first time through

G8D—global eight disciplines

GB—Green Belt

GD&T—geometric dimensioning and tolerancing

GE—General Electric Corporation

GLM—general linear model

GLP—good laboratory practice

GM—General Motors Corporation

GMP—good manufacturing practice

GPC—gage performance curve

GR&R—gage repeatability and reproducibility

GROW—goal, reality, options, way forward

GRPI—goals, roles, processes, interpersonal

GRR—gage repeatability and reproducibility

GQTS—global quality tracking system

GSQA—government source quality assurance

GUM—*Guide to the Expression of Uncertainty of Measurement*

Ha—alternative hypothesis

HA—hazard analysis

HACCP—hazard analysis and critical control points

HALT—highly accelerated life test

HARM—high-availability, reliability, and maintainability

HASA—highly accelerated stress audits

HASS—highly accelerated stress screening

HAZOP—hazard and operability study

HOQ—house of quality

HPT—human performance technology

HQS—high-quality screening

HR—human resources

HRM—human resources management

HSEQ—health safety environmental quality

HSPD—handling, storage, packaging, and delivery

HSSE—health safety security environment

HSSEQ—health safety security environment quality

IABLS—Institute of Advanced Business Learning Systems

IAQG—International Aerospace Quality Group

IATF—International Automotive Task Force

ICOV—identify–characterize–optimize–validate

ICT—information communication technology

ID—interrelationship digraph

IDDOV—identify–define–develop–optimize–verify (and validate)

IDEA—identify–design–evaluate–affirm

IDOV—identify–design–optimize–verify (and validate)

IEC—International Electrotechnical Commission

IEEE—Institute of Electrical and Electronics Engineers

IID—independent identically distributed

IIE—Institute of Industrial Engineers

ILT—instructor lead training

IMDS—International Material Data System

IMR—individuals and moving range

INT—interaction

IOBA—International Automotive Oversight Bureau

IPIP—improving performance in practice

IPO—input–process–output

IPS—innovative problem solving

IQA—Institute for Quality Assurance

IQCS—in-service quality control system

IQF—International Quality Federation

IQR—interquartile range

IQUE—in-plant quality evaluation

IRCA—International Register of Certified Auditors

IRR—internal rate of return

ISD—instructional system design

ISIR—Initial Sample Inspection Report

ISO—International Organization for Standardization

ISPI—International Society for Performance Improvement

ISSSP—International Society of Six Sigma Practitioners

IT—industrial technology

IT—information technology (computers)

IT—instructional technology (education)

ITU—International Telecommunication Union

JCAHO—Joint Commission on Accreditation of Healthcare Organizations

JDP—J. D. Power and Associates

JIS—Japan Industrial Standard

JIT—just in time

JUSE—Union of Japanese Scientists and Engineers

KBC—knowledge based community

KBF—key business factors

KBI—key business issue

KBR—key business requirement

KC—key characteristic

KCC—key control characteristic

KISS—keep it simple and specific *or* keep it simple statistician

KLT—key life test

KPC—key product characteristic

KPI—key performance indicator

KPI—key process indicator

KPIV—key process input variable

KPOV—key process output variable

KSN—knowledge sharing network

LACL—lower acceptance control limit

LCI—learner controlled instruction

LCL—lower control limit

LEO—listen (observe and understand), enrich (explore and discover), and optimize (improve and perfect)

LIFO—last in, first out

LLL—lower lot limit

LMS—learning management system

LOTO—lock out tag out

LQ—limiting quality

LQIP—laboratory quality improvement program

LQL—limiting quality level

LRU—line replaceable unit

LSA—logistic support analysis

LSD—least significant difference

LSL—lower specification limit

LSS—Lean Six Sigma

LTI—lost time injury

LTPD—lot tolerance percentage defective

LTR—long-term return rate

m—mean

M&A—manufacturing and assembly

M&TE—measurement and test equipment

MAIC—measure, analyze, improve, and control

MAR—maximum allowable range

MBB—Master Black Belt

MBO—management by objectives

MBNQA—Malcolm Baldrige National Quality Award

MBTI—Myers-Briggs Type Indicator

MBWA—management by walking around

MCF—mean cumulative function

MDR—Medical Device Report

MEDIC—map + measure, explore + evaluate, define + describe, implement + improve, control + conform

MFMEA—machinery failure mode and effects analysis

MIL-STD—United States military standard

MIS—management information systems

MIS—months in service

MMBF—mean miles between failures

MODAPTS—modular arrangement of predetermined time standards

MOS—management operating system

MOT—moment of truth

MPS—master production schedule

MQT—maintainability qualification test

MRA—mutual recognition arrangements

MRB—management review board

MRP—material requirements planning

MS—mean squares

MS (RES)—residual mean square

MSA—measurement systems analysis

MSB—mean square between treatments

MSD—maximum standard deviation

MSDS—Material Data Safety Sheet

MSE—mean squared error

MSI—mean square for interaction

MSW—mean square within treatments

MT&E—measuring tools and equipment

MTBF—mean time between failures

MTC—manage the change

MTTF—mean time to failure

MTTN—mean time to notification

MTTR—mean time to recover

MTTR—mean time to repair

NA—needs assessment

NA *or* **N/A**—not applicable

NACCB—National Accreditation Council for Certification Bodies

NADCAP—National Aerospace and Defense Contractors Accreditation Program

NATO—North Atlantic Treaty Organization

NCT—nonconformance ticket

ndc—number of distinct categories

NDE—nondestructive evaluation

NDT—nondestructive testing

NE *or* **N/E**—not evaluated

NGT—nominal group technique

NIH—not invented here

NIST—United States National Institute of Standards and Technology

NMI—near miss incident

NMQAO—Naval Materiel Quality Assessment Office

NPI—new product introduction

NPR—number of problem reports

NPV—net present value

NQCC—network quality control center

NTF—no trouble found

NTRM—NIST Traceable Reference Material

NVA—non-value-added

NVA-U—non-value-added, but unavoidable

NVH—noise, vibration, and harshness

O—occurrence

OBS—observation

OC—operating characteristic

OCAP—out-of-control action plan

OCC—operating characteristic curve

OCM—operating committee meeting

OCM—organizational change management

OCT—operations cost target

OD—organization development

OE—organizational excellence

OEE—overall equipment effectiveness

OEM—original equipment manufacturer

OFI—opportunity for improvement

OFM—outage frequency measurement

OFR—overdue fix responsiveness

OHS—occupational health and safety

OJT—on-the-job training

OLE—overall labor effectiveness

ORT—ongoing reliability test

OSHA—United States Occupational Safety and Health Administration

OSS—operational support system

OTD—on-time delivery

OTED—one touch exchange of dies

OTI—on-time item delivery

OTIS—on-time installed system delivery

OTS—on-time service delivery

P&L—profit and loss

P&S—products and services

P/T—precision/tolerance

PaR—patients at risk

PAR—preventive action report

PART—program assessment rating tool

PAT—part average testing

PBC—process behavior charts

PBIB—partially balanced incomplete block design

PC—physical contradiction

PCD—process control document

PCR—product change request

PDA—personal data assistant

PDC—product development cycle

PDCA—plan–do–check–act

PDM—precedence diagram method

PDPC—process decision program chart

PDSA—plan–do–study–act

PE—professional engineer

PERT—program evaluation review technique

PFMEA—process failure mode and effects analysis

PFQ—planning for quality

PI—principal inspector

PIPC—percent indices which are process capable

PISMOEA—part, instrument, standard, method, operator, environment, assumptions

PIST—percentage of inspection points satisfying tolerance

PIT—process improvement team

PM—preventive maintenance

PM—program management

PMA—premarket approval

PMA—president's management agenda

PMP—project management professional

PMS—planned maintenance system

PMTS—predetermined motion time system

PO—purchase order

PONC—price of nonconformance

P_p—long-term process capability measurement

PP&B—prototype planning and build

PP&DC—product planning and design committee

PP&TC—product planning and technology committee

PPAP—production part approval process

PPCC—normal probability plot correlation coefficient

PPF—production process and product approval

P_{pk}—long-term process capability measurement

ppm—parts per million

PPPPP—prior planning prevents piss-poor performance

PPPPPP—proper planning prevents particularly poor performance

PPR—patients per run

PPS—production preparation schedule

PQ—process qualification

PQA—President's Quality Award

Pr—capability performance ration

PR—production release

PRAT—production reliability acceptance test

PRR—problem reporting and resolution *or* product problem reporting

PSO—process sign-off

PSP—product support plan

PSW—part submission warrant

PTC—pass through characteristics

PTN—plant test number

PUMA—product usage measurements and applications

PV—part variation

PVP&R—production validation plan and report

PYR—pass yield rate

Q&R—quality and reliability

QA—quality assurance

QA—quick action

QAA—quality assurance analyst

QAA—quality assurance and assistance

QAA—quality assurance assessment

QAA—quality assurance audit

QAC—quality assurance checklist

QAC—quality assurance committee

QAD—quality assurance directorate

QAD—quality audit division

QADR—quality assurance discrepancy report

QAE—quality assurance engineer

QAE—quality assurance evaluation

QAE—quality assurance executive

QAER—quality acceptance equipment release

QAF—quality achievement factor

QAF—quality assurance fixture

QAF—quality assurance form

QAHB—Quality Assurance Program Handbook

QAI—quality assessment index

QAI—Quality Assurance Institute

QAI—quality assurance instruction

QALI—quality assurance letter of instruction

QAM—quality assurance manager

QAM—quality assurance monitoring

QAN—quality action notice

QAPI—quality assurance program index

QAPR—Quality Army Performance Review

QAR—quality acceptance report

QAR—quality assurance and reliability

QAR—quality assurance evaluator

QAR—quality assurance requirements

QAR—quality assurance review

QAR—quantitative analysis report

QAR—quarterly acceptance review

QARC—Quality Assurance Review Center

QAS—quality assurance, auditing, and security

QAS—quality assurance schedule

QAS—quality assurance screening program

QAS—quality assurance standard(s)

QAS—quality assurance study

QAS—quality assurance surveillance

QAS—quality assurance test system

QASP—quality assurance support plan

QATAP—quality assurance through attributes program

QATDP—quality assurance technical development program

QBP—quality and business planning

QC—quality center

QC—quality control

QCAI—quality control/assurance and inspection

QCCMM—quality control certified master model

QCE—quality control engineering

QCEM—quality control enforcement mechanism

QCI—Quality Circle Institute

QCI—quality control information

QCI—quality cost improve(ment)

QCI—Quality Council of India

QCI—Quality Council of Indiana

QCM—quality call monitoring

QCM—quality care monitoring

QCM—quality control manual

QCM—quality control master

QCP—quality commitment performance

QCP—quality control program

QCR—quality control reliability

QCR—quality control report

QCR—quality control representative

QCS—quality and customer satisfaction

QCS—quality customer service

QCT—quality, cost, timing

QCWF—quality, cost, weight, and function

QCWFT—quality, cost, weight, function, and timing attributes

QDR—quality, durability, reliability

QDR—quality deficiency report(s)

QEMS—quality and environmental management system

QEP—quality enhancement program

QEP—quality evaluation program

QF—quality form

QFD—quality function deployment

QFTF—quality function test fleet

QHC—quality in health care

QHNZ—Quality Health New Zealand

QHR—quality history records

QI—quality improvement

QI—quality increase

QIC—quality information using cycle time

QIES—quality improvement evaluation system

QIM—quality improvement meeting

QIP—quality improvement process

QIP—quality intervention plan

QIS—quality information system

QIT—quality in training

QIT—quality information and test

QITQM—*Quality Improvement Total Quality Management* (magazine)

QLA—quality level agreement

QLF—quality loss function

QLS—quality leadership system

QMAS—Quality Measurement Advisory Service

QMIS—quality management information system

QMMP—Quality Measurement and Management Project

QMP—quality, manufacturing, and purchasing

QMRP—Qantel manufacturing resource planning (MRP II) system

QMS—quality management system

QOS—quality of service

QOS—quality operating system

QP—quality procedure

QPC—quality and process control

QPC—quality performance consultant

QPI—quality performance indicator

QPIP—quality and productivity improvement program

QPM—quality and performance management

QPM—quality performance matrix

QPM—quality program manager

QPR—quality problem report

QPS—quality planning sheets

QPS—quality process sheets

QPS—quality process system

QPSS—quality process system sheets

QR—quality and reliability

QR—quality reject(s)

QR—quality report

QR—quantitative requirement

QR—quick response

QRA—quality and reliability assurance

QRA—quality reliability assurance

QRA—quick reaction assessment

QRA—quick readiness assessment

QRA—quick response audit

QRB—quality review board

QRC—quality record coordinator

QRC—quality risk and cost

QRD—quantitative risk management

QRO—quality review organization

QRS—quality review studies

QRT—quality responsible team

QS—quality systems

QS-9000—Quality System Requirements 9000

QSA—quality system analyst

QSC—quality strategy committee

QSDC—quality system document coordinator

QSF—quick service fix

QSHC—*Quality and Safety in Health Care* (magazine)

QSP—quality strategy and planning

QSR—quality system requirement(s)

QSRC—quality system record coordinator

QSS—quality support team

QSU—quality system update

QTS—quality tracking study

QUADS—quality document system

QUASAR—Quality and Safety Achievement Recognition

QUASAR—Quality Driven Software Architecture

QUEST—quality electrical systems test

QUEST—quality evaluation of settlement

QuEST—Quality Excellence for Suppliers of Telecommunications

QUGS—quality utilization generic screens

QUIP—quality assessment and improvement program

QUIP—quality assurance inspection procedure

QUIT—Quality in Training

QVI—quality verification inspection

QVP—quality vendor program

R—required

R²—coefficient of determination

R2R—runs to reject

R&A—reliability and availability

R&D—research and development

R&M—reliability and maintainability

R&M—reliability and maintenance

R&MWG—reliability and maintainability working group

R&R—repeatability and reproducibility (*see also* GR&R)

RA—risk analysis

RA—risk assessment

RAB—registrar accreditation board

RABQSA—RABQSA International (formerly the Registrar Accreditation Board and the Quality Society of Australasia)

RADHAZ—radio and radar radiation hazards

RAM—reliability, availability, and maintainability

RAMAS—reliability, availability, maintainability analysis system

RAMCAD—reliability and maintainability in computer-aided design

RAM-D—reliability, availability, maintainability, and durability

RAMDAS—reliability and maintainability data access system

RAMES—reliability, availability, maintainability, engineering system

RAMIS—reliability and maintainability information system

RAMS—range measurement system

RAMSH—reliability, availability, maintainability, safety, (and) human-factors (engineering)

RAMTIP—Reliability and Maintainability Technology Insertion Program

RAPID—rapid actions for process improvement deployment

RAS—reliability, availability, and serviceability

RBD—reliability block diagram

RBI—risk based inspection

RBM—risk based maintenance

RCA—root cause analysis

RCL—robustness checklist

RCM—reliability centered maintenance

RD/GT—reliability development/growth test

RDCOV—recognize–define–characterize–optimize–verify

REG—regression

REM—reliability engineering model

RES—residual

RF—radio frequency

RF—remaining float

RFI—radio frequency interference

RFP—request for proposal

RFQ—request for quote

RFTA—reverse fault tree analysis

RII—required inspection item

RIW—reliability improvement warranty

RM—reference material

RM&A—reliability, maintainability, and availability

RM&S—reliability, maintainability, and supportability

RMA—reliability, maintainability, and availability

RMMP—reliability and maintainability management plan

RMS—root mean square

ROA—report of analysis

ROA—return on assets

ROE—return on equity

ROI—return on investment

RONA—return on net assets

RPL—rejectable process level

RPM—revolutions per minute

RPN—risk priority number

RQL—rejectable quality level

RQMS—*Reliability and Quality Measurements for Telecommunications Systems*

RQT—reliability qualification test(ing)

RRA—residual risk assessment

RSM—repair station manual

RSM—response surface methodology

RTOK—retest OK

RTY—rolled throughput yield

S—satisfactory

S—severity

S3—safety and suitability for service

SAE—Society of Automotive Engineers *or* SAE International

SB—service bulletin

SBP—strategic business plan

SC—significant characteristic

SCOT—strengths, challenge, opportunities, threats

SCP—service control point

SDCA—standardize–do–check–act

SDE—supplier development engineer

SDS—safety data sheet

SDWT—self-directed work team

SE—simultaneous engineering

SE—standard error

SET—senior executive team

SF—secondary float

SIF—safety integrity analysis

SIPOC—supplier, input, process, output, and customer

SIT—systematic inventive thinking

SKSP—skip-lot sampling plan

SLACK—summary, learning objectives, application, context, knowledge base

SMART—specific, meaningful, agreed to, realistic, time-based

SMARTER—specific, measurable, acceptable, realistic, time-bound, evaluated, reviewed

SME—Society of Manufacturing Engineers

SME—small and medium enterprises

SME—subject matter expert

SMED—single-minute exchange of die

SMS—safety management system

SN—signal-to-noise ratio

SO—system outage measurement

SOP—standard operating procedure

SoPK—System of Profound Knowledge (Dr. W. Edwards Deming)

SOQ—service-oriented architecture

SOR—sign-off report

SOW—statement of work

SPA—second party audit

SPC—statistical process control

SPD—statistical process display

SPEAR—suppler performance and evaluation report

SPM—statistical process management

SPOF—single point of failure

SPOT—scope, purpose, overview, tangible benefits

SQC—statistical quality control

SQDCME—safety, quality, delivery, cost, moral, environment

SQE—software quality evaluation

SQE—supplier quality engineer

SQI—supplier quality improvement

SQP—strategic quality plan

SQR—supplier quality representative

SQRTF—Supplier Quality Requirements Task Force

SREA—supplier request for engineering approval

SRG—statistical research group

SRM—supplier relationship management

SRMR—security risk management review

SRP—strategic regulatory plan

SS—Six Sigma

SS—sum of squares

SSB—between-treatments sum of squares

SSBB—Six Sigma Black Belt

SSBoK—Six Sigma Body of Knowledge

SSC—column sum of squares

SSE—error sum of squares

SSGB—Six Sigma Green Belt

SSI—interaction sum of squares

SSMBB—Six Sigma Master Black Belt

SSOS—Six Sigma operating system

SSR—residual sum of squares

SSR—row sum of squares

SSRA—system safety risk assessment

SST—total sum of squares

SSW—within-treatments sum of squares

SSYB—Six Sigma Yellow Belt

STA—supplier technical assistance

STD—standard deviation

STOP—Safety Training Observation Program

STP—signaling transfer point

STS—synchronous transport signal

SWAG—statistical wild ass guess

SWIPE—standard, workpiece, instrument, person and procedure, environment

SWL—safe working load

SWOT—strengths, weaknesses, opportunities, threats

T—target

T&D—test and diagnostic

T&D—training and development

T&E—test and evaluation

T&EO—training and evaluation outline

T&M—time and materials

T&O—test and operation

TACT—total average cycle time

TAT—turnaround time

TBD—to be determined

TBE—to be established

TC—technical contradiction

TDR—technical design review(s)

TE—tooling and equipment

TF—total float

TGR—things gone right

TGW—things gone wrong

TIE—technical information engineer

TMAP—thought process map

TNA—training needs assessment

TOC—theory of constraints

TOPS—total operational performance system

TOU—terms of use

TPA—third-party audit

TPM—total productive maintenance

TPS—Toyota Production System

TQ—total quality

TQC—total quality control

TQHRM—total quality human resources management

TQM—total quality management

TRACE—total risk assessing cost estimate

TRACE—total risk assessing cost estimating

TRIZ—theory of inventive problem solving

TS—technical specification

TSS—total sum of squares

TV—total variation

TVM—total value management

UACL—upper acceptable control limit

UCL—upper control limit

UKAS—United Kingdom Accreditation Service

ULL—upper lot limit

UP—unit price

UPC—uniform parts code

UQL—unacceptable quality level

USL—upper specification limit

VA—value-added

VA/VE—value analysis/value engineering

VC—virtual container

VDA—Verband der Automobilindustrie (German)

VIM—*International Vocabulary of Metrology—Basic and General Concepts and Associated Terms*

VIN—vehicle identification number

VIPER—verifiable integrated processor for enhanced reliability

VOB—voice of the business

VOC—voice of the customer

VOE—voice of the employee

VOP—voice of the process

VQD—visual quality document

VSAS—vehicle situational awareness system

VSM—value stream mapping

WAG—wild ass guess

WBS—work breakdown structure

WCP—world class process

WGD—worldwide guidance documents

WI—work instructions

WIIFM—what's in it for me

WIP—work in process

WOW—worst of the worst

WQP—worldwide quality procedures

WQS—worldwide quality standards

WYSIWYG—What you see is what you get

x—average

X—cause or process variable

Y—effect or process output

YRR—one-year return rate

ZD—zero defects

Glossary

A

acceptance number—The maximum number of defects or defectives allowable in a sampling lot for the lot to be acceptable.

acceptance quality limit (AQL)—In a continuing series of lots, a quality level that, for the purpose of sampling inspection, is the limit of a satisfactory process average.

acceptance sampling—Inspection of a sample from a lot to decide whether to accept that lot. There are two types: attributes sampling and variables sampling. In *attributes sampling*, the presence or absence of a characteristic is noted in each of the units inspected. In *variables sampling*, the numerical magnitude of a characteristic is measured and recorded for each inspected unit; this involves reference to a continuous scale of some kind.

acceptance sampling plan—A specific plan that indicates the sampling sizes and associated acceptance or nonacceptance criteria to be used. In attributes sampling, for example, there are single, double, multiple, sequential, chain, and skip-lot sampling plans. In variables sampling, there are single, double, and sequential sampling plans. For detailed descriptions of these plans, see the standard ANSI/ISO/ASQ A3534-2-1993: *Statistics—Vocabulary and symbols—Statistical quality control.*

accuracy—The closeness of agreement between a test result or measurement result and the accepted/true value.[2]

activity based costing—An accounting system that assigns costs to a product based on the amount of resources used to design, order, or make it.

activity network diagram—A diagram that links tasks with direct arrows showing the path through the task list. Tasks are linked when a task is dependent on a preceding task.[3] (AKA *arrow diagram*.)

Advanced Product Quality Planning (APQP)—High-level automotive process for product realization, from design through production part approval.

affinity diagram—A management tool for organizing information (usually gathered during a brainstorming activity).

American National Standards Institute (ANSI)—A private, nonprofit organization that administers and coordinates the U.S. voluntary standardization and conformity assessment system. It is the U.S. member body in the International Organization for Standardization, known as ISO.

American Society for Quality (ASQ)—A global community of people dedicated to quality who share the ideas and tools that make our world work better. With individual and organizational members around the world, ASQ has the reputation and reach to bring together the diverse quality champions who are transforming the world's corporations, organizations, and communities to meet tomorrow's critical challenges.

analysis of means (ANOM)—A statistical procedure for troubleshooting industrial processes and analyzing the results of experimental designs with factors at fixed levels. It provides a graphical display of data. Ellis R. Ott developed the procedure in 1967 because he observed that nonstatisticians had difficulty understanding analysis of variance. Analysis of means is easier for quality practitioners to use because it is an extension of the control chart. In 1973, Edward G. Schilling further extended the concept, enabling analysis of means to be used with nonnormal distributions and attributes data in which the normal approximation to the binomial distribution does not apply. This is referred to as *analysis of means for treatment effects*.

analysis of variance (ANOVA)—A basic statistical technique for determining the proportion of influence a factor or set of factors has on total variation. It subdivides the total variation of a data set into meaningful component parts associated with specific sources of variation to test a hypothesis on the parameters of the model or to estimate variance components. There are three models: fixed, random, and mixed.

analytical (inferential) studies—A set of techniques used to arrive at a conclusion about a population based upon the information contained in a sample taken from that population.[1]

arrow diagram—A planning tool used to diagram a sequence of events or activities (nodes) and their interconnectivity. It is used for scheduling and especially for determining the critical path through nodes. (AKA *activity network diagram*.)

assignable cause—A name for the source of variation in a process that is not due to chance and therefore can be identified and eliminated. Also called "special cause."

attributes (discrete) data—Go/no-go information. The control charts based on attributes data include percent chart, number of affected units chart, count chart, count per unit chart, quality score chart, and demerit chart.

attributes, method of—Method of measuring quality that consists of noting the presence (or absence) of some characteristic (attribute) in each of the units under consideration and counting how many units do (or do not) possess it. Example: go/no-go gauging of a dimension.

audit—The on-site verification activity, such as inspection or examination, of a product, process, or quality system, to ensure compliance to requirements.

An audit can apply to an entire organization or might be specific to a product, function, process, or production step.

Automotive Industry Action Group (AIAG)—A global automotive trade association with about 1600 member companies that focuses on common business processes, implementation guidelines, education, and training.

average chart—A control chart in which the subgroup average, $\bar{x}$, is used to evaluate the stability of the process level.

average outgoing quality (AOQ)—The expected average quality level of an outgoing product for a given value of incoming product quality.

average outgoing quality limit (AOQL)—The maximum average outgoing quality over all possible levels of incoming quality for a given acceptance sampling plan and disposal specification.

average run length (ARL)—On a control chart, the number of subgroups expected to be inspected before a shift in magnitude takes place.

average sample number (ASN)—The average number of sample units inspected per lot when reaching decisions to accept or reject.

average total inspection (ATI)—The average number of units inspected per lot, including all units in rejected lots. Applicable when the procedure calls for 100 percent inspection of rejected lots.

B

balanced scorecard—A management system that provides feedback on both internal business processes and external outcomes to continuously improve strategic performance and results.

Baldrige Award—See *Malcolm Baldrige National Quality Award.*

baseline measurement—The beginning point, based on an evaluation of output over a period of time, used to determine the process parameters prior to any improvement effort; the basis against which change is measured.

batch and queue—Producing more than one piece and then moving the pieces to the next operation before they are needed.

Bayes's theorem—A formula to calculate conditional probabilities by relating the conditional and marginal probability distributions of random variables.

benchmarking—A technique in which a company measures its performance against that of best-in-class companies, determines how those companies achieved their performance levels, and uses the information to improve its own performance. Subjects that can be benchmarked include strategies, operations, and processes.

benefit–cost analysis—An examination of the relationship between the monetary cost of implementing an improvement and the monetary value of the benefits achieved by the improvement, both within the same time period.

bias—The influence in a sample of a factor that causes the data population or process being sampled to appear different from what it actually is, typically in a specific direction.[3]

binomial distribution—A discrete distribution that is applicable whenever an experiment consists of *n* independent Bernoulli trials and the probability of an outcome, say, success, is constant throughout the experiment.[1]

Black Belt (BB)—Full-time team leader responsible for implementing process improvement projects—define, measure, analyze, improve, and control (DMAIC) or define, measure, analyze, design, and verify (DMADV)—within a business to drive up customer satisfaction and productivity levels.

block diagram—A diagram that shows the operation, interrelationships, and interdependencies of components in a system. Boxes, or blocks (hence the name), represent the components; connecting lines between the blocks represent interfaces. There are two types of block diagrams: a *functional block diagram*, which shows a system's subsystems and lower-level products and their interrelationships and which interfaces with other systems; and a *reliability block diagram*, which is similar to the functional block diagram but is modified to emphasize those aspects influencing reliability.

brainstorming—A technique teams use to generate ideas on a particular subject. Each person on the team is asked to think creatively and write down as many ideas as possible. The ideas are not discussed or reviewed until after the brainstorming session.

breakthrough improvement—A dynamic, decisive movement to a new, higher level of performance.

business process reengineering (BPR)—The concentration on improving business processes to deliver outputs that will achieve results meeting the firm's objectives, priorities, and mission.

C

calibration—The comparison of a measurement instrument or system of unverified accuracy to a measurement instrument or system of known accuracy to detect any variation from the required performance specification.

capability—The total range of inherent variation in a stable process determined by using data from control charts.

causation—The relationship between two variables. The changes in variable *x* cause changes in *y*. For example, a change in outdoor temperature causes changes in natural gas consumption for heating. If we can change *x*, we can bring about a change in *y*.

cause—An identified reason for the presence of a defect, problem, or effect.

cause-and-effect diagram—A tool for analyzing process dispersion. It is also referred to as the "Ishikawa diagram," because Kaoru Ishikawa developed it, and the "fishbone diagram," because the completed diagram resembles a fish skeleton. The diagram illustrates the main causes and subcauses leading to an effect (symptom). The cause-and-effect diagram is one of the "seven tools of quality."

c-chart—See *count chart*.

centerline—A line on a graph that represents the overall average (mean) operating level of the process.

central limit theorem—A theorem that states that irrespective of the shape of the distribution of a population, the distribution of sample means is approximately normal when the sample size is large.[1]

central tendency—The tendency of data gathered from a process to cluster toward a middle value somewhere between the high and low values of measurement.

certification—The result of a person meeting the established criteria set by a certificate granting organization.

Certified Six Sigma Black Belt (CSSBB)—An ASQ certification.

Certified Six Sigma Green Belt (CSSGB)—An ASQ certification.

chain reaction—A chain of events described by W. Edwards Deming: improve quality, decrease costs, improve productivity, increase market share with better quality and lower price, stay in business, provide jobs, and provide more jobs.

chain sampling plan—In acceptance sampling, a plan in which the criteria for acceptance and rejection apply to the cumulative sampling results for the current lot and one or more immediately preceding lots.

champion—A business leader or senior manager who ensures that resources are available for training and projects, and who is involved in periodic project reviews; also an executive who supports and addresses Six Sigma organizational issues.

change agent—An individual from within or outside an organization who facilitates change in the organization; might be the initiator of the change effort, but not necessarily.

changeover—A process in which a production device is assigned to perform a different operation or a machine is set up to make a different part—for example, a new plastic resin and new mold in an injection molding machine.

changeover time—The time required to modify a system or workstation, usually including both teardown time for the existing condition and setup time for the new condition.

characteristic—The factors, elements, or measures that define and differentiate a process, function, product, service, or other entity.

chart—A tool for organizing, summarizing, and depicting data in graphic form.

charter—A written commitment approved by management stating the scope of authority for an improvement project or team.

check sheet—A simple data recording device. The check sheet is custom-designed by the user, which allows him or her to readily interpret the results. The check sheet is one of the "seven tools of quality."

checklist—A tool for ensuring that all important steps or actions in an operation have been taken. Checklists contain items important or relevant to an issue or situation. Checklists are often confused with check sheets.

chi square distribution—Probability distribution of sum of squares of n independent normal variables.[1]

classification of defects—The listing of possible defects of a unit, classified according to their seriousness. Note: Commonly used classifications: class A, class B, class C, class D; or critical, major, minor, and incidental; or critical, major, and minor. Definitions of these classifications require careful preparation and tailoring to the product(s) being sampled to ensure accurate assignment of a defect to the proper classification. A separate acceptance sampling plan is generally applied to each class of defects.

common causes—Causes of variation that are inherent in a process over time. They affect every outcome of the process and everyone working in the process. (AKA *chance causes*.) Also see *special causes*.

compliance—The state of an organization that meets prescribed specifications, contract terms, regulations, or standards.

conformance—An affirmative indication or judgment that a product or service has met the requirements of a relevant specification, contract, or regulation.

conformity assessment—All activities concerned with determining that relevant requirements in standards or regulations are fulfilled, including sampling, testing, inspection, certification, management system assessment and registration, accreditation of the competence of those activities, and recognition of an accreditation program's capability.

constraint—Anything that limits a system from achieving higher performance or throughput; also, the bottleneck that most severely limits the organization's ability to achieve higher performance relative to its purpose or goal.

consumer—The external customer to whom a product or service is ultimately delivered; also called end user.

continuous (variables) data—Data that vary with discontinuity across an interval. The values of continuous data are often represented by floating point numbers. In sampling, continuous data are often referred to as variables data.[3]

continuous flow production—A method in which items are produced and moved from one processing step to the next, one piece at a time. Each process makes only the one piece that the next process needs, and the transfer batch size is one. Also referred to as *one-piece flow* and *single-piece flow*.

continuous improvement (CI)—Sometimes called *continual improvement*. The ongoing improvement of products, services, or processes through incremental and breakthrough improvements.

continuous quality improvement (CQI)—A philosophy and attitude for analyzing capabilities and processes and improving them repeatedly to achieve customer satisfaction.

continuous sampling plan—In acceptance sampling, a plan, intended for application to a continuous flow of individual units of product, that involves acceptance and rejection on a unit-by-unit basis and employs alternate periods of 100 percent inspection and sampling. The relative amount of 100 percent inspection depends on the quality of submitted product. Continuous sampling plans usually require that each t period of 100 percent inspection be continued until a specified number i of consecutively inspected units is found clear of defects. Note: For single-level continuous sampling plans, a single d sampling rate (for example, inspect one unit in five or one unit in 10) is used during sampling. For multilevel continuous sampling plans, two or more sampling rates can be used. The rate at any given time depends on the quality of submitted product.

control chart—A chart with upper and lower control limits on which values of some statistical measure for a series of samples or subgroups are plotted. The chart frequently shows a central line to help detect a trend of plotted values toward either control limit.

control limits—The natural boundaries of a process within specified confidence levels, expressed as the upper control limit (UCL) and the lower control limit (LCL).

control plan (CP)—Written description of the systems for controlling part and process quality by addressing the key characteristics and engineering requirements.

corrective action—A solution meant to reduce or eliminate an identified problem.

corrective action recommendation (CAR)—The full cycle corrective action tool that offers ease and simplicity for employee involvement in the corrective action/process improvement cycle.

correlation (statistical)—A measure of the relationship between two data sets of variables.

cost of poor quality (COPQ)—The costs associated with providing poor-quality products or services. There are four categories: internal failure costs (costs associated with defects found before the customer receives the product or service), external failure costs (costs associated with defects found after the customer receives the product or service), appraisal costs (costs incurred to determine the degree of conformance to quality requirements), and prevention costs (costs incurred to keep failure and appraisal costs to a minimum).

cost of quality (COQ)—Another term for COPQ. It is considered by some to be synonymous with COPQ but is considered by others to be unique. While the two concepts emphasize the same ideas, some disagree as to which concept came first and which categories are included in each.

count chart—A control chart for evaluating the stability of a process in terms of the count of events of a given classification occurring in a sample; known as a "*c*-chart."

count per unit chart—A control chart for evaluating the stability of a process in terms of the average count of events of a given classification per unit occurring in a sample.

C_p—The ratio of tolerance to six sigma, or the upper specification limit (USL) minus the lower specification limit (LSL) divided by six sigma. It is sometimes referred to as the engineering tolerance divided by the natural tolerance and is only a measure of dispersion.

C_{pk} **index**—Equals the lesser of the USL minus the mean divided by three sigma (or the mean) minus the LSL divided by three sigma. The greater the C_{pk} value, the better.

C_{pm}—Used when a target value within the specification limits is more significant than overall centering.[3]

critical path method (CPM)—An activity-oriented project management technique that uses arrow-diagramming techniques to demonstrate both the time and the cost required to complete a project. It provides one time estimate: normal time.

critical to quality (CTQ)—A characteristic of a product or service that is essential to ensure customer satisfaction.[2]

cumulative sum control chart (CUSUM)—A control chart on which the plotted value is the cumulative sum of deviations of successive samples from a target value. The ordinate of each plotted point represents the algebraic sum of the previous ordinate and the most recent deviations from the target.

customer relationship management (CRM)—A strategy for learning more about customers' needs and behaviors to develop stronger relationships with them. It brings together information about customers, sales, marketing effectiveness, responsiveness, and market trends. It helps businesses use technology and human resources to gain insight into the behavior of customers and the value of those customers.

customer satisfaction—The result of delivering a product or service that meets customer requirements.

cycle time—The time required to complete one cycle of an operation. If cycle time for every operation in a complete process can be reduced to equal takt time, products can be made in single-piece flow. Also see *takt time*.

cyclical variation—Looks at the piece-to-piece changes in consecutive order. Patterns are identified in groups, batches, or lots of units.[3]

D

data—A set of collected facts. There are two basic kinds of numerical data: measured or variables data, such as "16 ounces," "4 miles," and "0.75 inches," and counted or attributes data, such as "go/no go" or "yes/no."

D-chart—See *demerit chart*.

decision matrix—A matrix teams use to evaluate problems or possible solutions. For example, a team might draw a matrix to evaluate possible solutions, listing them in the far left vertical column. Next, the team selects criteria to rate the possible solutions, writing them across the top row. Then, each possible solution is rated on a scale of 1 to 5 for each criterion, and the rating is recorded in the corresponding grid. Finally, the ratings of all the criteria for each possible solution are added to determine its total score. The total score is then used to help decide which solution deserves the most attention.

defect—A product's or service's nonfulfillment of an intended requirement or reasonable expectation for use, including safety considerations. There are four classes of defects: class 1, very serious, leads directly to severe injury or catastrophic economic loss; class 2, serious, leads directly to significant injury or significant economic loss; class 3, major, is related to major problems with respect to intended normal or reasonably foreseeable use; and class 4, minor, is related to minor problems with respect to intended normal or reasonably foreseeable use.

defective—A defective unit; a unit of product that contains one or more defects with respect to the quality characteristic(s) under consideration.

demerit chart—A control chart for evaluating a process in terms of a demerit (or quality score); in other words, a weighted sum of counts of various classified nonconformities.

Deming cycle—Another term for the plan–do–study–act cycle. Walter Shewhart created it (calling it the plan–do–check–act cycle), but W. Edwards Deming popularized it, calling it plan–do–study–act.

dependability—The degree to which a product is operable and capable of performing its required function at any randomly chosen time during its specified operating time, provided that the product is available at the start of that period. (Nonoperation related influences are not included.) Dependability can be expressed by the following ratio: time available divided by (time available + time required).

design for Six Sigma (DFSS)—Used for developing a new product or process, or for processes that need total overhaul. A process often used in DFSS is called DMADV: define, measure, analyze, design, verify.[4] See also *DMADV*.

design of experiments (DOE)—A branch of applied statistics dealing with planning, conducting, analyzing, and interpreting controlled tests to evaluate the factors that control the value of a parameter or group of parameters.

design record—Engineering requirements, typically contained in various formats; examples include engineering drawings, math data, and referenced specifications.

detection—The likelihood the failure will be caught by the current controls before it gets to the customer (usually a scale of 1-5 or 1-10).

deviation—In numerical data sets, the difference or distance of an individual observation or data value from the center point (often the mean) of the set distribution.

dissatisfiers—The features or functions a customer expects that either are not present or are present but not adequate; also pertains to employees' expectations.

distribution (statistical)—The amount of potential variation in the outputs of a process, typically expressed by its shape, average, or standard deviation.

DMADV—A data-driven quality strategy for designing products and processes; it is an integral part of a Six Sigma quality initiative. It consists of five interconnected phases: define, measure, analyze, design, and verify.

DMAIC—A data-driven quality strategy for improving processes, and an integral part of a Six Sigma quality initiative. DMAIC is an acronym for define, measure, analyze, improve, and control.

Dodge-Romig sampling plans—Plans for acceptance sampling developed by Harold F. Dodge and Harry G. Romig. Four sets of tables were published in 1940: single sampling lot tolerance tables, double sampling lot tolerance tables, single sampling average outgoing quality limit tables, and double sampling average outgoing quality limit tables.

downtime—Lost production time during which a piece of equipment is not operating correctly due to breakdown, maintenance, power failures, or similar events.

E

effect—The result of an action being taken; the expected or predicted impact when an action is to be taken or is proposed.

effectiveness—The state of having produced a decided on or desired effect.

efficiency—The ratio of the output to the total input in a process.

efficient—A term describing a process that operates effectively while consuming minimal resources (such as labor and time).

eight wastes—Taiichi Ohno originally enumerated seven wastes (muda) and later added *underutilized people* as the eighth waste commonly found in physical production. The eight are (1) overproduction ahead of demand, (2) waiting for the next process, worker, material, or equipment, (3) unnecessary transport of materials (for example, between functional areas of facilities, or to or from a stockroom or warehouse), (4) overprocessing of parts due to poor tool and product design, (5) inventories more than the absolute minimum, (6) unnecessary movement by employees during the course of their work (such as to look for parts, tools, prints, or help), (7) production of defective parts, (8) underutilization of employees' brainpower, skills, experience, and talents.

eighty–twenty (80–20)—A term referring to the Pareto principle, which was first defined by J. M. Juran in 1950. The principle suggests that most effects come from relatively few causes; that is, 80 percent of the effects come from 20 percent of the possible causes. Also see *Pareto chart*.

enumerative (descriptive) studies—A group of methods used for organizing, summarizing, and representing data using tables, graphs, and summary statistics.[1]

error detection—A hybrid form of error-proofing. It means a bad part can be made but will be caught immediately, and corrective action will be taken to prevent another bad part from being produced. A device is used to detect and stop the process when a bad part is made. This is used when error-proofing is too expensive or not easily implemented.

error-proofing—Use of process or design features to prevent the acceptance or further processing of nonconforming products. Also known as *mistake-proofing*.

experimental design—A formal plan that details the specifics for conducting an experiment, such as which responses, factors, levels, blocks, treatments, and tools are to be used.

external customer—A person or organization that receives a product, service, or information but is not part of the organization supplying it. Also see *internal customer*.

external failure—Nonconformance identified by the external customers.

F

failure—The inability of an item, product, or service to perform required functions on demand due to one or more defects.

failure cost—The cost resulting from the occurrence of defects. One element of cost of quality or cost of poor quality.

failure mechanism—Mechanism describing how the cause of the failure mode results in failure.

failure mode—Expressed as the inability to achieve the stated function.

failure mode analysis (FMA)—A procedure to determine which malfunction symptoms appear immediately before or after a failure of a critical parameter in a system. After all possible causes are listed for each symptom, the product is designed to eliminate the problems.

failure mode and effects analysis (FMEA)—A systematized group of activities to recognize and evaluate the potential failure of a product or process and its effects, identify actions that could eliminate or reduce the occurrence of the potential failure, and document the process.

F-distribution—A continuous probability distribution of the ratio of two independent chi-square random variables.[1]

first in, first out (FIFO)—Use of material produced by one process in the same order by the next process. A FIFO queue is filled by the supplying process and emptied by the customer process. When a FIFO lane gets full, production is stopped until the next (internal) customer has used some of that inventory.

first-pass yield (FPY)—Also referred to as the *quality rate*, the percentage of units that completes a process and meets quality guidelines without being scrapped, rerun, retested, returned, or diverted into an offline repair area. FPY is calculated by dividing the units entering the process minus the defective units by the total number of units entering the process.

first-time quality (FTQ)—Calculation of the percentage of good parts at the beginning of a production run.

fishbone diagram—See *cause-and-effect diagram*.

fitness for use—A term used to indicate that a product or service fits the customer's defined purpose for that product or service.

five S (5S)—Five Japanese terms beginning with "s" used to create a workplace suited for visual control and lean production. *Seiri* means to separate needed tools, parts, and instructions from unneeded materials and to remove the unneeded ones. *Seiton* means to neatly arrange and identify parts and tools for ease of use. *Seiso* means to conduct a cleanup campaign. *Seiketsu* means to conduct seiri, seiton, and seiso daily to maintain a workplace in perfect condition. *Shitsuke* means to form the habit of always following the first four S's.

five whys—A technique for discovering the root causes of a problem and showing the relationship of causes by repeatedly asking the question, "Why?"

flow—The progressive achievement of tasks along the value stream so a product proceeds from design to launch, order to delivery, and raw to finished materials in the hands of the customer with no stoppages, scrap, or backflows.

flowchart—A graphical representation of the steps in a process. Flowcharts are drawn to better understand processes. One of the "seven tools of quality."

force-field analysis—A technique for analyzing what aids or hinders an organization in reaching an objective. An arrow pointing to an objective is drawn down the middle of a piece of paper. The factors that will aid the objective's achievement, called the driving forces, are listed on the left side of the arrow. The factors that will hinder its achievement, called the restraining forces, are listed on the right side of the arrow.

G

gage repeatability and reproducibility (GR&R)—The evaluation of a gauging instrument's accuracy by determining whether its measurements are repeatable (there is close agreement among a number of consecutive measurements of the output for the same value of the input under the same operating conditions) and reproducible (there is close agreement among repeated measurements of the output for the same value of input made under the same operating conditions over a period of time).

Gantt chart—A type of bar chart used in process planning and control to display planned and finished work in relation to time.

geometric dimensioning and tolerancing (GD&T)—A set of rules and standard symbols to define part features and relationships on an engineering drawing depicting the geometric relationship of part features and allowing the maximum tolerance that permits full function of the product.

go/no-go—State of a unit or product. Two parameters are possible: go (conforms to specifications) and no-go (does not conform to specifications).

Green Belt (GB)—An employee who has been trained in the Six Sigma improvement method at a Green Belt level and will lead a process improvement or quality improvement team as part of his or her full-time job.

H

Hawthorne effect—The concept that every change results (initially, at least) in increased productivity.

heijunka—A method of leveling production, usually at the final assembly line, that makes just-in-time production possible. It involves averaging both the volume and sequence of different model types on a mixed-model production line. Using this method avoids excessive batching of different types of product and volume fluctuations in the same product.

histogram—A graphic summary of variation in a set of data. The pictorial nature of a histogram lets people see patterns that are difficult to detect in a simple table of numbers. One of the "seven tools of quality."

hoshin kanri—The selection of goals, projects to achieve the goals, designation of people and resources for project completion, and establishment of project metrics.

hoshin planning—Breakthrough planning. A Japanese strategic planning process in which a company develops up to four vision statements that indicate where the company should be in the next five years. Company goals and work plans are developed based on the vision statements. Periodic submitted audits are then conducted to monitor progress. Also see *value stream*.

house of quality—A product planning matrix, somewhat resembling a house, that is developed during quality function deployment and shows the relationship of customer requirements to the means of achieving these requirements.

I

in-control process—A process in which the statistical measure being evaluated is in a state of statistical control; in other words, the variations among the observed sampling results can be attributed to a constant system of chance causes (common causes). Also see *out-of-control process*.

incremental improvement—Improvement implemented on a continual basis.

indicators—Established measures to determine how well an organization is meeting its customers' needs and other operational and financial performance expectations.

inputs—The products, services, and material obtained from suppliers to produce the outputs delivered to customers.

inspection—Measuring, examining, testing, and gauging one or more characteristics of a product or service and comparing the results with specified requirements to determine whether conformity is achieved for each characteristic.

inspection, normal—Inspection used in accordance with a sampling plan under ordinary circumstances.

inspection, 100 percent—Inspection of all the units in the lot or batch.

inspection cost—The cost associated with inspecting a product to ensure that it meets the internal or external customer's needs and requirements; an appraisal cost.

inspection lot—A collection of similar units or a specific quantity of similar material offered for inspection and acceptance at one time.

internal customer—The recipient (person or department) within an organization of another person's or department's output (product, service, or information). Also see *external customer.*

internal failure—A product failure that occurs before the product is delivered to external customers.

International Organization for Standardization—A network of national standards institutes from 157 countries working in partnership with international organizations, governments, industry, business, and consumer representatives to develop and publish international standards; acts as a bridge between public and private sectors.

interrelationship diagram—A management tool that depicts the relationship among factors in a complex situation; also called a *relations diagram.*

Ishikawa diagram—See *cause-and-effect diagram.*

J

jidoka—The deliberate effort to automate a process with a human touch. It means that when a problem occurs on a production line, a worker or machine is able to stop the process and prevent defective goods from being produced.

just-in-time (JIT) manufacturing—An optimal material requirement planning system for a manufacturing process in which there is little or no manufacturing material inventory on hand at the manufacturing site and little or no incoming inspection.

K

kaizen—A Japanese term that means gradual unending improvement by doing little things better and setting and achieving increasingly higher standards. Masaaki Imai made the term famous in his book *Kaizen: The Key to Japan's Competitive Success.*

kanban—A Japanese term for one of the primary tools of a just-in-time system. It maintains an orderly and efficient flow of materials throughout the entire manufacturing process. It is usually a printed card that contains specific information such as part name, description, and quantity.

key performance indicator (KPI)—A statistical measure of how well an organization is doing in a particular area. A KPI could measure a company's financial performance or how it is holding up against customer requirements.

key process characteristic—A process parameter that can affect safety or compliance with regulations, fit, function, performance, or subsequent processing of product.

key product characteristic—A product characteristic that can affect safety or compliance with regulations, fit, function, performance, or subsequent processing of product.

L

leadership—An essential part of a quality improvement effort. Organization leaders must establish a vision, communicate that vision to those in the organization, and provide the tools and knowledge necessary to accomplish the vision.

lean—Producing the maximum sellable products or services at the lowest operational cost while optimizing inventory levels and eliminating waste.

lean enterprise—A manufacturing company organized to eliminate all unproductive effort and unnecessary investment, both on the shop floor and in office functions.

lean manufacturing/production—An initiative focused on eliminating all waste in manufacturing processes. Principles of lean manufacturing include zero waiting time, zero inventory, scheduling (internal customer pull instead of push system), batch to flow (cut batch sizes), line balancing, and cutting actual process times. The production systems are characterized by optimum automation, just-in-time supplier delivery disciplines, quick changeover times, high levels of quality, and continuous improvement.

lean migration—The journey from traditional manufacturing methods to one in which all forms of waste are systematically eliminated.

linearity—Refers to measurements being statistically different from one end of the measurement space to the other. For example, a measurement process may be very capable of measuring small parts but much less accurate measuring large parts, or one end of a long part can be measured more accurately than the other.[3]

lot—A defined quantity of product accumulated under conditions considered uniform for sampling purposes.

lot, batch—A definite quantity of some product manufactured under conditions of production that are considered uniform.

lot quality—The value of percentage defective or of defects per hundred units in a lot.

lot size (also referred to as *N*)—The number of units in a lot.

lower control limit (LCL)—Control limit for points below the central line in a control chart.

M

maintainability—The probability that a given maintenance action for an item under given usage conditions can be performed within a stated time interval when the maintenance is performed under stated conditions using stated procedures and resources.

Malcolm Baldrige National Quality Award (MBNQA)—An award established by the U.S. Congress in 1987 to raise awareness of quality management and recognize U.S. companies that have implemented successful quality management systems. Awards can be given annually in six categories: manufacturing, service, small business, education, healthcare, and nonprofit. The award is named after the late Secretary of Commerce Malcolm Baldrige, a proponent of quality management. The U.S. Commerce Department's National Institute of Standards and Technology manages the award, and ASQ administers it.

Master Black Belt (MBB)—Six Sigma or quality expert responsible for strategic implementations in an organization. An MBB is qualified to teach other Six Sigma facilitators the methods, tools, and applications in all functions and levels of the company, and is a resource for using statistical process control in processes.

matrix diagram—A planning tool for displaying the relationships among various data sets.

mean—A measure of central tendency; the arithmetic average of all measurements in a data set.

mean time between failures (MTBF)—The average time interval between failures for repairable product for a defined unit of measure; for example, operating hours, cycles, and miles.

measure—The criteria, metric, or means to which a comparison is made with output.

measurement—The act or process of quantitatively comparing results with requirements.

median—The middle number or center value of a set of data in which all the data are arranged in sequence.

metric—A standard for measurement.

MIL-STD-105E—A military standard that describes the sampling procedures and tables for inspection by attributes.

mistake-proofing—Use of production or design features to prevent the manufacture or passing downstream of a nonconforming product; also known as *error-proofing*.

mode—The value occurring most frequently in a data set.

muda—Japanese for *waste*; any activity that consumes resources but creates no value for the customer.

multivariate control chart—A control chart for evaluating the stability of a process in terms of the levels of two or more variables or characteristics.

multivoting—Typically used after brainstorming, multivoting narrows a large list of possibilities to a smaller list of the top priorities (or to a final selection) by allowing items to be ranked in importance by participants. Multivoting is preferable to straight voting because it allows an item that is favored by all, but not the top choice of any, to rise to the top.[4]

N

n—The number of units in a sample.

N—The number of units in a population.

nominal group technique (NGT)—A technique, similar to brainstorming, used to generate ideas on a particular subject. Team members are asked to silently write down as many ideas as possible. Each member is then asked to share one idea, which is recorded. After all the ideas are recorded, they are discussed and prioritized by the group.

nonconformity—The nonfulfillment of a specified requirement.

nondestructive testing and evaluation (NDT, NDE)—Testing and evaluation methods that do not damage or destroy the product being tested.

nonlinear parameter estimation—A method whereby the arduous and labor-intensive task of multiparameter model calibration can be carried out automatically under the control of a computer.

nonparametric tests—All tests involving ranked data (data that can be put in order). Nonparametric tests are often used in place of their parametric counterparts when certain assumptions about the underlying population are questionable. For example, when comparing two independent samples, the Wilcoxon Mann-Whitney test (see entry) does not assume that the difference between the samples is normally distributed, whereas its parametric counterpart, the two-sample *t*-test, does. Nonparametric tests can be, and often are, more powerful in detecting population differences when certain assumptions are not satisfied.

non-value-added—A term that describes a process step or function that is not required for the direct achievement of process output. This step or function is identified and examined for potential elimination. Also see *value-added*.

normal distribution (statistical)—The charting of a data set in which most of the data points are concentrated around the average (mean), thus forming a bell-shaped curve.

O

occurrence—The likelihood of a cause resulting in the occurrence of a failure mode. This may be based on historical data with other similar processes (usually a scale of 1–5 or 1–10).

operating characteristic curve (OC curve)—A graph to determine the probability of accepting lots as a function of the lots' or processes' quality level when using various sampling plans. There are three types: type A curves, which give the probability of acceptance for an individual lot coming from finite production (will not continue in the future); type B curves, which give the probability of acceptance for lots coming from a continuous process; and type C curves, which (for a continuous sampling plan) give the long-run percentage of product accepted during the sampling phase.

operations—Work or steps to transform raw materials to finished product.

out of spec—A term that indicates a unit does not meet a given requirement or specification.

out-of-control process—A process in which the statistical measure being evaluated is not in a state of statistical control. In other words, the variations among the observed sampling results can not be attributed to a constant system of chance causes. Also see *in-control process*.

outputs—Products, materials, services, or information provided to customers (internal or external), from a process.

P

paired-comparison tests—Examples are two-mean, equal variance *t*-test; two-mean, unequal variance *t*-test; paired *t*-test; and *F*-test.

Pareto chart—A graphical tool for ranking causes from most significant to least significant. It is based on the Pareto principle, which was first defined by Joseph M. Juran in 1950. The principle, named after 19th-century economist Vilfredo Pareto, suggests that most effects come from relatively few causes; that is, 80 percent of the effects come from 20 percent of the possible causes. One of the "seven tools of quality."

parts per million (ppm)—A method of stating the performance of a process in terms of actual nonconforming material, which can include rejected, returned, or suspect material in the calculation.

p-chart—See *percent chart*.

percent chart—A control chart for evaluating the stability of a process in terms of the percentage of the total number of units in a sample in which an event of a given classification occurs. Also referred to as a *proportion chart*.

plan–do–check–act (PDCA) cycle—A four-step process for quality improvement. In the first step (plan), a way to effect improvement is developed. In the second step (do), the plan is carried out, preferably on a small scale. In the third step (check), a study takes place comparing what was predicted and what was observed in the previous step. In the last step (act), action is taken on the causal system to effect the desired change. The plan–do–check–act cycle is sometimes referred to as the Shewhart cycle, because Walter A. Shewhart discussed the concept in his book *Statistical Method from the Viewpoint of Quality Control,* and as the Deming cycle, because W. Edwards Deming introduced the concept in Japan. The Japanese subsequently called it the Deming cycle. Also called the *plan–do–study–act (PDSA) cycle*.

point of use—A technique that ensures people have exactly what they need to do their jobs—work instructions, parts, tools, and equipment—where and when they need them.

Poisson distribution—A discrete probability distribution that expresses the probability of a number of events occurring in a fixed time period if these events occur with a known average rate and are independent of the time since the last event.

poka-yoke—Japanese term that means mistake-proofing. A poka-yoke device is one that prevents incorrect parts from being made or assembled, or easily identifies a flaw or error.

positional variation—Type of variation frequently within-piece, but can also include machine-to-machine variation, line-to-line or plant-to-plant variation, within-batch variation, and test positioning variation.[3]

P_p **(process performance index)**—An index describing process performance in relation to specified tolerance.[2]

P_{pk} **(minimum process performance index)**—The smaller of upper process performance index and lower process performance index.[2]

practical significance—At least as important as the question of statistical significance, practical or economic significance determines whether an observed sample difference is large enough to be of practical interest.

precision—The aspect of measurement that addresses repeatability or consistency when an identical item is measured several times.

prevention cost—The cost incurred by actions taken to prevent a nonconformance from occurring; one element of cost of quality or cost of poor quality.

preventive action—Action taken to remove or improve a process to prevent potential future occurrences of a nonconformance.

prioritization matrix—An L-shaped matrix that uses pairwise comparisons of a list of options to a set of criteria in order to choose the best option(s). First, the importance of each criterion is decided. Then, each criterion is considered separately, with each option rated for how well it meets the criterion. Finally, all the ratings are combined for a final ranking of options. Numerical calculations ensure a balance between the relative importance of the criteria and the relative merits of the options.[4]

probability (statistical)—The likelihood of occurrence of an event, action, or item.

procedure—The steps in a process and how these steps are to be performed for the process to fulfill a customer's requirements; usually documented.

process—A set of interrelated work activities characterized by a set of specific inputs and value-added tasks that make up a procedure for a set of specific outputs.

process average quality—Expected or average value of process quality.

process capability—A statistical measure of the inherent process variability of a given characteristic. The most widely accepted formula for process capability is six sigma.

process capability index—The value of the inherent tolerance specified for the characteristic divided by the process capability. The several types of process capability indices include the widely used C_{pk} and C_p.

process control—The method for keeping a process within boundaries; the act of minimizing the variation of a process.

process decision program charts (PDPC)—A variant of tree diagrams, a PDPC can be used as a simple alternative to FMEA.[3]

process flow diagram—A depiction of the flow of materials through a process, including any rework or repair operations; also called a *process flow chart*.

process improvement—The application of the plan–do–check–act cycle (see entry) to processes to produce positive improvement and better meet the needs and expectations of customers.

process management—The pertinent techniques and tools applied to a process to implement and improve process effectiveness, hold the gains, and ensure process integrity in fulfilling customer requirements.

process map—A type of flowchart depicting the steps in a process and identifying responsibility for each step and key measures.

process owner—The person who coordinates the various functions and work activities at all levels of a process, has the authority or ability to make changes in the process as required, and manages the entire process cycle to ensure performance effectiveness.

process performance management—The overseeing of process instances to ensure their quality and timeliness; can also include proactive and reactive actions to ensure a good result.

process quality—The value of percentage defective or of defects per hundred units in product from a given process. Note: The symbols "p" and "c" are commonly used to represent the true process average in fraction defective or defects per unit, and "$100p$" and "$100c$" the true process average in percentage defective or in defects per hundred units.

production part approval process (PPAP)—A "Big Three" automotive process that defines the generic requirements for approval of production parts, including production and bulk materials. Its purpose is to determine during an actual production run at the quoted production rates whether all customer engineering design record and specification requirements are properly understood by the supplier and that the process has the potential to produce product consistently meeting these requirements.

program evaluation and review technique (PERT) charts—Developed during the Nautilus submarine program in the 1950s, a PERT chart resembles an activity network diagram in that it shows task dependencies. It calculates best, average, and worst expected completion times.[3]

project management—The application of knowledge, skills, tools, and techniques to a broad range of activities to meet the requirements of a particular project.

project team—Manages the work of a project. The work typically involves balancing competing demands for project scope, time, cost, risk, and quality, satisfying stakeholders with differing needs and expectations, and meeting identified requirements.

proportion chart—See *percent chart*.

pull system—An alternative to scheduling individual processes in which the customer process withdraws the items it needs as at a supermarket, and the supplying process produces to replenish what was withdrawn; used to avoid push. Also see *kanban*.

Q

quality—A subjective term for which each person or sector has its own definition. In technical usage, quality can have two meanings: 1. the characteristics of a product or service that bear on its ability to satisfy stated or implied needs; 2. a product or service free of deficiencies. According to Joseph M. Juran, quality means "fitness for use"; according to Philip Crosby, it means "conformance to requirements."

quality assurance/quality control (QA/QC)—Two terms that have many interpretations because of the multiple definitions for the words "assurance" and "control." For example, "assurance" can mean the act of giving confidence, the state of being certain, or the act of making certain; "control" can mean an evaluation to indicate needed corrective responses, the act of guiding, or the state of a process in which the variability is attributable to a constant system of chance causes. (For a detailed discussion on the multiple definitions, see ANSI/ISO/ASQ A3534-2, *Statistics—Vocabulary and symbols—Statistical quality* *control.*) One definition of quality assurance is: all the planned and systematic activities implemented within the quality system that can be demonstrated to provide confidence that a product or service will fulfill requirements for quality. One definition for quality control is: the operational techniques and activities used to fulfill requirements for quality. Often, however, "quality assurance" and "quality control" are used interchangeably, referring to the actions performed to ensure the quality of a product, service, or process.

quality audit—A systematic, independent examination and review to determine whether quality activities and related results comply with plans and whether these plans are implemented effectively and are suitable to achieve the objectives.

quality costs—See *cost of poor quality.*

quality function deployment (QFD)—A structured method in which customer requirements are translated into appropriate technical requirements for each stage of product development and production. The QFD process is often referred to as listening to the voice of the customer.

quality loss function—A parabolic approximation of the quality loss that occurs when a quality characteristic deviates from its target value. The quality loss function is expressed in monetary units: the cost of deviating from the target increases quadratically the farther the quality characteristic moves from the target. The formula used to compute the quality loss function depends on the type of quality characteristic being used. The quality loss function was first introduced in this form by Genichi Taguchi.

quality management (QM)—The application of a quality management system in managing a process to achieve maximum customer satisfaction at the lowest overall cost to the organization while continuing to improve the process.

quality management system (QMS)—A formalized system that documents the structure, responsibilities, and procedures required to achieve effective quality management.

queue time—The time a product spends in a line awaiting the next design, order processing, or fabrication step.

quick changeover—The ability to change tooling and fixtures rapidly (usually within minutes) so multiple products can be run on the same machine.

R

random cause—A cause of variation due to chance and not assignable to any factor.

random sampling—A commonly used sampling technique in which sample units are selected so all combinations of n units under consideration have an equal chance of being selected as the sample.

range (statistical)—The measure of dispersion in a data set (the difference between the highest and lowest values).

range chart (R chart)—A control chart in which the subgroup range R evaluates the stability of the variability within a process.

rational subgrouping—Subgrouping wherein the variation is presumed to be only from random causes.[2]

regression analysis—A statistical technique for determining the best mathematical expression describing the functional relationship between one response variable and one or more independent variables.

relations diagram—See *interrelationship diagram.*

reliability—The probability of a product's performing its intended function under stated conditions without failure for a given period of time.

repeatability—The variation in measurements obtained when one measurement device is used several times by the same person to measure the same characteristic on the same product.

reproducibility—The variation in measurements made by different people using the same measuring device to measure the same characteristic on the same product.

requirements—The ability of an item to perform a required function under stated conditions for a stated period of time.

risk management—Using managerial resources to integrate risk identification, risk assessment, risk prioritization, development of risk handling strategies, and mitigation of risk to acceptable levels.

risk priority number (RPN)—The product of the severity, occurrence, and detection values determined in FMEA. The higher the RPN, the more significant the failure mode.

robustness—The condition of a product or process design that remains relatively stable, with a minimum of variation, even though factors that influence operations or usage, such as environment and wear, are constantly changing.

root cause—A factor that caused a nonconformance and should be permanently eliminated through process improvement.

run chart—A chart showing a line connecting numerous data points collected from a process running over time.

S

sample—In acceptance sampling, one or more units of product (or a quantity of material) drawn from a lot for purposes of inspection to reach a decision regarding acceptance of the lot.

sample size (n)—The number of units in a sample.

sample standard deviation chart (s-chart)—A control chart in which the subgroup standard deviation s is used to evaluate the stability of the variability within a process.

scatter diagram—A graphical technique to analyze the relationship between two variables. Two sets of data are plotted on a graph, with the *y*-axis being used for the variable to be predicted and the *x*-axis being used for the variable to make the prediction. The graph will show possible relationships (although two variables might appear to be related, they might not be; those who know most about the variables must make that evaluation). One of the "seven tools of quality."

seven tools of quality—Tools that help organizations understand their processes to improve them. The tools are the cause-and-effect diagram, check sheet, control chart, flowchart, histogram, Pareto chart, and scatter diagram.

seven wastes—See *eight wastes*.

severity—The severity of the failure mode is based on the worst-case effect of the failure mode. Severity may range from safety concern (very high) to no effect (very low) (usually a scale of 1-5 or 1-10).

Shewhart cycle—See *plan–do–check–act cycle*.

sigma—One standard deviation in a normally distributed process.

single-piece flow—A process in which products proceed one complete product at a time, through various operations in design, order taking, and production without interruptions, backflows, or scrap.

SIPOC diagram—A tool used by Six Sigma process improvement teams to identify all relevant elements (suppliers, inputs, process, outputs, customers) of a process improvement project before work begins.

Six Sigma—A method that provides organizations tools to improve the capability of their business processes. This increase in performance and decrease in process variation lead to defect reduction and improvement in profits, employee morale, and quality of products or services. Six Sigma quality is a term generally used to indicate that a process is well controlled (±6σ from the centerline in a control chart).

six sigma quality—A term generally used to indicate process capability in terms of process spread measured by standard deviations in a normally distributed process.

special causes—Causes of variation that arise because of special circumstances. They are not an inherent part of a process. Special causes are also referred to as *assignable causes*. Also see *common causes*.

specification—A document that states the requirements to which a given product or service must conform.

stages of team growth—Four stages that teams move through as they develop maturity: forming, storming, norming, and performing.

standard deviation (statistical)—A computed measure of variability indicating the spread of the data set around the mean.

standard work—A precise description of each work activity, specifying cycle time, takt time, the work sequence of specific tasks, and the minimum inventory of parts on hand needed to conduct the activity. All jobs are organized around human motion to create an efficient sequence without waste. Work organized in such a way is called standard(ized) work. The three elements that make up standard work are takt time, working sequence, and standard in-process stock.

standard work instructions—A lean manufacturing tool that enables operators to observe a production process with an understanding of how assembly tasks are to be performed. It ensures that the quality level is understood and serves as an excellent training aid, enabling replacement or temporary individuals to easily adapt and perform the assembly operation.

statistical process control (SPC)—The application of statistical techniques to control a process; often used interchangeably with the term *statistical quality control.*

statistical quality control (SQC)—The application of statistical techniques to control quality. Often used interchangeably with the term *statistical process control,* although statistical quality control includes acceptance sampling, which statistical process control does not.

statistical significance—Level of accuracy expected of an analysis of data. Most frequently it is expressed as either a "95 percent level of significance" or "five percent confidence level."[5]

strengths, weaknesses, opportunities, threats (SWOT) analysis—A strategic technique used to assess an organization's competitive position.

Student's *t*-distribution—A continuous distribution of the ratio of two independent random variables—a standard normal and a chi-square.[1]

supplier—A source of materials, service, or information input provided to a process.

supplier quality assurance—Confidence that a supplier's product or service will fulfill its customers' needs. This confidence is achieved by creating a relationship between the customer and supplier that ensures that the product will be fit for use with minimal corrective action and inspection. According to Joseph M. Juran, nine primary activities are needed: (1) define product and program quality requirements, (2) evaluate alternative suppliers, (3) select suppliers, (4) conduct joint quality planning, (5) cooperate with the supplier during the execution of the contract, (6) obtain proof of conformance to requirements, (7) certify qualified suppliers, (8) conduct quality improvement programs as required, (9) create and use supplier quality ratings.

supply chain—The series of suppliers to a given process.

system—A group of interdependent processes and people that together perform a common mission.

T

Taguchi methods—The American Supplier Institute's trademarked term for the quality engineering methodology developed by Genichi Taguchi. In this engineering approach to quality control, Taguchi calls for off-line quality control, online quality control, and a system of experimental design to improve quality and reduce costs.

takt time—The rate of customer demand, takt time is calculated by dividing production time by the quantity of product the customer requires in that time. Takt is the heartbeat of a lean manufacturing system. Also see *cycle time*.

team—A group of individuals organized to work together to accomplish a specific objective. Also see *stages of team growth*.

temporal variation—The time-to-time or shift-to-shift variation—that is, variation across time.[3]

theory of constraints (TOC)—A lean management philosophy that stresses removal of constraints to increase throughput while decreasing inventory and operating expenses. TOC's set of tools examines the entire system for continuous improvement. The current reality tree, conflict resolution diagram, future reality tree, prerequisite tree, and transition tree are the five tools used in TOC's ongoing improvement process. Also called *constraints management*.

throughput—The rate at which the system generates money through sales, or the conversion rate of inventory into shipped product.

tolerance—The maximum and minimum limit values a product can have and still meet customer requirements.

total productive maintenance (TPM)—A series of methods, originally pioneered by Nippondenso (a member of the Toyota group), to ensure that every machine in a production process is always able to perform its required tasks so production is never interrupted.

total quality management (TQM)—A term coined by the Naval Air Systems Command to describe its Japanese-style management approach to quality improvement. Since then, TQM has taken on many meanings. Simply put, it is a management approach to long-term success through customer satisfaction. TQM is based on all members of an organization participating in improving processes, products, services, and the culture in which they work. The methods for implementing this approach are found in the teachings of such quality leaders as Philip B. Crosby, W. Edwards Deming, Armand V. Feigenbaum, Kaoru Ishikawa, and Joseph M. Juran.

Toyota Production System (TPS)—The production system developed by Toyota Motor Corp. to provide best quality, lowest cost, and shortest lead time through eliminating waste. TPS is based on two pillars: just-in-time and jidoka. TPS is maintained and improved through iterations of standardized work and kaizen.

tree diagram—A management tool that depicts the hierarchy of tasks and subtasks needed to complete an objective. The finished diagram bears a resemblance to a tree.

trend—The graphical representation of a variable's tendency, over time, to increase, decrease, or remain unchanged.

trend control chart—A control chart in which the deviation of the subgroup average, $\bar{x}$, from an expected trend in the process level is used to evaluate the stability of a process.

TRIZ—A Russian acronym for a theory of innovative problem solving.

t-test—A method to assess whether the means of two groups are statistically different from each other.

type I error—An incorrect decision to reject something (such as a statistical hypothesis or a lot of products) when it is acceptable.

type II error—An incorrect decision to accept something when it is unacceptable.

U

u-chart—Count-per-unit chart.

unit—An object for which a measurement or observation can be made; commonly used in the sense of a "unit of product," the entity of product inspected to determine whether it is defective or nondefective.

upper control limit (UCL)—Control limit for points above the central line in a control chart.

V

validation—The act of confirming that a product or service meets the requirements for which it was intended.

validity—The ability of a feedback instrument to measure what it was intended to measure; also, the degree to which inferences derived from measurements are meaningful.

value stream—All activities, both value-added and non-value-added, required to bring a product from raw material state into the hands of the customer, bring a customer requirement from order to delivery, and bring a design from concept to launch. Also see *hoshin planning*.

value stream mapping—A pencil and paper tool used in two stages. First, follow a product's production path from beginning to end and draw a visual representation of every process in the material and information flows. Second, draw a future state map of how value should flow. The most important map is the future state map.

value-added—A term used to describe activities that transform input into a customer (internal or external)–usable output.

variables (attributes) data—Measurement information. Control charts based on variables data include average ($\bar{x}$) chart, range (R) chart, and sample standard deviation (s) chart.

variation—A change in data, characteristic, or function caused by one of four factors: special causes, common causes, tampering, or structural variation.

verification—The act of determining whether products and services conform to specific requirements.

voice of the customer—The expressed requirements and expectations of customers relative to products or services, as documented and disseminated to the providing organization's members.

W

waste—Any activity that consumes resources and produces no added value to the product or service a customer receives. Also known as *muda*.

Wilcoxon Mann-Whitney test—Used to test the null hypothesis that two populations have identical distribution functions against the alternative hypothesis that the two distribution functions differ only with respect to location (median), if at all. It does not require the assumption that the differences between the two samples are normally distributed. In many applications, it is used in place of the two-sample t-test when the normality assumption is questionable. This test can also be applied when the observations in a sample of data are ranks, that is, ordinal data, rather than direct measurements.

X

x-bar ($\bar{x}$) chart—Average chart.

Z

zero defects—A performance standard and method Philip B. Crosby developed, which states that if people commit themselves to watching details and avoiding errors, they can move closer to the goal of zero defects.

Endnotes

Source: Except where noted, definitions reproduced with permission of ASQ, http://www.asq.org/glossary/index.html. The glossary was compiled by *Quality Progress* magazine editorial staff members Dave Nelsen, Assistant Editor, and Susan E. Daniels, Editor at Large. Volunteers James Bossert, R. Dan Reid, and James Rooney reviewed the content.

1. Reproduced by permission of Bhisham C. Gupta and H. Fred Walker, *Applied Statistics for the Six Sigma Green Belt* (Milwaukee: ASQ Quality Press, 2005).
2. Reproduced by permission of the ASQ Statistics Division, *Glossary and Tables for Statistical Quality Control,* 4th ed. (Milwaukee: ASQ Quality Press, 2004).
3. Reproduced by permission of Kim H. Pries, *Six Sigma for the Next Millennium* (Milwaukee: ASQ Quality Press, 2006).
4. Reproduced by permission of Nancy R. Tague, *The Quality Toolbox,* 2nd ed. (Milwaukee: ASQ Quality Press, 2005).
5. Reproduced by permission of Donald L. Siebels, *The Quality Improvement Glossary.* (Milwaukee: ASQ Quality Press, 2004).

Notes

CHAPTER 1

1. ASQ, "History of Quality," http://asq.org/learn-about-quality/history-of-quality/overview/overview.html.

2. Donald J. Wheeler, *Understanding Statistical Process Control*, 3rd ed. (Knoxville, TN: SPC Press, 2010).

3. *Wikipedia*, s.v. "Joseph M. Juran," last modified May 5, 2016, https://en.wikipedia.org/wiki/Joseph_M._Juran.

4. *Wikipedia*, s.v. "Noriaki Kano," last modified April 24, 2016, https://en.wikipedia.org/wiki/Noriaki_Kano; *Wikipedia*, s.v. "Genichi Taguchi," last modified May 31, 2016, https://en.wikipedia.org/wiki/Genichi_Taguchi.

5. Joseph Juran, *Managerial Breakthrough: A New Concept of the Manager's Job* (New York: McGraw Hill, 1964).

CHAPTER 2

1. Anna Gorman, "Hospitals Seeking an Edge Turn to Unlikely Adviser: A Carmaker," *State of Health* (blog), KQED News, July 30, 2015, http://ww2.kqed.org/stateof-health/2015/07/30/hospitals-seeking-an-edge-turn-to-unlikely-adviser-a-carmaker.

2. James P. Womack, Daniel T. Jones, and Daniel Roos, *The Machine That Changed the World: How Japan's Secret Weapon in the Global Auto Wars Will Revolutionize Western Industry* (New York: HarperPerennial, 1991).

CHAPTER 4

1. B. W. Tuckman, "Developmental Sequence in Small Groups," *Psychological Bulletin* 63, no. 6 (November–December, 1965): 384–99.

2. Peter R. Scholtes, Brian L. Joiner, and Barbara J. Streibel, *The Team Handbook,* 3rd ed. (Madison, WI: Oriel, 2003), http://rube.asq.org/2003/01/teams/the-team-handbook-3rd-edition.pdf.

3. Microsoft, "Survey Finds Workers Average Only Three Productive Days per Week," March 15, 2005, http://news.microsoft.com/2005/03/15/survey-finds-workers-average-only-three-productive-days-per-week/.

CHAPTER 5

1. D. W. Benbow and T. M. Kubiak, *The Certified Six Sigma Black Belt Handbook* (Milwaukee, WI: ASQ Quality Press, 2005).
2. An example Six Sigma calculator can be found at http://www.isixsigma.com/process-sigma-calculator/. Try both the manufacturing example and the service example in the advanced mode with Six Sigma shift = 0.
3. Benbow and Kubiak, *The Certified Six Sigma Black Belt Handbook*.
4. Ibid.

CHAPTER 6

1. ASQ, "Six Sigma Project Assignment: Know Your Black Belts," http://rube.asq.org/six-sigma/2007/02/project-management/know-your-black-belts.pdf.

CHAPTER 7

1. H. Kerzner, *Project Management: A Systems Approach to Planning, Schedule, and Controls,* 8th ed. (New York: John Wiley & Sons, 2003).
2. ASQ, "Beyond the Basics," ASQ *Quality Progress*, April 2012, http://asq.org/quality-progress/2012/04/basic-quality/beyond-the-basics.html.

CHAPTER 8

1. For risks associated with sample sizes, see power and sample concepts explained in Roderick A. Munro, Govindarajan Ramu, and Daniel J. Zrymiak, *The Certified Six Sigma Green Belt Handbook,* 2nd ed. (Milwaukee, WI: ASQ Quality Press, 2015).

CHAPTER 9

1. Govindarajan Ramu, "Measurement System Analysis—Tutorial" (slide show presentation), presented at ASQ Silicon Valley Conference, October 21, 2010, http://www.slideshare.net/govindramu/measurement-system-analysis-5731384/.

CHAPTER 10

1. AIAG, *Measurement System Analysis*, 4th ed. (DaimlerChrysler Corporation, Ford Motor Company, General Motors Corporation, 2010).
2. Ibid.
3. Larry B. Barrentine, *Concepts for R&R Studies,* 2nd ed. (Milwaukee, WI: ASQ Quality Press, 2003).

CHAPTER 11

1. AIAG, *Potential Failure Mode and Effects Analysis (FMEA) Reference Manual,* 4th ed. (DaimlerChrysler Corporation, Ford Motor Company, General Motors Corporation, 2008).

2. ISO 9001:2015 *Quality Management System—Requirements* (International Organization for Standardization, 2015), http://asq.org/quality-press/display-item/index.html?item=T1040.

3. Govindarajan Ramu, "FMEA Minus the Pain," ASQ *Quality Progress* (March 2009), http://asq.org/quality-progress/2009/03/risk-management/fmea-minus-the-pain.html.

CHAPTER 12

1. Taiichi Ohno, "Ask 'Why' Five Times about Every Matter," *Toyota Traditions* (March 2006), http://www.toyota-global.com/company/toyota_traditions/quality/mar_apr_2006.html.

2. Bjørn Andersen, Tom Fagerhaug, and Marti Beltz, *Root Cause Analysis and Improvement in the Healthcare Sector: A Step-by-Step Guide* (Milwaukee, WI: ASQ Quality Press, 2010): 93–94.

3. ASQ, "Seven New Quality Tools: The Prioritization Matrix Webcast," February 2014, http://asq.org/2014/02/quality-tools/seven-new-quality-tools-the-prioritization-matrix-webcast.html?ctx=kc.

CHAPTER 15

1. "Minitab Statistical Software—Help Guide," https://www.minitab.com/en-us/support/.

CHAPTER 16

1. Wikipedia, "Net Present Value," accessed March 9, 2016, https://en.wikipedia.org/wiki/Net_present_value.

2. Douglas C. Wood, ed., *Principles of Quality Costs: Financial Measures for Strategic Implementation of Quality Management,* 4th ed. (Milwaukee, WI: ASQ Quality Press, 2012): 4, http://asq.org/quality-press/display-item/?item=H1438.

3. Joseph A. DeFeo, "The Tip of the Iceberg," ASQ *Quality Progress* 34, no. 5 (May 2001), http://asq.org/qic/display-item/?item=14608.

4. Wood, *Principles of Quality Costs*, 9.

CHAPTER 17

1. ASQ, "Quality Glossary—C," http://asq.org/glossary/c.html.

2. Mary Walton, *The Deming Management Method* (New York: Perigree Books, 1988).

Bibliography

AIAG (Automotive Industry Action Group). *Statistical Process Control*, 4th ed., https://www.aiag.org/products/products-list/product-details?ProductCode=SPC-3

Alra, Pablo. "Evaluating Repeatability." ASQ *Quality Progress* (November 2014). http://asq.org/quality-progress/2014/11/expert-answers.html.

Andersen, Bjørn, and Tom Fagerhaug. *Root Cause Analysis: Simplified Tools and Techniques*, 2nd ed. Milwaukee, WI: ASQ Quality Press, 2006. http://asq.org/quality-press/display-item/?item=H1287.

ASQ. Lean Enterprise Division Resources. http://www.asqled.org.

———. "Plan-Do-Check-Act (PDCA) Cycle." http://asq.org/learn-about-quality/project-planning-tools/overview/pdca-cycle.html.

———. "Scatter Diagram." http://asq.org/learn-about-quality/cause-analysis-tools/overview/scatter.html.

———. "The 7 Basic Quality Tools for Process Improvement." http://asq.org/learn-about-quality/seven-basic-quality-tools/overview/overview.html.

———. "Seven New Quality Tools: The Prioritization Matrix Webcast" (webinar). February 2014. http://asq.org/2014/02/quality-tools/seven-new-quality-tools-the-prioritization-matrix-webcast.html?ctx=kc.

———. "SIPOC (Suppliers, Inputs, Process, Outputs, Customers) Diagram." http://asq.org/service/body-of-knowledge/tools-sipoc/.

———. "Six Sigma Belts, Executives and Champions—What Does It All Mean?" http://asq.org/learn-about-quality/six-sigma/overview/belts-executives-champions.html.

———. "SOP It Up." ASQ *Quality Progress* (August 2011). http://asq.org/quality-progress/2011/08/expert-answers.html.

———. "What Is a Process Flowchart?" http://asq.org/learn-about-quality/process-analysis-tools/overview/flowchart.html.

Bialek, Ron, Grace L. Duffy, and John W. Moran. "SIPOC+CM Diagram." ASQ. http://asq.org/healthcare-use/why-quality/sipoc.html.

Chartered Quality Institute (CQI). "The Evolution of Quality Thinking, post c1970." http://www.thecqi.org/Knowledge-Hub/Knowledge-portal/Concepts-of-quality/Evolution-of-quality-thinking/.

Deming, W. Edwards. "System of Profound Knowledge." The W. Edwards Deming Institute. https://deming.org/theman/theories/profoundknowledge/.

Duffy, Grace, Scott A. Laman, Pradip Mehta, Govind Ramu, Natalia Scriabina, and Keith Wagoner. "Beyond the Basics." ASQ *Quality Progress* (April 2012). http://asq.org/quality-progress/2012/04/basic-quality/beyond-the-basics.html.

Juran, Joseph. *Managerial Breakthrough: A New Concept of the Manager's Job.* New York: McGraw Hill, 1964.

Juran, Joseph M., and Joseph A. DeFeo. *Juran's Quality Handbook: The Complete Guide to Performance Excellence*, 6th ed. New York: McGraw-Hill, 2010.

Lean Enterprise Institute. Knowledge Center. http://www.lean.org.

Manos, Anthony, and Chad Vincent, eds. *The Lean Handbook: A Guide to the Bronze Certification Body of Knowledge*. Milwaukee, WI: ASQ Quality Press, 2012.

"Minitab Statistical Software—Help Guide." https://www.minitab.com/en-us/support/.

Moen, Ronald D., and Clifford L. Norman. "Circling Back." ASQ *Quality Progress* (November 2010). http://asq.org/quality-progress/2010/11/basic-quality/circling-back.html.

Montgomery, Douglas C. *Introduction to Statistical Quality Control*, 2nd ed. New York: John Wiley & Sons, 1991.

Pyzdek, Thomas. "101 Things Every Six Sigma Black Belt Should Know." Pyzdek Institute, 2003. http://www.sixsigmatraining.org/101-things-a-black-belt-should-know/.

Ramu, Govindarajan. "Innovative Approach to FMEA Facilitation" (slide show presentation). May 2009. http://www.slideshare.net/govindramu/innovative-approach-to-fmeaasq/.

———. "Measurement System Analysis—Tutorial" (slide show presentation). Presented at ASQ Silicon Valley Conference. 2010. http://www.slideshare.net/govindramu/measurement-system-analysis-5731384/.

———. "Metrics That Trigger Actionable Discussions: Prioritize Process Improvements Using Gauge R&R and SPC Capability." *ASQ Six Sigma Forum* (December 2007). http://rube.asq.org/sixsigma/2007/12/metrics/metrics-that-trigger-actionable-discussions-prioritize-process-improvements-using-gauge-rr-and-spc-capability.pdf.

Rooney, James J., and Lee N. Vanden Heuvel. "Root Cause Analysis for Beginners." ASQ *Quality Progress* (July 2004). http://asq.org/quality-progress/2004/07/quality-tools/root-cause-analysis-for-beginners.html.

Stamatis, D. H. *Failure Mode and Effect Analysis: FMEA from Theory to Execution*, 2nd ed. Milwaukee, WI: ASQ Quality Press, 2003. http://asq.org/quality-press/display-item/?item=H1188/.

Tague, Nancy R. *The Quality Toolbox*, 2nd ed. Milwaukee, WI: ASQ Quality Press, 2005. http://asq.org/quality-press/display-item/index.html?item=H1224.

Toyota. "Toyota Production System." http://www.toyota-global.com/company/vision_philosophy/toyota_production_system/.

Triola, Mario F. *Elementary Statistics*, 12th ed. Boston: Pearson, 2012.

Westcott, Russell T., and Grace L. Duffy, eds. *The Certified Quality Improvement Associate Handbook: Basic Quality Principles and Practices*, 3rd ed. Milwaukee, WI: ASQ Quality Press, 2015.

Wood, Douglas C., ed. *Principles of Quality Costs*, 4th ed. Milwaukee, WI: ASQ Quality Press, 2012. http://asq.org/quality-press/display-item/?item=H1438/.

Index

Note: Page numbers followed by *f* or *t* refer to figures or tables, respectively.

The Knowledge Center
www.asq.org/knowledge-center

Learn about quality. Apply it. Share it.

ASQ's online Knowledge Center is the place to:

- Stay cn top of the latest in quality with Editor's Picks and Hot Topics.

- Search ASQ's collection of articles, books, tools, training, and more.

- Connect with ASQ staff for personalized help hunting down the knowledge you
  need, the networking opportunities that will keep your career and organization
  moving forward, and the publishing opportunities that are the best fit for you.

Use the Knowledge Center Search to quickly sort through hundreds of books, articles,
and other software-related publications.

www.asq.org/knowledge-center

The Global Voice of Quality®

Ask a Librarian

Did you know?

- The ASQ Quality Information Center contains a wealth of knowledge and information available to ASQ members and non-members

- A librarian is available to answer research requests using ASQ's ever-expanding library of relevant, credible quality resources, including journals, conference proceedings, case studies and Quality Press publications

- ASQ members receive free internal information searches and reduced rates for article purchases

- You can also contact the Quality Information Center to request permission to reuse or reprint ASQ copyrighted material, including journal articles and book excerpts

- For more information or to submit a question, visit **http://asq.org/knowledge-center/ ask-a-librarian-index**

Visit www.asq.org/qic for more information.

TRAINING   CERTIFICATION   CONFERENCES   MEMBERSHIP   **PUBLICATIONS**

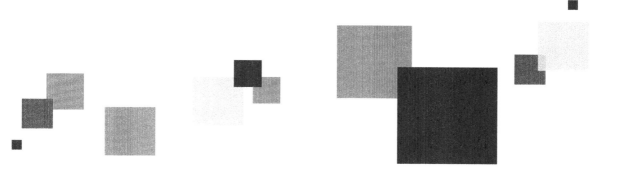

Belong to the Quality Community!

Established in 1946, ASQ is a global community of quality experts in all fields and industries. ASQ is dedicated to the promotion and advancement of quality tools, principles. and practices in the workplace and in the community.

The Society also serves as an advocate for quality. Its members have informed and advised the U.S. Congress, government agencies, state legislatures, and other groups and individuals worldwide on quality-related topics.

Vision

By making quality a global priority, an organizational imperative, and a personal ethic, ASQ becomes the community of choice for everyone who seeks quality technology, concepts, or tools to improve themselves and their world.

ASQ is...

- More than 90,000 individuals and 700 companies in more than 100 countries

- The world's largest organization dedicated to promoting quality

- A community of professionals striving to bring quality to their work and their lives

- The administrator of the Malcolm Baldrige National Quality Award

- A supporter of quality in all sectors including manufacturing, service, healthcare, government, and education

- YOU

Visit www.asq.org for more information.

PUBLICATIONS

The Global Voice of Quality®

ASQ Membership

Research shows that people who join associations experience increased job satisfaction, earn more, and are generally happier*. ASQ membership can help you achieve this while providing the tools you need to be successful in your industry and to distinguish yourself from your competition. So why wouldn't you want to be a part of ASQ?

Networking

Have the opportunity to meet, communicate, and collaborate with your peers within the quality community through conferences and local ASQ section meetings, ASQ forums or divisions, ASQ Communities of Quality discussion boards, and more.

Professional Development

Access a wide variety of professional development tools such as books, training, and certifications at a discounted price. Also, ASQ certifications and the ASQ Career Center help enhance your quality knowledge and take your career to the next level.

Solutions

Find answers to all your quality problems, big and small, with ASQ's Knowledge Center, mentoring program, various e-newsletters, *Quality Progress* magazine, and industry-specific products.

Access to Information

Learn classic and current quality principles and theories in ASQ's Quality Information Center (QIC), *ASQ Weekly* e-newsletter, and product offerings.

Advocacy Programs

ASQ helps create a better community, government, and world through initiatives that include social responsibility, Washington advocacy, and Community Good Works.

Visit www.asq.org/membership for more information on ASQ membership.

*2008, The William E. Smith Institute for Association Research

TRAINING   CERTIFICATION   CONFERENCES   **MEMBERSHIP**   **PUBLICATIONS**   The Global Voice of Quality®